Computer
Performance
Optimization

Computer Performance Optimization

Martin A. W. Nemzow

McGraw-Hill, Inc.

New York   San Francisco   Washington, D.C.   Auckland   Bogotá
Caracas   Lisbon   London   Madrid   Mexico City   Milan
Montreal   New Delhi   San Juan   Singapore
Sydney   Tokyo   Toronto

Library of Congress Cataloging-in-Publication Data

Nemzow, Martin A. W.
    Computer performance optimization / Martin A. W. Nemzow.
        p.   cm.
    Includes index.
    ISBN 0-07-911689-2 (paper)
    1. Electronic digital computers—Evaluation. I. Title.
QA76.9.E94N46 1994
004.2′4—dc20   93-42960
                                                  CIP

1 2 3 4 5 6 7 8 9 0 DOC/DOC 9 0 9 8 7 6 5 4

P/N 046343-3
PART 0F
ISBN 0-07-911689-2

The sponsoring editor for this book was Jeanne Glasser, the editing supervisor was David E. Fogarty, and the production supervisor was Donald Schmidt.

Printed and bound by R. R. Donnelley & Sons Company.

Contents

Chapter 5   Application Enhancement   113

Chapter 6   Client/server optimization   139

Chapter 8   Tools Disk   193

Special thanks to all those people who provided help for this book, and particularly to Carol Weingrod.

Martin Nemzow
October 1993

Computer
Performance
Optimization

Chapter

1

Overview

Introduction

This book is for speed demons. It is for computer group managers and users with speed-limiting budgets. It is for all those seeking to improve computer application performance and computer system results. *Computer Performance Optimization* comprehensively explains how to make computer systems run faster and provide better results. It is designed to help you detect performance bottlenecks, analyze the root causes of these obstructions, determine how to choose the best action, and then implement practical and effective computer performance optimization. The tools disk included with this book contains a hypertext help file with the table of contents, text, index, and hot links to related topics and definitions. The disk also contains published software benchmarks and other tools and information sources which are indispensable for analyzing system performance.

This book is about expanding the performance of computers. It is about making computers perform beyond the norm. It is about getting the best return on investment for computer system investments. It is about getting the fastest results. It is about getting the best quality results. It is about doing the most within financial or other resource limitations. It is about normalizing performance expectations and developing a practical methodology for enhancing performance. It is about optimizing both stand-alone, server, host, and enterprise computer systems and overall operations performance.

As such, *Computer Performance Optimization* shows how to optimize the system architecture, configuration, the communications environment, hardware, and software. This book is not about specifics of optimizing the performance of just one tool, just one operating system, or just one network operating system. As soon as you optimize so specific a factor, a new revision or software upgrade is released, hardware changes incrementally, and a new set of tips, tricks, traps, and help is suddenly available. Rather than just focus specifically, this book aims to define the underlying methods and detail the thought processes for effectively optimizing computer operations and making them go faster.

But optimization is more than simply going fast. Going fast nowhere, going fast blindly, or choosing the wrong route is unproductive; too many users and managers choose dead-end paths and lose sight of the real mission. This book retains the image of the real mission and suggests ways to go faster with purpose. Optimization is a means to achieve your destination by the most economical route, with the least work and the best results. Solutions are presented with a mind to practicality and feasibility; organizations do not want Star Wars solutions for industrial age problems. Coverage includes computing platforms, supplemental component hardware, operating systems, networks, application software, and utility software. The following list gives the performance targets covered:

- Computer platforms
- Operating systems
- Graphic user interfaces
- Network operating systems
- Supplemental hardware components
- Application software
- User activities
- Multitasking and threading
- Device drivers
- Utility hardware
- Graphic accelerators
- Coprocessors
- Bus mastering interfaces
- Benchmark tools
- System and performance analysis tools

Computer Performance Optimization describes common techniques for optimizing performance, but also provides prolific examples specific to various platforms or operating systems. This comprehensive coverage is provided because multiple-platform computing is the norm rather than the exception for most corporate and organizational data-processing activities. Computing platforms include Intel-compatible CPU-based computers (IBM-compatible personal computers), RISC-based engineering workstations, superservers, PowerPC machines, and Motorola-based Apple Macintoshes. Some of the material in this book refers to mainframes and minicomputers, and is relevant to them as well. Operating systems include MS DOS (and PC DOS), OS/2, UNIX, AIX, SunOS, VMS, Macintosh System 6.x and 7, and PowerOpen, while Sun NFS, Novell NetWare,

Banyan Vines, LAN Manager, LAN Server, NT Advanced Server, and PC LAN are representative of network operating systems, servers, and networked clients. This book includes abundant coverage of Microsoft Windows and Windows NT.

Additionally, *Computer Performance Optimization* discusses the relative merits of graphic accelerators; bus-mastering network and disk controllers; ISA, MCA, EISA, and local bus data-communication channels; network transmission protocols; coprocessors; network devices; and other special hardware that is positioned by vendors to improve computer system performance. *Computer Performance Optimization* includes extensive coverage of software, including end-user applications, client/server databases and procedures, utility software, and benchmarking tools. Utilities are represented by disk compression and optimization tools, workload analyzers, tools that analyze system and software configuration and optimize it, keyboard macros, at-specified-times execution tools, antivirus tools, backup machinery, and memory management tools.

Purpose of book

Although magazines have published many articles about tuning and performance optimization, the material is usually focused to a single operating system and very limited in depth. Trade articles basically define a scattershot approach. Few books are available on this topic; most exist as specialized technical reference manuals from the vendor or third-party publishers. The information on benchmarks and tools is more limited and insufficient. Furthermore, the mathematics for performance modeling are well-developed although not sufficiently practical yet. This book targets these gaps and provides information on benchmarks, analysis tools, performance tuning kits, and the methodology for optimizing performance.

The goal of *Computer Performance Optimization* is to show you how to squeeze more work throughput from the computer environment. Primarily, this means improving processing speed with faster systems, coprocessing, better device drivers, and optimized system configuration; secondarily, it means reviewing what you use the computer for, how you use the computer, and how you split workload and redirect work to secondary machines. It also means evaluating alternatives for improving computer system results. This means that many tasks can be dramatically improved with better techniques, presentation, and applications. In other words, tasks may be optimized by finding better routes, avoiding misleading or dead-end paths, and synchronizing computer activity to the real, underlying mission. There are always better ways to get things done; sometimes we become inflexible and forget to realize, consider, or try other methods. In effect, *Computer Performance Optimization* delivers insight into other ways—some obvious, usually practical—to improve productivity.

Intended audience

The intended audience includes MIS directors, industry consultants, network managers, work-group managers, software developers building client/server and networking applications, support technicians, computer professionals, and anyone who uses a computer and wants to optimize computer performance. Anyone who is intending to upgrade even one system will find this material valuable for its tricks and tips, new ways of looking at performance problems, and realistic views about performance. This book is also a useful teaching tool; it covers many systems from the vantage point of specific technical details but also with the perspective of general problem-solving methods.

Since the possible return on investment of resources is very great when optimization is performed over a large base, the material in this book is clearly useful to managers in large computing environments that include stand-alone PCs, client workstations, and network servers. Network managers tend to work within more modest and limited budgets. Therefore, the replacement of servers and workstations with the latest and fastest systems is strictly not feasible. The alternative is to tune performance and find better ways to achieve comparable results.

Book content

The content of *Computer Performance Optimization* is straightforward. This book defines typical performance bottlenecks, addresses methods for quantifying and assessing performance, and suggests methods of improving performance. Suggestions include general and persistent guidelines for optimizing performance that are applicable to most platforms. Additionally, this book presents specific techniques, tools, and methods for tuning DOS, UNIX, OS/2, MS Windows, database, and client/server processes. Moreover, *Computer Performance Optimization* goes beyond solving the obvious and immediate bottlenecks to review common difficulties; suggestions include reviewing the purposes of computing, assessing the mission as it should be, and trying to find shortcuts, better solutions, and new approaches. Such suggestions range from performance tips and tricks to better commercial solutions that can be found in the marketplace.

About the included tools disk

The tools disk incorporated with this book is a 3½-in IBM PC-compatible diskette. It contains software, text, benchmarks, and other tools pertinent for computer system performance optimization. Most of the included programs are operating system-specific, whether UNIX, OS/2, DOS, or MS Windows. Since most operating systems have native or extensible facilities for reading a DOS-based diskette, all files, regardless of the operating system, are in DOS format. Refer to Chapter 8 for tools disk contents, file details, and installation instructions.

Structure of book

Chapter 1, this overview, presents the topics and the framework for *Computer Performance Optimization*. As an acknowledgment of the reader's limited time, Figure 1.1 shows the table of contents in a visual presentation.

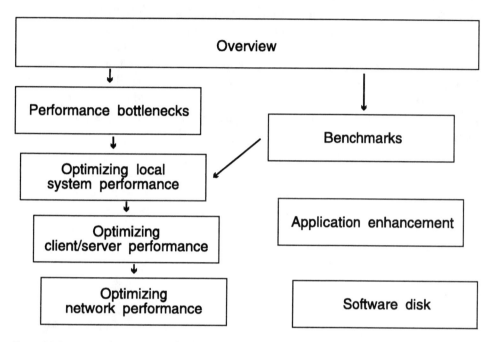

Figure 1.1 Organization of *Computer Performance Optimization*.

Chapter 2 details typical computer system performance bottlenecks. Coverage includes CPU, bus, disk hardware, network, and configuration problems. It defines a bottleneck both in rigorous technical terminology and through practical examples. Less obvious bottlenecks, such as complexity, user training, and reliability, are described here as well.

Chapter 3 explains benchmarks and defines a benchmark as an applicable measuring system based upon performance criteria. This chapter elaborates on commercial tools and published, free circulation measurement applications, some of which are included on the disk. Other common tools are referred to.

Chapter 4 demonstrates how to optimize single-user stand-alone PC performance with improved hardware, more memory, and disk and video substitutions or additions, and suggests methods to minimize unnecessary overhead or divert processing to other systems.

Chapter 5 exposes methods to enhance the computer process with different equipment and software including unexpected substitutions and the reassessment of goals and realistic options for achieving them.

Chapter 6 reviews client/server applications. It elaborates on why it is that these applications represent so complex a processing environment and why they are so difficult to optimize. Nonetheless, this chapter discusses concise and practical techniques to improve client/server access and results.

Chapter 7 explores network bottlenecks and procedures suitable for optimizing local area, wide area, and enterprise network operations. This chapter discusses some of the common approaches, and shows which perform best.

Chapter 8 describes the contents of tools disk, how to run each utility, and how to apply each to common computer performance bottlenecks.

The appendixes contain acknowledgments to the people and organizations that helped with this book, as well as numerous references to benchmarks, white papers, textbooks, other tuning guides, and tools. Additionally, *Computer Performance Optimization* contains a large glossary of acronyms and common terms. These are included on the disk in hypertext format and are automatically referenced with hot links when they appear in the text.

Chapter
2

Performance
Bottlenecks

Introduction

Many bottlenecks can be addressed and resolved. Some cannot be. They must first be discovered, interpreted, and recognized for what they are. This chapter defines typical computer performance bottlenecks. These bottlenecks are representative of those found on most platforms, operating systems, network operating systems, device drivers, and applications. This includes DOS, Windows, UNIX, UNIX derivatives, OS/2, NetWare and other network services, the Macintosh user interface, and System 7. They are also representative of those found on mainframe and workgroup operating systems.

Definition of performance bottleneck

A computer *bottleneck* can be caused by any system component—hardware, software, subcomponent, process, task, or person—that delays the results beyond the expected completion time. Formally, a bottleneck represents the critical path on a *performance evaluation and review technique* (PERT) called the *critical path method* (CPM). The bottleneck is the path without *slack time*, which is the path that is holding up the completion of the project or the path which causes follow-on activities to wait until it has completed. The path lacking slack time is the limiting performance factor in the system, as Figure 2.1 illustrates.

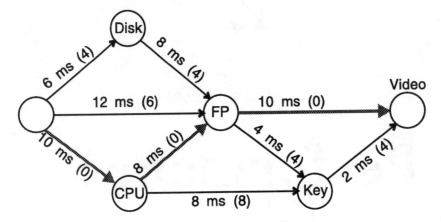

Figure 2.1 A critical path in CPM shows no slack time. Paths with slack time are narrow; those paths that constrain completion time are thicker. Numbers in parentheses represent the amount of slack time.

The bottleneck is the critical path. Therefore, while there is usually one, there also could be many active and in-force bottlenecks on the system at any time. Adding slack time to the critical path—that is, speeding up that path or simplifying that task so that it completes sooner—generally shortens project completion times; when the critical path can be relocated elsewhere with minor model adjustments, the system is very sensitive to tuning and perhaps not sufficiently stable for effective optimization. Improving performance on paths that are not so engaged—are not critical paths—does not affect performance, as the inconsequential performance improvements in Figure 2.2 show.

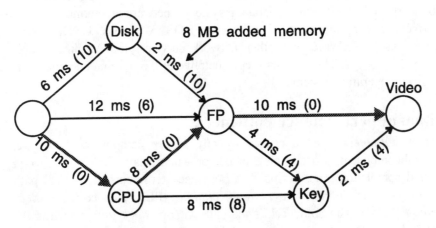

Figure 2.2 Adding slack to paths with slack time does not affect overall performance. Paths with slack time are narrow; those paths that constrain completion time are thicker.

For example, improving graphics display speeds with accelerator cards when floating-point processing is the bottleneck (as with most spreadsheet models) will have no overall effect on performance. If tasks are sequential or parallel (as in most CAD applications), improving both floating-point processing speeds and video refresh times is effective. (Note, however, that these critical path diagrams are an oversimplification of the interaction in a computer system.)

Bottlenecks are limitations, restrictions, choke points, blockages, constrictions, impediments, slowdowns, constraints, qualifications, and protocols. It is important to recognize that there are tradeoffs and compromises that often must be made between performance, speed, functionality, reality, time, and, of course, the availability of resources, financial or otherwise, to resolve the bottlenecks. Bottlenecks are not always obvious. What may masquerade as a performance problem may be in fact a training issue or a problem of misuse, mismanagement, poor configuration, or other similar flaws. Lack of qualified personnel, cost or difficulty in upgrading to a new software release or hardware platform, and the time required to retrain users for new operations and software can represent bottlenecks. System integration, component compatibility, and lack of documentation and support from a vendor can severely restrict performance. This is an interaction issue. The typical view of a system in terms of performance is that of a complex mechanism reduced to encapsulation layers. Specifically, the layers of a computer system can be broken down into the following components:

- People—skill levels, training, support facilities, and experience
- Operations—people, complexity of task, time-criticality of task, and management
- Network—protocol, complexity, hardware, tuning, and loads
- CPU—processor, motherboard design, and operating system
- Window/graphic interface—system, library, accelerators, and device drivers
- Disk—controller speed, size, number, type, driver algorithms, cache, and load balance
- Memory—cache type, size, cost, speed
- Database—buffer sizes, lock time-outs, number of users, and caches
- System kernel—base size, efficiency, buffer size, paging, tuning, and configuration
- Executable code—runtime or compile, native or interpreted, environment, and file system
- Source code—algorithms, languages, programming method, and compiler

While some people—in particular designers and engineers tuning systems—find it useful to view a computer system in terms of its fundamental components, most readers seem to find it is more useful for optimization to view it in terms of the functional components that actually create bottlenecks. Some of the limitations this chapter directly raises include those listed on the next page:

- Reliability
- Cost
- Speed
- Sophistication
- Environment
- Disk space
- Maintainability
- Ease of use
- Time
- Priorities for optimization

- Compatibility
- Performance
- Memory
- Functionality
- Network
- Efficiency
- Platform independence
- Complexity
- Life span
- Organizational culture

Reliability

Reliability is usually not viewed as a performance issue. Rather, it is viewed as an environmental factor or an infrastructure issue. Unfortunately, it is often viewed as something beyond the control of users and managers alike. However, reliability is a performance issue, and should be pursued as one. If computer systems are unreliable, overall performance is poor. If you cannot count on a system, it seems pointless to make it work faster—when it works.

For example, the loss of a morning's work, plus the loss of half an hour restoring the network or just one damaged system, represents more than a 50 percent loss of performance. Even the sporadic and intermittent failure of a computer system is a substantial bottleneck. Work flow is disrupted, time is wasted, while losses may be difficult to retrieve or even reconstruct. Fast systems, like race cars that break down, do not win races; they merely hold empty promises. Optimizing these systems without addressing the reliability issues *first* represents a bad use of resources and a mistake in judgment. The lack of reliability should be viewed as a fundamental bottleneck. Any suggestions that performance can be optimized with a tradeoff in reliability should be evaluated by a cost/benefit analysis; it rarely wins, as any performance gains are eroded by loss in reliability.

Compatibility

Compatibility is as serious a performance issue as reliability. It is not only an environmental factor, it is also a performance issue, and should be pursued as one. If the results of computer system tuning, enhancement cards, recompiling software for special CPU features, or conflicts over memory, address space, or drivers create computing surprises, you probably have some thinking to do. If you cannot count on your system and have applications, operating system, and hardware which fail to work together, it seems pointless to make the system work faster. Strange, inaccurate results and sporadic reliability problems are the hallmark of compatibility flaws.

As with reliability, even the sporadic and intermittent failure of a computer system is a substantial bottleneck. Work flow is disrupted, time is wasted, and losses may be difficult to retrieve or even reconstruct. Fast systems, like race cars that go the wrong way do not win races; they merely look ridiculous. Optimizing these systems without maintaining compatibility is poor judgment. The lack of compatibility should be a fundamental bottleneck.

Financial bottlenecks

The most obvious barrier when enhancing computer performance is financial restrictions, not simple performance bottlenecks. Many performance problems are attacked and resolved most easily by throwing money at them. More memory, faster and more processors, added coprocessors, faster storage media, and wider network channels will correct most performance bottlenecks. More money will hire people to improve or replace bad software. If time and people resources are more restricting than money for new hardware, the best solution is to buy faster hardware. Intel Pentium- and 80486-based systems tend to be faster than 80386 and 80286 systems. Sun Microsystems SparcStations and DEC Alpha AXP systems run faster with faster CPUs, more CPUs, and more memory; these computers also are faster than most Intel-based PCs.

Scope

However, most organizations do not solve problems only with money. Budgets are limited. Furthermore, some problems defy solution by financial fiat. Limitations of available technology may prevent obvious solutions. Some bottlenecks cannot be solved head on by the most obvious and desirable method. Some require re-trenchment, a rebuilding of the infrastructure, business reengineering, or even fundamental redesign or a different approach. This is true not only of networks and client/server operations, but of small-scale single-user tasks.

Also, note that bottlenecks move. As you fix one choke point, the problem is apt to move elsewhere. Consider all the issues presented in this chapter. The odds are that you will solve one bottleneck, only to be faced with a new and different one a month or two later. However, moving bottlenecks is not as grim as it may appear. It is not endless and all-encompassing. It is not pointless either. Each bottleneck resolved tends to increase overall performance. It is not as though you optimized one problem but created another of the same magnitude. You should have tuned up computer system performance. While the new problem may be as serious and threatening as a server capacity constraint or as minor as a shortage of RAM, more likely you are just pushing the limitations of application software.

Typical performance bottlenecks

The most common causes of computer performance problems are applying loads in excess of computer capacity, installation and configuration errors, an I/O bottleneck, inadequate resources, or software and processes that are excessively complex. The rest of this chapter describes these categories and defines each in greater detail. The following list outlines the typical performance bottlenecks by category:

- Workload
- CPU speed
- GUI video demands
- Configuration and installation errors
- Network

- Random access memory
- I/O overloads
- Software
- Background processes
- Reliability

Although this may seem self-evident, it is not always clear that the typical performance constraint for most computer processes is the workload itself. By that, I mean that the computer is slow because it is doing something that applies load to the computer. It is important to realize that hardware alone does not cause a bottleneck. Operating systems are rarely so burdensome as to overwhelm a single stand-alone system, a server, or a whole network. Operating system load is typically 4 to 7 percent without secondary processes. SNMP or CMIP network device management support on a system can add 10 percent load. NetWare NLMs should require no more than 10 percent of system resources when idled. Not until users start processes, tasks, and software applications will the computer system become a bottleneck. Furthermore, you cannot assess computer system performance until you apply a load to the computer. An idle computer has no load and represents no bottleneck until it has some task to perform.

There are true performance bottlenecks; you should have no doubts about that. However, the underlying cause of the most commonly observed bottlenecks is nothing more than a user's expectation that the process should go faster. In other words, the processing of that load is occurring more slowly than you expect. "I think the computer is slow" or "I think this isn't working very well" represents the typical first indications of a performance issue.

Before you attempt to optimize a computer system, it is important that you ascertain that something is indeed wrong lest you embark upon a significant effort to repair a nonexistent problem. The task of fixing something that isn't wrong is perhaps the most infuriating, unsuccessful, and time-consuming task you will undertake. You will expend time with no results and nothing to show for it.

Before spending time fruitlessly, examine the complaint. Does the user have objective or subjective reasons to complain about computer performance? Objective information, such as job timings, is more useful than subjective speculation. Consider whether the user has used different machines for these tasks and may have assessed *relative* performance correctly. Consider whether ancillary or background tasks have increased. Within a network environment variable task performance is very probable, since client performance is often as dependent upon server and network operation as it is upon the local processor. Also, consider the external factors—a network server or network link may be performing poorly, or the server load may be high.

If a complaint is subjective, it cannot be so easily ignored. Run benchmarks. Test the performance of a task on different systems. Compare results against prior timings. Do not perform multiple tests after a problem is observed—you will get the same results. This will not provide you with independent baseline information. If necessary, run the task on different computers, and computers that are known to have different performance levels. Should you ascertain that the task is indeed performing slowly, run standard benchmarks, as described in Chapter 3, on these computers to corroborate that one computer is indeed slow. One important thing to consider is that a computer virus may be the cause of these problems; therefore, take precautions to isolate machines and media so as not to spread the virus.

Even when the benchmarks seem to show that performance is adequate and similar on different computers and even different types of computers, you must understand the implications. Load represents many factors, such as CPU speed, I/O bus width and load, disk speed and disk throughput, and network service speed, among others. Timings can appear the same on different machines, but these results may have occurred for different reasons. Performance on a system with a slow video display could mimic the results on a system with an older CPU or defective hard disks.

The illustration in Figure 2.3 shows the logical composition in a typical computer system. Notice the data transmission channels between named devices. Those channels and devices would correspond to the paths in the previously illustrated critical path models when projects are converted into their fundamental tasks.

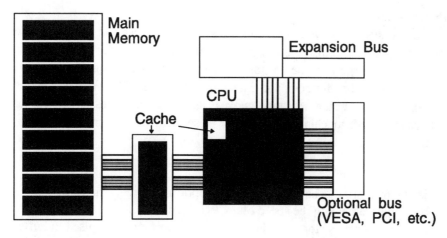

Figure 2.3 A logical view of the typical computer system showing the parallels to the critical path models.

Random access memory

Every computer system has memory; *random access memory* (RAM) is the memory used for holding applications, parts of the operating system, and user data. It is the most important component which affects computer performance. It may be built into the CPU for truly single-purpose computers, as in microwave ovens. However, the computers here have RAM apart from the CPU. This memory is rarely as fast as cache built into the CPU or directly wired to the CPU. Furthermore, it does not need to be that fast, since bus contention and other timing issues generally slow access to this memory. Memory limitations are based upon the following:

- Quantity
- Operating system
- Caches and spoolers
- Allocation
- CPU cache buffers
- File space and buffers
- Refresh speed
- Configuration

Quantity

The most obvious RAM bottleneck is an insufficient amount. Although many MS DOS application will not load without sufficient memory, this is a simple and primitive operating system. Applications for MS Windows, Macintosh, UNIX, and other similar operating systems expect a minimum configuration, but will use disk space in lieu of RAM—so-called *virtual RAM* (VRAM), *swap files*, or *memory paging*. Simply stated, when the operating system or applications relying upon it require more memory than is available, they page to a swap file. Basically, there is a tradeoff here between the faster RAM, which is accessible in times from 50 to 100 ns, and the slower disk, which is accessible in times from 4 to 40 ms. The RAM is thus about 100 times faster than the disk.

CPU cache buffers

Many PC-based systems have options for static RAM buffers and caches. These are expensive computer chips with fast refresh times—on the order of 10 ns. It is pertinent to get as large a cache as possible for the faster systems because this cache increases the buffer for code and data available to the CPU. The CPU is less apt to stop and wait for memory moves and disk accesses. Engineering workstations and RISC machines tend to have these facilities built into the system, not optional.

Cache

A *cache* is any memory mechanism generally supporting a higher speed than main memory but comparable with the speed of a CPU or controller. The name refers to the fact that the memory is stored for later use. Cache memories are used to buffer CPU operations so that application instructions or data are always available or to contain information for short periods of time in order to minimize contention over the bus and access to devices. Caches are used to buffer the CPU and to buffer data media and application code. The lack of a cache or a cache that is large enough represents a performance bottleneck. Most power management software for laptops and desktop machines with miserly energy usage precludes the use of caches since they are not refreshed often enough to maintain their contents.

The use of multiple caches, as with a hardware controller disk cache, operating system cache, and an application cache, can create a contention problem and decreases performance. Multiple caches also increase the number of steps required to complete a process, and thus represent a series of inefficient steps that impede performance. Additionally, untuned caches represent a possible performance hit. Caches support different data management schemes; these include LIFO, FIFO, most frequently read data, assigned priority, and sector/cluster read ahead. Timing of cache operation with respect to bit refresh, bus operations, and CPU loads are relevant tuning parameters but usually beyond the scope of most users.

Operating system

The choice of operating system has a significant effect on computer system performance. It provides device management, basic flow of control management, memory mapping, overhead, and support facilities for user applications. In general, MS DOS does not manage RAM well. Although MS DOS 3.3 is faster than PC DOS 4.0 and MS DOS 5.0, comparisons between operating systems are generally pointless. Even though the newer releases of MS DOS are moving away from the early 256-kB-based PC architecture toward a flat RAM address space as supported by Macintosh, OS/2, and UNIX, comparison between them is pointless. Applications, computing platforms, network environments, and user applications tend to mandate the use of a particular operating system.

File space and buffers

All operating systems require preset RAM or allocate it on the fly to provide the necessary space to contain the file structures that define the files accessed from disk or other devices, and buffer space to contain segments of that file. Most operating systems provide a means to establish a minimum amount as a default, and then increase it automatically as demanded. While an insufficient amount may represent a serious limitation for DOS because applications may crash, perform erratically, or merely run slowly, most other operating systems do not locate and delete extra space once it is allocated. This is usually a minor issue. It is an issue for OS/2 and NetWare because insufficient space impedes performance.

Caches and spoolers

Computer operating systems buffer slow I/O operations so that other tasks can continue without being delayed by printers and other simple output tasks. If the software is designed in such a way that it waits for completion of these operations before continuing, the application itself is the bottleneck. When the application can continue without waiting for the slower operations to complete, you have circumvented the I/O bottleneck. Specifically, a print spooler is a block of memory that may reside in computer memory, disk, or both that accepts all the printed output at once. It then doles out information at the slower rate of the printer. The *print spooler* is a structure in memory that buffers output destined for the printer. Thus, the *print queue* is the list of print jobs in the print spooler.

Caches are another technique to buffer both input and output from various devices, including the CPU, printers, CD-ROMs, video controllers, and disks, and thus provide better performance. Information is stored to a temporary electronic memory area and written to the disk when the CPU is idle. Similarly, a cache may contain information never explicitly requested by the CPU, but read into memory at a previous time or read ahead by the disk controller. If this information is useful, it saves I/O time that would otherwise be required for the CPU to request the information from the disk. Additionally, background multitasking as available with DCA Crosstalk under MS Windows or through most UNIX systems provides a means to download files as fast as possible (usually limited by the speed of the serial link) while continuing to perform other tasks. It is also possible to maintain multiple sessions and download and upload from different sources simultaneously. Multitasking, like parallel processing within the CPU, is a powerful technique for getting more work completed within a fixed time frame.

Refresh speed
The refresh speed represents the time between each cycle when memory values are checked or changed. If memory were not refreshed, the values in RAM would flicker and decay, causing a parity error. The CPU and platform architecture usually determine the requisite refresh speed for RAM. Some PCs, however, can use various speeds of RAM. Some systems will function with 50- to 80-ns memory chips, although generally not all of these. Older PCs use 220-ns chips. The CPU and its supporting hardware expect different wait states depending upon the RAM speed. Slower RAM may require more wait states, and thus provide less performance. Faster does not necessarily mean better unless the CPU can support the faster memory.

Data path width
Some systems provide data bus widths of 8 bits, while others provide 64-bit path widths. These bus width differences are most pronounced in PC architecture. ISA buses provide only 8-bit widths, while some PC-based superservers provide 64-bit channels to increase performance. The analogy to consider is that it is faster to build with larger building blocks—32-bit ones—than with smaller blocks. It is also easier to move more data with larger building blocks than with the smaller units—and do so in a shorter period of time. Sixty-four-bit addresses can be handled by eight 8-bit addresses. That represents the same amount of actual work, but it is completed in eight (or more) times as many CPU cycles. Conversion between these different "byte" sizes is handled by operating systems and the compilers which build them and the applications. This is why the same software compiled for 32-bit systems runs faster than compilations in a 16-bit format.

Allocation

How RAM is allocated is very pertinent. RAM can be used for application code, the operating system, caches and buffers, RAM disks, and data areas. While adding more RAM may make this issue moot, it is not always possible. A SparcStation can address gigabits of RAM, but organizations may not spring for the cost. Eventually, memory will not be the primary bottleneck; it will move somewhere else. Allocation is a configuration and installation issue.

CPU speed

The central processing unit (CPU) is the brains behind the computer and an important component which affects computer performance. Every task on a computer is coordinated through the CPU. When you type a letter on the keyboard, the operating system interprets that key and sees how it should be processed. Internally, software directs processes and waits for responses from these tasks. Peripheral devices and other tasks may send messages which initiate other events and CPU activity. When comparing computer systems with similar configurations, the unit with the faster CPU will complete the task faster.

CPUs are available in various types and from many manufacturers. The most prevalent are the Intel 8086 series in the original IBM PC. Since that time, Intel has brought the 8088, 80286, 80386, 80486, and Pentium chips to market. Intel also markets different chips within those categories, namely the SX, the DX, and the IBM-licensed SLC chip lines. Motorola has produced the 68000, 68010, 68020, 68030, 68040, and 68050 chips, and various other chips as well. Sun Microsystems produces its own reduced instruction set chips (RISC). AMD, Texas Instruments, and Cyrix produce chips compatible with the Intel chips but with different performance characteristics. This includes chips with lower energy demands and special power management features.

CPU chips are becoming increasingly complex in order to perform computer operations faster than their predecessors and with fewer sequential instructions. Primarily, this allows operations being handled as a 64-bit operation to be handled in a single operation rather than as iterative or complex assignments, such as the eight 8-bit memory address. Additionally, the clock cycles have increased from the original 2 million cycles per second (1.8 MHz) to more than 66 MHz. A typical 8086 (as found in an IBM PC XT) operation may require from 1 to 30 instructions; CPU performance is enhanced by reducing an operation performing 30 CPU instructions—which require at least 30 cycles—to an operator performing a fewer number at a higher clock rate. Thus, a 80386 chip running at 25 MHz will tend to be 20 percent faster than a 80386 chip running at 20 MHz. Additionally, better chip design can mean that a step requiring those same 30 instructions can be solved with parallel tasking so that only 6 cycles are required, for example. The result is that the newer chips tend to perform tasks faster. Figure 2.4 illustrates iComp performance benchmarks for various Intel CPU models.

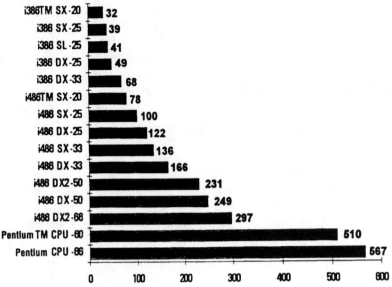

Figure 2.4 The Intel iComp benchmark index (Intel Corporation).

However, the CPU model, speed, and complexity are not the only measures of whether a task is a bottleneck at the CPU. You need only review the performance timings and benchmarks in an issue of *PC Magazine, MAC User, UNIX World,* or *UNIX Review* to see that systems which are built with the same CPU and the same components can vary in performance by more than 20 percent. Note that for reasons discussed in Chapter 3, the machine with the fastest benchmark time does not necessarily provide the best overall performance within *your* environment.

I/O overloads

The third most important influence upon task performance and the next most likely performance bottleneck is an input or output (I/O) overload. The CPU cannot run at full speed if it cannot get information from a disk storage unit and has to wait for that disk to spin at full speed and seek the information. Similarly, even the slowest CPU can send information to a printer faster than the printer can process it; as a result, the CPU will wait for the printer to send an acknowledgment that it can accept more information. This is directly analogous for all computer devices, including video displays, information storage, network interface cards (NICs), coprocessors, serial links, modems and other linkage devices, and even memory.

Furthermore, consider a Pentium chip that can perform 66 million memory moves in 64-kbit units per second. Despite that enormous speed, it nonetheless must access only 32 Mbits of main memory over a 24-MHz communication bus, and thus may manage to move 16 Mbits/s under the best circumstances. Some systems components can reduce the PC bus speeds to 6.88 MHz for compatibility. What is that chip doing during the slack time? It may be sharing CPU cycles with background processes, managing the use of the communication bus, or, more likely, waiting for the internal message from the memory management processor that it can send more bits to memory. The most likely I/O constraints are those listed below:

- Disk space
- Disk speed
- I/O channel limitations
- Wait cycles
- Resynchronization

- Data organization on disk
- Disk controller speed
- Video speed
- Time-outs

The available disk space has an enormous effect upon computer performance. Insufficient disk space when information must be written to disk is a serious bottleneck. If processing requires information to be written to disk and the system cannot find available disk space, it cannot continue. If it takes a long time for sufficient disk space to be allocated, the CPU must wait for a signal that the space is free. However, disk operations include disk writes that are not so obvious. Most complex operating systems—this includes MS Windows, NetWare, Mach, UNIX, and Macintosh System 7—use the disk storage medium not only for file and data storage, but also for storage of temporary files and configurations and as a second-order disk-based cache. The computer system thrashes when there is insufficient disk space or disk space that is insufficiently accessible because it is fragmented into many small units.

In situations where disk space and speed of disk access are the limiting performance factor, the system is said to be disk-bound. When this limitation is overcome, the bottleneck tends to revert back to the CPU.

Disk speed

The speed at which the disk rotates—called the *disk rotation speed*—and the speed at which the read/write heads move from point to point across the spinning media—called the *seek time*—also affect system performance. The seek time is generally the more important component since it limits how quickly the computer system can locate a requested piece of information and how quickly it can begin to write information. The computer system generally waits for disk operations. Disk rotation time is more a factor affecting how much information can be sustainably transferred into memory continuously; this is called the *disk transfer rate*. Faster transfer rates are important for graphic- or data-intensive operations, such as image scanning, storage and retrieval operations, file services, and client/server databases. Transfer rates are a factor of not only disk speed, but also the disk controller speed.

Disk controller speed

Performance of the disk controller can vary substantially. Some controllers require that the CPU control their operations; as such they are "slaves" to the CPU requests and subtract from overall system performance. Some *bus-mastering* controllers "master" the bus to bypass the CPU and require little or no CPU overhead for disk operations. Other controllers can sustain multiple disk drives to read and write data streams simultaneously. This coprocessing technology increases the effective disk speed several-fold. *Caching controllers* buffer disk operations. They either *buffer* by storing the last accessed data in their own memory (previous read or written information) on the chance that it will be requested again, or *read ahead* by reading more data than requested by the CPU into a memory area on the chance that it will be requested later, or *cache write* by deferring writing data to the disk until such time as the disk is idle (or when forced to do so because the cache memory space is required for new information).

The benefit from the cache is determined by the *hit rate,* which is defined as the number of times requested information is found in the cache divided by the number of requests made to the disk, expressed as a percentage. The effectiveness of a caching controller is determined by the system or user applications. Cache with word processing is useful only when the document is already in memory or is scrolled through top to bottom frequently. Other examples of when caches are effective include the calling of application code overlays and dynamic link libraries (DLLs), referencing a spelling dictionary, or scrolling through database master index records.

Cache tends to be more effective for database and simple file operations. The hit rate can be improved by increasing the size of the available cache; eventually, improvements in the hit rate will have negligible effects on system performance.

I/O channel limitations
The I/O channel itself can become a bottleneck because it is not fast enough, it is not wide enough, or it becomes saturated with system communication traffic. Most control signals for peripheral devices are routed through this computer system "backbone." The I/O channel in a computer system is often a single focal point, called the *bus*. The bus varies in width from 8 bits up to 64 bits, and in speed from 3 Mbits/s to 40 Mbits/s for IBM PC Microchannel Architecture (MCA), to hundreds of Mbits/s for engineering workstations and special superserver architectures. VESA VL bus architecture provides full communication at the CPU speed. Limitations and problems with VL do exist in that the adapters must be fully compliant and the bus will support one and maybe two adapters before performance degrades *below* a comparable ISA-based system.

Even for computers with true bus speeds above 30 MHz, it is still possible to overwhelm the bus. In most cases, the bus is a single-direction communication path. In other words, the CPU can direct a disk controller, or the controller can talk to the CPU, but not both at the same time. Communication must be sequential. Furthermore, the CPU cannot talk to two controllers or to one controller and the VGA controller at the same time. For that matter, while the bus-mastering controller does not require much CPU for managing memory exchanges, it does prevent the CPU from accessing the bus while it masters it. While contention over the bus lasts mere milliseconds, its frequency detracts from performance out of proportion to its duration.

DMA

Direct memory access (DMA) is not only a function of bus-mastering controllers, it is also a feature of operating systems, network operating systems, device drivers, and application software. It is faster if memory is directly manipulated rather than being referenced indirectly through a table lookup or negotiated through the CPU, as Figure 2.5 illustrates.

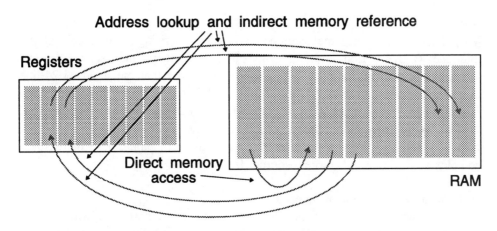

Figure 2.5 Direct memory access is faster than indirect memory references.

Wait states

Some CPUs are so fast that they outstrip the capacity of the bus to transmit a control signal and receive the acknowledgment. Similarly, the CPU may be able to process information faster than it can address and reference memory. Therefore, it must wait some number of clock cycles before continuing with processing operations. As a result, many operations are delayed by the slower bus or memory speeds. In fact, the Intel DX2/66 processors run at 66 MHz for internal operations while maintaining only 33 MHz externally. Internal operations must wait one cycle (at least) for memory transfers. It is for this reason that the faster CPUs include immediately accessible caches built into the chip.

Contention

Contention over bus access or access to devices represents a performance traffic jam. The CPU is the arbiter and controls what accesses devices and when. Contention management is becoming more of an issue as CPUs support true multitasking and parallel computing. Some computer systems off-load the management of bus and device access to a secondary processor.

Device population

An excessive number of devices can decrease performance. The CPU must poll devices periodically—whether they are directly wired to the CPU or attached through the bus—to see if they require access to the bus and main memory. More devices increase the poll time. Additionally, controllers can support multiple devices themselves. So while a SCSI disk controller represents a single poll to the CPU, a fully populated daisy chain with seven devices attached represents a possible traffic obstruction for the controller itself. It also matters on loaded buses whether SCSI communication is synchronous or asynchronous.

Video

Video has only lately become a serious bottleneck. The rising use of graphical user interfaces (GUI) as front ends for many operating systems and user applications increases the demand for faster video speeds. Consider that the standard 24-line, 80-character-width terminal represents only 1920 bytes. Contrast this with the low resolution 480 x 640-pixel VGA display, which represents 38,400 bytes, the 1640 x 1280 24-bit true-color display, which represents over 6 MB. The time and computer resources needed to interpret, construct, and paint these increasingly complex screens demands more resources from the CPU.

Installation and configuration errors

Computer systems are no longer simple collections of hardware with a small operating system like MS DOS. The hardware has become complex and must be tuned well. Although an 80486-based PC is quite similar to the original IBM PC, the comparisons really end outside the case. The hardware represents a phenomenal increase in complexity. The CPU is more complex. Secondary processors are standard. The need to better time and tune the exchange of information between multiple processors is more pressing. The mere assembly of the fastest components is no assurance of a high-performance system. In fact, such a system will probably be suboptimal. Operations which occur millions of times per second must mesh in terms of timing, bus access, memory speeds, and signal contention. However, hardware may represent a performance range of 20 percent from the fastest to the slowest system in the same class. Even a processor that is faster by an order of magnitude will not necessarily yield the performance gains imagined unless it is supported by infrastructure geared to that CPU.

Installation errors are profoundly more affecting. Switch settings, jumpers, wait state settings, and placement of devices in the wrong order or with the wrong priorities can slow performance dramatically. Conflicts that are not adequately resolved may be invisible to the user but may cause a loss of a few CPU cycles every time the conflict occurs. The only way to detect these problems is when devices will not work, with special test software, or by applying a known benchmark.

The effects of installation and configuration errors are more pronounced with software. Software is more complicated than hardware. Although the latest CPU may contain 4 million circuits and more, the range of software functions is more imaginative and complex. Typically, the use of the wrong drivers, the wrong operating system, and the wrong applications create performance problems. Also, conflicts between these can cause outright system failure or something as subtle as a slowdown. For example, consider the case of a Matrox-manufactured enhanced VGA controller, called the Impression 1024. Screen performance was faster with a PC's native-mode VGA at 640 x 480. While the native VGA board supported 800 x 600 resolution, the Matrox board was marginally faster at displaying images. Note also that 1024 x 768 drivers supporting 24 bits are faster than the drivers for the less information-intensive 256 colors. Why? Because the software developers tuned the 24-bit drivers, since the thrust of the product was the high-end display market.

Devices are not only hardware objects. Devices can include caches and buffers of various types, memory reallocations, memory configurations, print spoolers, and logical device reassignments. The simple MS DOS supports these functions, as do DR DOS, UNIX, OS/2, and most other operating systems. While outright logical device conflicts create immediate failures, you can expect to see subtle and even not so subtle performance problems. The installation of unnecessary devices wastes memory and time. The lack of sufficient buffers and cache space will cause a system to thrash, while the allocation of too much memory to these structures wastes precious resources and tends to create a path without slack resources somewhere else.

While device drivers are integral components of operating systems, they are not the only components that can represent bottlenecks. For example, the "simple" MS DOS can cause problems when available free memory drops below 570 kB (out of the available 640 kB of standard memory space). The installation of long search paths, keyboard command stack space, alias names for devices and disk locations, and device drivers that are not really needed uses memory resources. Although newer versions of MS DOS allow you to load and map these structures into the high memory anomalies of DOS, there is a performance hit. Also, other operating systems do not have these contrived memory structures; logical devices and system facilities just reduce memory and generally provide a filter which intercepts and redirects many system operations.

Software

Software is the most serious and likely bottleneck. Applications now embody graphic interfaces, complex processing, and significant demands for data and data structures. A significant application might have represented 64 kB on a PC, or 256 kB on UNIX, or 640 kB on a mainframe ten years ago. Now, user applications can easily require 2 MB just to load and swap through another 10 MB of code and utilities. Operating systems also are becoming more complex.

Basic graphic support, file management, task management, coprocessing, multitasking, threading, and utility support are expected as basic facilities of the software. Data communications and networking increasingly are perceived as standard operating system functions.

The line between operating system, network operating system, database server, and application is fading. Applications bypass and replace fundamental processes in the operating system with drivers, redirecters, and temporary patches. Figure 2.6 illustrates the intertwining of the operating system kernel, network operating systems, device drivers, and applications.

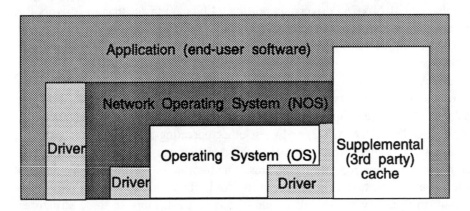

Figure 2.6 The division between software components is disappearing as applications become more intertwined and seamless with the operating system kernel.

As a result, the days of a simple operating system are fading too. The complexity of software—all types—increases, resulting in new bottlenecks. While it may seem that prepackaged software provides less of an opportunity for optimization, the diversity of the software and the ease with which specialty software can now be created just move the issue from the interactions between software and hardware to the issues of selection. The items below represent significant opeating system bottlenecks:

- Device drivers
- Operating system
- Bus and signal synchronization
- Applications

- Message response
- Network operating system
- System wait times
- Utilities

Device drivers

CPU operations tend to be delayed by devices. These may be disks, printers, network interfaces, or graphic video displays. The software drivers that control these devices are part of the operating system, but generally replaceable. Device drivers are generally small modules that run frequently. They control the disks, the printer output, and the video display. They may control other devices as well.

Device drivers may be included as part of an operating system because, well, devices are quite common for computers. However, they are not a monolithic part of the operating system because the functions and features of devices vary. Also, because they tend to run so frequently—a disk device driver is invoked every time the CPU reads or writes information to disk—minor tuning can make substantial differences. Saving a loop iteration or a handful of CPU cycles represents a dramatic performance improvement.

A suboptimal driver may have a performance effect out of proportion to its code size. It runs so frequently, perhaps a hundred times per second, that it slows performance in proportion to its usage.

Operating system

Operating systems manage memory, device access, and application execution. Devices and applications tend to use the resources of the operating system to get tasks completed. Disk access, report printing, video display, and file management are generally passed to the operating system. It is always there, always running and supporting the overlaid user applications. It represents more RAM and CPU overhead than anything but the device drivers and applications. As such, it represents a significant performance bottleneck.

The selection of different versions or releases of an operating system for performance reasons may not be practical. You may be unable to get adequate support for the older, smaller systems and more performance-optimal systems. Even if support is available, it may not be as good. An older version may not provide a stable or acceptable platform for new applications. Furthermore, selection among AIX, Berkeley, XENIX, SCO, SunOS and Solaris on UNIX 5, Venix, OSF, and other dialects of UNIX is not necessarily a relevant performance issue. The choice of MS DOS or Solaris may be a pertinent issue when considering user applications and processor scalability. If the task is clerical data entry and transcription, an MS DOS-based word processor may represent sufficient performance and better financial optimization. In short, the CPU (and possibly the attached network) does not represent an impeding performance bottleneck; the speed of the typist does. On the other hand, a client/server database application may grow to consume the resources of the computer system and yet be fully optimized for the current platform.

Network operating system

Data and applications are migrating from stand-alone systems to networks. The controlling software for network operations is called the *network operating system* or NOS. It overlays the operating system; it may even replace it. For example, an MS DOS network may not have an MS DOS server, but rather a NetWare, NFS, or Banyan replacement. NetWare, NFS, and Banyan do not require an MS DOS foundation; they substitute for it and provide their own OS functionality. The operating system intercepts commands and reinterprets them. For example, a simple request for a file catalog may be trapped and redirected over the network to a server or a peer. As such, the NOS represents a processing filter for every command. Even user applications, which may merely request a file or print a report, are reinterpreted in light of the network. This represents a CPU load.

Furthermore, the network is not part of the client computing system. The connecting link is a data communication channel with a limited bandwidth shared by many other clients and network stations. Access to the network is by contention resolution—a problem just like that handled by the CPU to allocate the bus among devices—or by some token-based bandwidth allocation protocol. This network channel thus imposes its own bottleneck. A busy network can slow the fastest computer system to a crawl. In fact, a suboptimal network has a disproportionate effect on the fastest computer systems; the system spends more time just waiting for the network rather than processing.

On the other hand, network data storage and print facilities represent both an opportunity and a bottleneck. Network storage tends to be faster than local devices. First, network managers tend to install better components as global network devices. Second, network storage requirements are usually significant. Therefore, devices are chained or replicated. Disk striping and redundancy decreases access times and improves performance. Read operations are distinctly improved, an important consideration for network databases. Network printers tend to be faster than personal printers, if only for the reason that the workload tends to be concentrated here.

However, such network services can be significant bottlenecks. When the load becomes high and arrival times of that load overlap, network disks and printers become performance obstructions. Combine that with client systems hammering away at the network bandwidth, and you have the formula for network performance disaster.

Applications

The purpose of the computer system is to run the applications as people see them and apply them. The underlying device drivers, operations systems, and network components are merely the foundation for these tools. Applications tend to be the most significant workload bottlenecks. They require nearly constant disk access, keep repainting the display, calculate complex algorithms, and create full-page graphic reports. To achieve these results, they stress the operating system, demand that the network redirect their requests to network devices, and keep the user waiting for the CPU.

Utilities

Software utilities are special applications. They tend to run frequently, hide in the background as a background task, or provide special services. Examples include a keyboard macro interpreter, a free system resource monitor, and resident time management tools, calendars, thought organizers, E-mail notices, and Rolodexes.

They should be noted as separate from other typical user applications because they are concurrent or multitasked processes.

Background processes

Background processes are applications that run concurrently and share system resources. They are thus called *shared tasks*. This may include peer-to-peer networking services, utilities running as icons, or user applications running in the lulls between more important foreground applications. A system with sufficient resources can create reports from databases, print a document with embedded graphics, and perform other similar tasks while at the same time providing high-priority service to the user on an active task. Background tasks become bottlenecks when they clash over devices, memory, CPU, or other resources.

Viruses

Viruses are a special type of background process, certainly one that is unwarranted and undesired. They corrupt memory, data files, and even hardware. Some merely slow performance without overt damage; the Internet Worm is one example. In any event, they cause poor or erratic performance—because they represent a background application, a modified operating system process, or a rogue program that diddles with memory, code, and disk-based data—and even halts any performance completely.

Network bottlenecks

A network bottleneck is a serious one because the network is a global resource. It is not always easily resolved. Networks become bottlenecks through improper architecture, poor installation, bad configuration, insufficient resources, and overloads. The network also becomes a bottleneck for the reasons described previously under "Software: Network operating system". Also, you might refer to the McGraw-Hill/Windcrest book *LAN Performance Optimization*, for information specific to local area networks. Improper architecture includes the selection of the wrong protocol, use of the wrong materials, a logical network structure with choke points, and just poor design. Poor installation is a network killer; performance can be erratic or simply slow. Bad configuration is not an issue of improper architecture. It is possible to have designed and installed a sufficient network, but not configured it properly.

The most obvious examples might be the separation of a server from its clients by a bridge or a router, the designation of addresses with duplicates or with different network segment addresses, establishing critical stations with insufficient resources, or setting the wrong buffer sizes and protocol for the network. The network as a entity can have insufficient resources when key components are overloaded. For example, a 4-page/minute printer can get backlogged quickly. The printer spooler can fill up all available free disk space with this backlog and thus halt all other operations until the disk space is released.

Networks also saturate with traffic load. A "network" as in a client/server network is not just the principal resource but also the data communication link. Such links become bottlenecks not only because the level of traffic exceeds bandwidth, but for two other reasons as well. First, the access delay can grow because the network has too many nodes. Second, in the case of Ethernet, contention over access to the channel can create *collision saturation* where no traffic moves.

Conclusion

Either you can throw money at the problem and usually get the problem resolved, or you make concessions and select what you want to optimize. Performance optimization is generally a tradeoff. Some bottlenecks are so new that no amount of money can solve the problem. Optimizing one performance aspect requires a different resource. Networks faster than FDDI are as yet unavailable. A computer with a PC architecture faster than 100 MHz is not available. Instead, you accept the limitations. Or you could switch platforms. You might redesign a database. You might reengineer the entire process. You might switch operating systems and architecture and select a mainframe with terminals. You might give up on the concept of a true multitasking GUI front end for a telemarketing organization. One of the important things to know about performance optimization is that there are limits of one kind or another. Some will not be under your control, and you will need to recognize them. The next chapter addresses the issue of benchmarks and the methods to root out underlying causes of computer performance bottlenecks.

3

Benchmarking Bottlenecks

Introduction

Benchmarks are standardized software programs or manual comparisons used to test processor power and component functionality of different computers. Benchmarks measure an applied workload. A benchmark may consist of a generalized processing problem, a random access file routine, a sorting problem, generation of prime numbers, a matrix inversion, a mathematical problem, or a repetitive screen display. It might be a specific set of instructions compiled under different compilers and languages to test how each machine, each compiler, and the software performs.

Benchmarks include commercial products that are formalized tools, copyrighted public domain measuring systems, and ad hoc tests created without peer review, marketplace acceptance, or basis for comparison with other benchmarks. The source of benchmarks in no way minimizes their importance.

It is important to recognize that computer systems are general-purpose machines and that benchmarks can test either very specific conditions or generalized performance. A *benchmark* is a measuring stick of a workload. What matters is not so much what the scale for measurement is, but that the scale is useful, can be repeated and replicated, and provides a history for comparison. It is sometimes important to test similar applications on vastly different computing platforms, or different applications on similar platforms. While it may seem unimportant what that workload is, how it is applied, or how generalized the work is, it will matter to you. The workloads which you benchmark should approximate your actual working conditions. Although this may not be practical, consider this ideal concept as you read through this chapter.

Therefore, for practical reasons, *workload* represents a generalized performance. As such, most benchmarks abstract, measure, and define a "generalized" or "theoretical" workload. *Workload classification* is the amount of work assigned to or done by a person, group, workstation, client, workgroup, server, or internetwork in a given time period. Therefore, *workload characterization* is the science that observes, identifies, and explains the phenomena of work in a manner that simplifies how resources are being used.[1]

The abstracted benchmark results are actual completion, time trials, timings, and resource comparisons. Benchmarks are usually precise in the answers they provide. For example, a benchmark can be a statement that the computer either completed the task or failed. Another example is the count of *millions of instructions per second* (MIPS). Typically, benchmarks are combined into suites for better coverage and comparison of different types of applications, assessments, or processing speed measurements. Some, like the BAPCo test, compile the results of six different automated macros into a single number. Such formal benchmarks are useful for evaluating the best method to free up a critical path. The Ziff-Davis WinMark tests how many millions of pixels can be displayed on screen within a single second (averaged over a longer test period). The usefulness of this particular benchmark for simple comparison purposes has been distorted for the pivotal decision maker by vendors who have included optimized video routines to specifically enhance the performance of this benchmark.

The value of any benchmark or the results from any test application should be considered carefully against the context in which it was designed and against which it was applied. Consider the following analysis: "Unnatural workloads generate unnatural results." The author continues, "Tests using synthetic workloads are a favorite of hardware manufacturers because they so easily demonstrate the need for bigger and faster hardware."[2]

Benchmarks also may be subjective and evaluative, such as "the computer completed the task as expected and to satisfaction." Examples include, "the color is better," "the screen jitters less," or "the software is easier to use." Although subjective benchmarks lack the precision and formality of numerical answers, they are as useful as "2.03 MIPS" for locating and evaluating performance bottlenecks. Recall from Chapter 2 that bottlenecks are not just deterministic critical paths;

[1]*An Introduction to Workload Characterization*, Novell Research APPNotes, Ron Lee, Senior Consultant, Novell, May 1991.
[2]*Identifying Test Workloads in LAN Performance Evaluation Studies*, NetWare APP Note, Ron Lee, Senior Consultant, Novell, May 1992.

they can include the more subtle issues of finance, user qualifications, system and network architecture, and quality of results. Some bottlenecks which are a factor of performance and time are not always subject to comparison by benchmarks. (Exceptions to this are products available for multiple platforms.)

For example, a software application with bloated code may be best examined with a *source code profiler* to see what delays activity and where this happens. On the other hand, process time comparison of a software application on a machine with a floating-point coprocessor may indicate that the computer lacking this feature is a bottleneck.

Variety of benchmarks

Now that it seems that benchmarks are so simple, here are some complications. Benchmarks not only gauge the speed of performance; they indicate other factors as well. At least three families of performance benchmarks are covered in this book. Clearly, the strongest benchmarks are those designed to measure task performance times on various platforms and types of CPUs. Second, functional performance methods that compare and contrast the different hardware, software, components, and application paradigms provide a means to evaluate how applications perform a given task. Third, operational performance transcends the computing platform, the operating and network operating systems, and the user applications; this relates to how well and quickly people perform a given task using different tools. These three types of benchmarks are categorized below:

- Speed of performance
- Functional performance
- Operational performance

Speed of performance

Speed of performance benchmarks are the most common. They tend to appear more credible and scientific because they represent number of operations during a fixed time interval. Performance benchmarks are easily designed to compare disparate platforms and CPUs. As such, they are very useful. The utility of such numerical benchmarks should not outweigh the other benchmarks because they describe only the exact condition for which they were defined. For example, the Dhrystones and Whetstones benchmarks, which are common for UNIX testing, show only floating-point and other similar computational speeds. The same is true for the WinMark megapixels per second. They provide a small and perhaps precise view of one aspect of performance issues.

Functional performance

Functional performance relates to what a system or application actually does. Some people call the functions *features*. Measuring functions and features is relevant in most computer systems and applications. For example, consider the feature difference between Wordstar 3-31 (released in 1983) and Word for Windows release 2.0c (released in 1992). Wordstar is a character-based word processor limited to a screen of 132 columns and 50 lines. It can open only one file at a time. Cutting and pasting between files is awkward at best. It prints to a variety of printers supporting variable-width character spacing and microspacing. It has a spell checker and synonym library. It creates indexes and tables of contents, and merges databases into a master file for output. Microsoft Word for Windows (WinWord) does all that Wordstar does and more. It is a graphically based word desktop publishing system and shows exactly how a printed page will appear. It supports multiple documents at a time and supports a cut-and-paste facility as well as a glossary feature, enables dynamic data exchange (DDE) between different programs, and will even open other applications to update a graph, a spreadsheet, or an image through object linking and embedding (OLE). It typesets output by supporting most known typefaces at almost any size. It has more features. Is it therefore better?

It is not necessarily better. WinWord requires an Intel 80386 or 80486 microprocessor to run well and quickly. Alternatively, in fact, under most conditions Wordstar will run as quickly on a slow 80286 as it will on a high-performance PC. The reason for this anomaly is that the 80286 is fast enough for most typists; the processing speed of the CPU, bus, and disk is faster than most printers. On the other hand, WinWord is a graphically based word processor supporting complex image operations. WinWord benefits from speed optimization. Many trade magazine articles create multipage tables in order to compare features for like applications. Typically, word processors, spreadsheets, databases, and even untraditional applications are contrasted by features. While speed of operation is usually the primary optimization target after process integration, a functional issue is more important in the primary decision stages. For example, Wordstar is excellent for text entry—in fact, this book was written first in Wordstar for several performance reasons and because it fit on a laptop computer—but Wordstar 3.31 could not support the rich text format (RTF) or WexTech's Doc-to-Help Word Basic macros used to create the MS Windows hypertext help file which accompanies the book.

Functional issues include such requirements as inner and outer database joins, network-wide fax phone books with privacy features, network fax broadcast capabilities, and automatic spreadsheet 3-D presentation templates. Such lists are specific to the platform, the goal, and the applications.

Operational benchmarks

The last benchmark category that is referenced in *Computer Performance Optimization* is the operational issues for computing. Operational issues reflect platform, OS, NOS, and speed of performance issues. They include such factors as the complexity of the system, the reliability of the system, the costliness of a particular solution, and how well it performs and completes the given tasks. Consider Wordstar and WinWord again. Wordstar has complex command keystroke sequences. This is a moot issue if you learned it in 1978, because the alternative text processors at that time had fewer features. The same holds true for users of EMACS, an early and powerful UNIX editor. However, the command syntax is baffling to users trained on systems with pulldown menus and instant on-line help.

Nonetheless, there is a significant learning curve to understanding the WinWord word processing tools. WinWord requires at least 5 MB of disk space and as much as 10 MB, while Wordstar 3.31 fits onto a single 360 kB-floppy disk. It requires substantial system resources to run. Although it does indeed keep up with a proficient typist, some people find the screen display and formatting options more complex and unnecessary for simple text entry.

Operational issues for databases might include multiplatform availability and interoperability, processor scalability, ease of programming and maintaining, reliability of the data set, and accuracy of transaction rollbacks or restitution of disjointed databases after a system failure. By the way, *transactions per second* (TPS) provides speed of performance measurements. Network fax server operational issues include how E-mail is integrated as a delivery option, how incoming faxes are routed, how security for sensitive documents is handled, what happens to incoming faxes when fax storage space is filled, and how faxes are routed for lowest transmission rates. Certainly, cost is a relevant benchmark.

Necessity for benchmarks

Here is a paraphrase about the perceived value, to some, of benchmarks: "Lies, damn lies, and benchmarks." Keep this in perspective as you make performance assessments based upon benchmarks. Vendors selling equipment and software primarily on the basis of benchmark speed choose benchmarks that favor their presentation. They will choose the benchmarks they refer to in order to show their products in the best light. They will even reverse-engineer benchmarks and include specialized hardware or software to improve the benchmark scores as part of the product. Benchmarks are routinely subverted. This does not detract from the importance of benchmarks. They provide information for making intelligent assessments of computer performance. If you lack such information—and merely guess at it—it is difficult to accurately optimize performance. You are apt, instead, to degrade performance and create new bottlenecks. You need a starting point. The benchmark indicates relative and absolute performance changes. Figure 3.1 shows some numerical results with annotation. The magnitude of the numerical values is irrelevant; the changes and steps are more interesting.

Consider a client/server environment that has grown from 20 to 55 users. The initially immediate response times have since degraded to 17 seconds with that growth. Typically, the servers, the clients, and the network transmission channel are all prime candidates for review and upgrade. Most situations are financially limited. Replacement of all the hardware is unrealistic. Furthermore, it is genuinely possible that the hardware is not the problem. Do you really want to find that out after committing to the upgrade and system replacement path? What if the server's disk storage were merely so badly fragmented that writes to the disk consumed over 75 percent of all server processing and waiting time? What if the database were built with true normalized table, record, and key structures, so that as the workload grew, the record search time grew exponentially?

```
Program Started : Thu Nov 11, 1993      15:16:26.73


Program Segment Address is at           : 2CC0H
Environment Space begins at             : 2CB3H
Bytes left in current segment           : FEF0H
...Running database access macros and upon completion
    also running a data backup procedure as a sample of
    typical performance loading.


Program Ended : Thu Nov 11, 1993      16:43:03.57
```

Figure 3.1 A sample benchmark which provides numerical results.

The bottleneck here is disk access time, record lookup, and space for the lookup tables. Recall the effects of adding capacity to a segment with slack time, as shown in Figure 2.2. Any changes to a process or system architecture do not affect the overall process time unless those changes affect the critical path. Effects on the critical path, however marginal, affect performance. If you make the servers, clients, or network transmission channel faster and that is not the problem, you have only added slack time to the system as a whole and noncritical task overcapacity; it will not affect performance. You need benchmarks and other tools to provide useful information so that you can find the critical path and move performance in the right direction.

Commercial tools

There are commercial benchmark tools. Examples include the Auerbach Information Systems EPD Reports, the previously mentioned BAPCo macros, the iCOMP (Intel Comparative Microprocessor Performance) Index, and tools provided with operating systems. There are also a large number of hardware inventory tools that analyze the configuration of the system. While inventory tools are not per se benchmarks, they can provide useful information for discovering sources of performance bottlenecks.

iCOMP

Intel designed a relative measurement tool to compare the performance of its own chip sets with each other and with competitors' chip sets. It is a horsepower rating without a measurement scale based upon anything physical; there is no horse. It is merely a *comparative* or *logical* scale. This benchmark is called the *iCOMP index*. The index was designed to reflect typical workload characteristics. As such, iCOMP includes the Ziff-Davis CPU benchmarks, Whetstone, and BAPCo SPECmark92 tests and weights eight different numerical results to form a composite value. The weighting method is not generally available. Refer to Figure 2.4 to see the iCOMP index for various Intel processors.

BAPCo SYSmark 92

Business Application Performance Corporation (BAPCo) is an independent research firm funded by hardware and software leaders, including Intel, Lotus, and WordPerfect. Based upon its own research, BAPCo created a benchmark that executes a series of keyboard macros to invoke standard and popular business applications, including spreadsheets, word processing, and databases. These results are converted into integer, floating-point, and overall system performance benchmarks. Again, these values are only relative assessments; they provide no ultimate and natural measurement system.

BMC Software

Many mainframe data collection, analysis, and performance optimization tools are available. BMC is one vendor. Basically, the requirement for computer performance optimization has always existed and vendors have sought to fill this niche. They have had more time to meet the requirement for mainframe operations than they have for PCs, workstations, servers, networks, and database engines. The availability of such products for older platforms speaks to the need for similar tools on the platforms addressed in this book. BMC Software provides at least two products of relevance. These are Activity Monitor for DB2, which traces DB2 database block and record operations, and Opertune for DB2, which helps you configure buffers, threads, free space, log files, and RAM utilization.

Power Meter

Power Meter is a subset of the DiagSoft QA Plus/FE diagnostic software for PCs. The QA Plus software mostly provides hardware inventory information and system configuration. While this information is not overtly pertinent for performance optimization, it does provide insight on interrupt settings, memory conflicts, and hard disk configuration.

When adapter boards have interrupt settings that conflict with other adapters or with motherboard devices, in the best cases system operation will be unreliable. At least with diagnostic software you will know you have a performance problem. In the worst case, the operating system will overcome these invisible errors at a cost of lost CPU cycles each time there is a conflict. This tool, and others like it such as Check It, DIAG, and Skylight, do provide clear insight toward optimizing the hard disk interleaving or locating marginal sectors, clusters, and tracks. The Power

Meter subset performs a number of performance tests, including workload simulation, disk performance tests, standardized CPU and memory speed tests, video display speeds and capacities, as well as tests on the performance of laptop batteries and recharger timings.

Macintosh tools

Snooper from MAXA detects hardware flaws, bad RAM, CPU problems, and disk flaws. This kit contains a NuBus card to use when the system will not even boot. Furthermore, This tool provides some basic performance testing tools, tools which form the first level for analyzing Macintosh system performance. Alert! also from MAXA diagnoses software and network conflicts over a network connection. This tool is interesting in so far as it contains an on-line help file with diagnostic information.

MacEKG from MicroMat is is an interesting tool for diagnosing Apple Macintosh computers because it actually talks through the speaker to you. This is basically a diagnostic tool for a system engineer. However, the pertinent utilities are useful for establishing system-level performance benchmarks. On the other hand, Help! from Technosys represents many of the new tools that analyze system configuration and then generate an analysis of how computer performance can be improved. This tool detects interrupt conflicts, incompatibilities, and duplicate files. It is relevant for tuning system configuration.

Skylight

This MS Windows diagnostic tool from the Renasonce Group extracts configuration information for display and also interprets it with graphical displays and identification labels. In many ways it is similar to QA Plus, Check It, MEM, PSTAT, MAXA, MacEKG, and other diagnotic tools. However, Skylight is different because it identifies WIN.INI and SYSTEM.INI settings, extracts and parses system resource utilitization, and color codes memory conflicts and addresses in use. Although Skylight also provides some predefined tuning suggestions, the most useful aspect of this tool is the accurate and consistent presentation of DOS and MS Windows configuration information.

WinSense

WinSense from SoftLogic Solutions is not the ordinary benchmark. In fact, it is not a benchmark, per se. Rather it analyzes the MS Windows configuration settings as currently defined, interviews the user about how MS Windows is used, and then automatically tunes the configuration. Some items it cannot change; nonetheless, it provides some suggestions on these for a manual reconfiguration. This type of tool is available for OS/2 (Clear & Simple Performance 2.x) and for the Macintosh (Help!), and represents how tuning knowledge can be incorporated into software tools. Given the complexity of most GUI interfaces, we will probably see more tools such as these which automate the configuration and performance tuning process. Figure 3.2 shows WinSense.

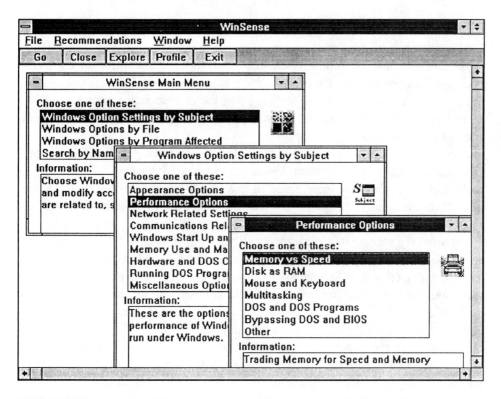

Figure 3.2 WinSense measures MS Windows performance in terms of system configuration settings.

Virus checkers

Viruses can cause system failure or less obvious performance problems. Computer viruses have been created to damage most operating systems, platforms, and even postscript printers. Tools that search for viruses or damage from them are called *virus checkers*. Virus checkers are the tools to "benchmark" and locate infecting viruses, if they exist on the network or computer system. There are a number of shareware and commercial tools that look for specific computer viruses, search for *virus signatures,* or create checksums and verify them against executable file dates and sizes. The variety and complexity of virus checkers is only matched by the complexity and confusion caused by viruses.

Some anti-virus tools *innoculate* the operating system by creating a constantly running filter or background process which checks all disk write activity for the presence of viruses. Norton Utilities provides one such program, while Intel and Western Digital have created controllers with hardware-based algorithms. It is important to realize that such computer programs reduce overall system performance and may also cause other side effects which decrease performance.

Source code profiler

It is worthwhile to test applications that are frequently run and command a significant portion of computing resources. Tools that analyze where the CPU time goes when an application is run are called *source code profilers*. These tools run the actual executable code while showing you the corresponding source code line by line as it is run. Obviously, in order to profile the application, you need to have access to the source code.

Code profilers are available for most dialects of C language, COBOL, and significant database programming languages, such as Sybase and Oracle. Some tools may even chart the percentage of time each module is executed. This is important information because you want to optimize the performance of the functions, subroutines, and modules that run most frequently. You rarely want to spend time on a module that is clearly inefficient, but runs only once per day. That is, of course, unless that single module runs once all day and takes all day to run. The typical methods of tuning application performance are to use code force reduction, minimize the number of data file relations, assign file indexes rather than do sequential record lookups, and build more unique indexes to improve application performance. Chapter 5 details application tuning methods.

One note to remember about source code profilers, and also debuggers and debugging statements is that they themselves require system resources. These tools will change how the system functions and how quickly an application will work. They tend to slow both down. More importantly, however, realize that any special features added to an application to profile its operation should be *removed* before the application is returned to the operational environment. Otherwise, unnecessary code may further degrade what had been already deemed a performance problem.

Trace

Trace shows what system calls are made and the value of the parameters passed. This tool is useful for exploring how the kernel is used, what calls are made to libraries, and how the shared libraries start up. This is a primitive command, but it is generally available on all versions of UNIX. It works with any application but provides only information available at the OS-level.

Quantify

If you have the source code, Quantify from Pure Software is an enhanced version of the UNIX trace command for Sun Microsystems SunOS. You must have the source code, or at least the unlinked code modules to use Quantify. This benchmarking tool profiles the portions of an application that dominate its execution time. Output is in two formats; percentages of execution time by procedure, and a graphical display showing the path through the program with the critical performance path displayed in greater thickness. It extracts call sequences, machine cycles consumed for each function, and time spent while the operating system services the application. The graphical display is useful because it shows where performance time is spent. It is not a true critical path since it does not show performance limitations and paths lacking slack time. Nonetheless, this is an unrivaled tool for tuning application performance.

For example, as Chapter 5 details, you should explore where applications are bottlenecks. That is not always feasible. As a proxy, you can discover where an application uses the most resources and optimize there. Quantify certainly shows that. Quantify will show the effects of optimizing compilers—which do not always optimize—and it will show the effects provided by RISC processing instruction scheduling where asynchronous operations are performed in parallel for performance gain. Lastly, Quantify will also let you model other platforms or computers still years away from availability to explore the performance effects of different performance designs, caches, disk speeds, and software architectures.

Shareware and public domain tools

Many trade magazines create benchmarks in order to review platforms and operating systems within an unbiased format. These benchmarks are published and made freely available so that vendors and users can compare their systems with the published results. The free availability is important to the process and to maintaining the fairness and honesty of the benchmark. On the other hand, if a benchmark becomes an important measuring stick, as the WinMark millions of pixels per second in MS Windows has become, vendors modify their products to skew the results. In fact, several Windows video accelerator card manufacturers have already included code in hardware that dramatically improves WinMark benchmark results without providing any significant performance advantage.

Although it would be desirable to renew and upgrade these important benchmarks frequently to defeat attempts at bypassing or subverting them, the reality is that the benchmarks must be freely available for assessment and provide a useful life span so that measurements made today can be compared faithfully with those of a year ago. One important example that endured for about eight years as the PC compatibility benchmark was Flight Simulator from SubLogic. At its introduction it was just a fun game that many people had, it was widely available, and it refused to run on many PC clones. This software application wrote directly to memory, to screen, and to disk in order to bypass the slow parts of the operating system. It was useful as a compatibility test because it would not run on many machines with data bus speeds, clock-doubled or CPU "turbo" modes, and other special features.

WinMark and WinBench

Ziff-Davis Laboratories provides a standard benchmark suite for measuring the performance of MS Windows on a PC, the performance of CPUs, and the performance of networks. These tests are called *WinBench, CPU benchmarks*, and *NetBench*. The WinBench tests are designed specifically to measure the performance capacities of the computer components. This includes CPU throughput and capacity, disk, and video. The *WinMark* subset of WinBench results specifically refers to the video speed; it is represented by the millions of pixels per second that can be displayed under MS Windows. The CPU benchmark measures the relative capacity of different Intel-compatible CPUs. NetBench is protocol-independent and generates block reads and writes across the network to ascertain its speed and performance.

Dhrystones

The Dhrystone test is a standardized program that stresses the calculation capability of the CPU and the speed of RAM. It was initially designed as a means to test UNIX systems, but the source code has been ported to different platforms so that reasonable comparisons can be made between different types of hardware and software environments. This test performs integer-based calculations iteratively and counts the number of completed Dhrystone calculations per second. Results are usually presented in thousands. The Dhrystone benchmark is included on the tools disk both as a DOS and MS Windows executable program and as C source code for compiling on other platforms. Note that the source code includes some benchmark values for about 60 different systems, including VAX 11/785 and Pyramid 90x.

Whetstones

The Whetstone test is another traditional test that stresses the calculation capability of the CPU and the speed of RAM. It was initially designed as a means to test UNIX systems, but the source code has been ported to different platforms so that reasonable comparisons can be made between different types of hardware and software environments. While similar to the Dhrystone test, it differs in that emphasis is placed upon floating-point operations rather than upon integer arithmetic. Results are provided in terms of thousands of calculations per second.

MacMeter

This graphical tool displays CPU utilization and load statistics much as PS and STAT do on many UNIX systems. This desk accessory is for Apple Macintosh computers only. The most recent version of this shareware is found on many dial-in bulletin board services, such as CompuServe.

MIPS

The number of instructions per second is sometimes useful as a rough measure of system performance. Since most computers can perform *millions of instructions per second* (MIPS), results are usually presented in this scale. Since this is a CPU and memory test, other tests, such as a Dhrystone or Whetstone, are usually normalized to provide a MIPS benchmark. This test is interesting in that you can make some cross-platform comparisons, but it does not account for the bus speeds and architectural designs of different platforms. Comparison of a PC and a VAX 11/760 is really not too useful when comparing server throughput or execution of CAD software. The bus and data storage capacities are very different, and the applications which run on each type of platform tend to be different. On the other hand, comparison of a 486 SX, 486 DLC, and a 486 DX/2 is relevant.

Network performance index

The network performance index is a good statistic to compare NIC, server (or workstation), and CPU performance. The network performance index is network bandwidth utilization divided by the CPU utilization. This statistic is primarily referenced when manufacturers or magazines are profiling bus-mastering network adapters because statistic shows whether the NIC or the CPU is the bottleneck.

Sieve of Erastosthenes

This is a traditional test which uses a well-known algorithm to generate a sequence of prime numbers. This test usually completes too quickly on most computers to be of practical utility. Completion times are under a second, and the granularity and accuracy of the results is insufficient to provide meaningful information.

Speedometer

This utility tests most aspects of Apple Macintosh performance and contracts these to other stock Apple computers. This tool provides a graphic comparison of different machine speeds, much the same way as the Dhrystones only with very intuitive bar graphs. The most recent version of this shareware is found on many dial-in bulletin board services, such as CompuServe.

UNIX SPEC SDM

The SPEC (System Performance Evaluation Cooperative) Software Development Multitasking benchmark suite measures overall system capacity within a multitasking UNIX environment. It exercises CPU, memory, disk I/O, and operating system services. It tests a workload on a server and increases that workload to characterize the addition of more clients or processes. Results show peak performances and a relative measure of throughput. The workload does not necessarily correspond to a realistic workload as might be observed in your organization; this is merely a measure to compare and contrast the qualities of different UNIX systems.

Ghardenstone

Novell Laboratories has released a benchmark based upon actual workload characteristics in a LAN environment. This network benchmark deviates from the application of simple and repetitive block transfers and file copies to stress and test the networks, as is common in network testing with tools like Ziff-Davis

NetBench. This tool aims to overcome the shortcomings of most performance testing based upon CPU horsepower and simple and repetitive operations; instead, this benchmark creates bursts and fluctuating test loads. The goal of the Ghardenstone benchmark is to assess the performance of servers and the network channel within the framework of the LAN. The object is to test performance on a day in the true life of a LAN and its servers.

IBM LAN Performance Group

The LAN Server and LAN Performance Group have a test "engine" that runs actual client scripts (macros) on graphical stations and text-based stations to compare the performance of servers. These scripts invoke Lotus 1-2-3, WordPerfect, FoxBase, cc:Mail, and other common office environment applications. They also perform the traditional block transfers and file copies, although the scripts are expected to get more complex and to be representative of real-world server and network workloads.

SCSI Evaluator

This Apple Macintosh tool tests raw disk speeds and SCSI disk transfer rates. This utility is similar to the DiagSoft Power Meter, the Quantum disk test tool, and other disk seek, latency, and transfer performance analysis tools. This shareware is found on many dial-in bulletin board services which specialize in Apple Macintosh computers, or large commercial services such as Online America, Genie, and CompuServe.

EXESIZE

Another useful C/C++ code profiler is called EXESIZE.EXE. This tool searches for unreferenced functions, compiler or linker oversights, use of functions, features, or modes not necessary with MS Windows, and internal memory management. Best of all, this utility is available from many dial-in bulletin board services which specialize in applications development. Since this application was profiled in a Microsoft System Journal article,[3] you can locate this utility on CompuServe in the Microsoft Developers Forum.

Other benchmarks

Other interesting benchmarks include SPEC SDM, AIM Milestone, AIM III, X11, and PERF for measuring CASE-built applications; Linpack for assessing CAD; TPC-A, TPC-B, and TPC-C for measuring relative database performance; AIM III, NHfsstone, and AIM Milestone for assessing server performance; and SPECrate_int, SPECint, SPECfp, SPECrate_fp, and Linpack for general-purpose relative calculation capacities.

---

[3]*Liposuction Your Corpulent Executables and Remove Excess Fat,* Pietrek, Matt, Microsoft Systems Journal, July 1993.

Multiuser systems

Typically, multiuser systems include useful and informative performance measuring tools. While such tools are generally lacking in personal and single-user systems, this is not so for AS/400, AIX, or UNIX. Basically, these systems were designed for time-sharing, multiuser, multiprocessing, time-slicing, or threaded operations. As such, there has always been substantial need to track active processes, virtual memory, paging faults, and CPU activity. Almost every factor of these operating systems can be documented, measured, and analyzed.

If anything, too much performance information can be gathered for these operating systems. In such cases, establish clear objectives before trying the many different data capture and analysis tools. You do not want to be overwhelmed or sidetracked by power of tools, such as IOSTAT, NFSSTAT, TIME, TRACE, VMSTAT, PSTAT, PS, PROF, SAR, and MBUF. These tools track CPU utilization, I/O statistics, virtual memory and paging utilization, network usages, active processes, process priorities, what processes are actually using CPU resources, disk reads, writes, kernel processes, queue lengths, and activity logs.

System settings

Some of the software on the included tools disk tests system configurations. This information can be useful to ascertain how memory is configured, the reliability of that memory, what types of hard disks and controllers are in the system, the speed of the disk subsystem, and the quality of the hard disks. While most of the system tests are basically diagnostic in nature, they are nonetheless useful. A system that has bad memory and causes parity errors will tend to provide poor performance. A system with disks that are developing bad sectors will decrease other performance. Commercial tools that do this include Micro House's *DrivePro*, Norton Utilities *Calibrate* and *Disk Doctor*, and the previously mentioned DiagSoft *QA Plus/FE*.

Since it is far easier to fix a real system problem than to improve performance, it is worthwhile trying the software included with this book to check your system, or acquiring a commercial diagnostic package to qualify your systems. Test your systems. These tools are also useful for creating system and disk performance benchmarks for different configurations. This may include how RAM is split between device drivers, caches, spoolers, RAM disks, and other system configurations. The results can tell you which disk cache works better, whether a hardware disk cache is faster than a software cache, and what effects having a large cache can have on computer system performance.

UART tests

Older model PCs, including the original IBM PC XT, came with a serial controller port chip called the 8250 series *Universal Asynchronous Receiver/Transmitter* (UART). This chip has a small data buffer—1 byte. This was subsequently changed to the 14550 series chip with the introduction of the IBM PC AT to support a wider bandwidth. Unfortunately, this chip has a design defect and has been installed by most PC-compatible manufacturers because it is significantly less expensive than other alternatives. The newer 16550 series chip includes a 16 kB buffer which best for high-speed communications in a multitasking environment.

If your system is a PC and you connect to other modems at speeds above 9600 bits/s from within a multitasking environment, this might be a valid concern. If you frequently find the connection dropped, consider testing for the older chips. Commercial services at 1200 to 9600 bits/s generally do not warrant the newer chip. Note that many internal modems bypass the system's built-in serial ports. See the CHK_UART utility on the included tool disk to test the UART configuration of a PC without opening up the case.

Conclusion

Benchmarks and testing tools are critical for defining the important performance characteristics, gathering performance information, building relative and comparable benchmark data, and providing the means to make applicable performance evaluations. You will need to confirm your bottleneck hypotheses before embarking on the process of tuning a computer or network. Benchmarks provide the underlying information to pinpoint them. It will help you differentiate slow networks from slow client/server processing, a bus-bound server from a disk-bound client, and an overloaded server from overloaded clients.

If you are building a PERT or critical path model, the model will need path information, timings, and purposes. Those path values do not come from thin air. Furthermore, benchmarks provide the only effective means to assess the optimization effort. You will need to know if the computer system performance is actually better, that performance levels are going in the right direction—or for that matter, actually changing. Too often, optimization based upon improper performance evaluations yields minimal or even negative effects.

Without the benchmark measuring stick, you will be unable to gauge computer system changes. Chapter 4 now explains when to use benchmarks, which benchmarks to use, and how to gather information to locate computer system performance bottlenecks, and optimize single-user stand-alone performance.

4

Optimizing Performance

Introduction

This chapter presents general techniques of performance optimization as well as some specific methods for improving local station (stand-alone) performance. Because bottlenecks on local stations may relate specifically to server delays and network problems, the next three chapters present both general and concise methods for computers running client (requester) processes and networked applications. This chapter focuses strictly on issues of stand-alone, single-user performance improvement. The key topics presented in this chapter are listed here.

- Generalized optimization techniques
- Optimization tools
- Optimizing hard disks
- Increasing I/O channel speed
- Increasing CPU speed
- Memory allocation and management
- Improving work methods

The process of optimizing a local station—whether it is a DOS-based PC, a UNIX workstation, or some other similar computer—depends significantly on configuration, purpose, and goal. Here is a word of caution: You optimize what you seek to optimize. This is true whether or not you have picked the correct goal, interpreted the benchmarks results correctly, or identified true sources of performance bottlenecks.

For example, if you assume that video display and refresh is the bottleneck because of all the published WinMark benchmark scores and vendor video-card promotion, and therefore install one highly rated enhanced display adapter, the result may disappoint you. Simply because a system's video performance is faster in a standard benchmark, it does not follow that your application will run faster. Video redisplay will be faster for specialized tasks (which you may not need at all) and perhaps even slower than originally observed for your application because of tradeoffs made to optimize certain types of performance over others.

If you optimize a process path that is not the bottleneck, you will see no performance improvement. If you optimize a process path that is an active bottleneck and expect a 10 percent speed gain because you increase that component's speed by 10 percent, consider these two qualifications. First, adding slack to the current bottleneck may only cause another component to become the active bottleneck. Second, improving performance of a single component by 10 percent does not always provide a direct correlation with computational results. It is true that this component will perform a task 10 percent faster. Since this component represents one path of many and is only a linking path, the project is unlikely to be 10 percent faster. More likely, while this previously critical path may possibly complete 10 percent faster, some of the 10 percent path savings may become slack time. In other words, other paths may become critical paths with this enhancement. Figure 4.1 illustrates this concept.

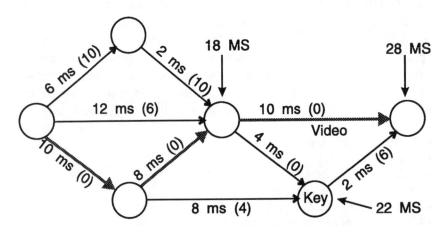

Figure 4.1 Enhancing a component creating a bottleneck on a project may provide full or partial benefits depending upon whether that affected path now has slack time. A 10 percent improvement on the video path may reflect a 1-ms performance boost to that path—from 10 ms to 9 ms—and lower overall project completion time from 28 ms to 27 ms. This is only a 3.5 percent boost to overall project completion time.

Before haphazardly tuning a system, consider that there are always other options that may yield better results. You should know what results to expect from your efforts. Correlate that with the effort undertaken to improve performance. You should answer the questions of why you need to tune the system if it is not broken, and who will provide the time and materials for the tuning process.

Generalized optimization techniques

The most effective technique—bar none—for optimizing overall computer system performance is to minimize the workload on the system. You will find it easier to reduce the load on the system than to make a current set of tasks run significantly faster. Stop background tasks. Run batch operations after peak hours. Hire a person to perform data backup early in the morning, late at night, or on weekends. Consider moving multitasked operations to another computer. The slower, older, hand-me-down models with $300 or less resale value may no longer be suitable at all for anyone lower in the hardware food chain in your organization. Alternatively, they may be perfect for making distribution floppies, driving a plotter or printer, managing the incoming faxes or E-mail, or providing the on-line services that were running as resource-consuming background icons. An enhanced computer system may not perform better than the original *and* a second, slow system together. The rest of this section summarizes generalized techniques for optimizing various systems to help you get started quickly; it may replicate some of the information detailed in the other major sections later in this chapter.

Increase RAM

Random access memory (RAM) is the large block of main memory in a computer system. Increase it. Memory is inexpensive relative to other performance optimizing methods; adding more memory provides the most bang for the buck. This is true for PCs, Macintoshes, engineering workstations, and proprietary platforms. Operations bound by memory include GUI-intensive paging, image processing, sorting and database operations, and multiprocessing and threaded applications. The working set of memory in most GUI or multitasking systems applies a linear model of memory (unlike the partitioned 640-kB, 384-kB, and above 1024-kB segments on MS and PC DOS) with system resources, nonresident operating system kernels, heaps, and demand-load blocks. These blocks contain transient code, data, and memory objects. Even word processing and spreadsheets may be limited by the extent of the document or formulas which fit within memory at any one time.

For example, while a 30-kB document is not an issue, a 1.6-MB magnum opus will not fit within the 585-kB working memory available to DOS word processing code and data. If the application can support expanded or extended memory, perhaps adding 2 MB of memory will improve performance substantially. Also, consider the most effective alternative of reducing the workload; break the mammoth document into manageable chapters. Do not keep multiple documents open in different windows or keep multiple instances of an application running simultaneously.

On engineering workstations, sufficient memory will speed processing of software compilation by maintaining the full symbol tables in memory. Processing of CAD objects and graphic images is significantly enhanced when all the entities or the entire image can be retained in RAM rather than on the disk. Paging to disk to swap portions from memory and replace them with other portions is at least 200 times slower.

When that is not possible, as with large CAD designs, databases, or graphic images, adding memory is the correct approach. If a large database or CAD image can be cached in memory, effective performance may improve more than three times. More memory improves performance. There is a decreasing utility for adding more memory, as Figure 4.2 illustrates. Eventually, more memory will yield no further measurable benefits. Benchmarks show you when adding more memory has no further utility.

Performance

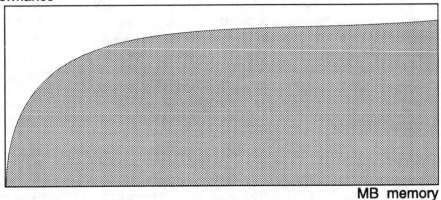

MB memory

Figure 4.2 Performance improves dramatically when memory is first added, but adding further memory has a declining utility.

Lack of usable RAM is characteristic of MS DOS. After the 67 kB operating system is loaded, about 580 kB is free. Special device drivers, network operating systems, and TSRs for file and print redirection take a toll too. Often, about 380 kB is all that is left for a DOS application, far too little for many applications and the in-progress large data sets or documents. Many memory managers, such as QEMM, Headroom, 386MAX, ToTheMAX, MEMMaker (which comes with MS DOS 6.0), and others will free an additional 100 MB of RAM. Also, by loading DOS HIGH and loading drivers or TSRs into high memory—that 384 kB space between 640 kB and 1 MB—it is possible to create a contiguous DOS segment as large as 736 kB. Some vendors claim as much as 801 MB with older versions of MS DOS. If you raise the DOS ceiling with memory from the VGA ranges, attempts to access the VGA graphics mode tend to crash the system. Since MS Windows is not really functional without at least the minimum VGA resolution (EGA is very restricting), raising the DOS ceiling to 600 kB is quite good. You can minimize the use of STACKS, LASTDRIVE, FILES, and BUFFERS. Eliminate the EMS page frame. Add the UMBFILES to increase DOS space by about 2 kB.[1]

This memory limbo dancing is extraordinary when it works. The configuration is complex and the likelihood for conflicts and compatibility problems is significant. There also is a question about reliability and system stability. Frequently, MS Windows and DOS applications will cease suddenly or behave erratically when memory usage overlaps the same ranges. This is the hallmark of the risk embodied by memory managers. When RAM limitations severely constrain your operations, consider these tools as a last resort. However, consider that their complexity is suboptimal and while they may create more free RAM, this usually comes with a tradeoff in speed of performance. Furthermore, the segmented memory structure of DOS is a historical artifact that will disappear as operating systems become more complex and inclusive of the basic system utilities, applets, and facilities.

Restart the computer system

Heap management, garbage collection, and working set coalescence or compaction represent the process of recycling and rearranging system resources into the largest single free memory space. While UNIX and OS/2 are quite efficient at this, and allocate memory without vestiges that hang around, Windows 3.x is not. Furthermore, many applications—including applications for DOS, OS/2, UNIX, Windows, and particularly X Windows—do not return allocated resources and release all reserved memory areas when they terminate. They *leak* memory. This is a problem with Beta software and operating system releases and upgrades when compatibility is not perfect. This is true in Windows, and it is true of complex MS DOS applications as well. If you notice that memory seems to be lost, that the largest free memory block is smaller than at system initialization, or that system resources are low, restart the computer. Reboot the computer after running resource-intensive applications and before running other resource-intensive applications. Figure 4.3 shows the 200,000-kB artifact gaps in memory utilization.

Before reaching the conclusion that memory is fragmented and cannot be recovered, ascertain that all tasks are terminated, including resident and background tasks. Halt operations as required by the operating system. Then, reboot. You do not want to leave files and buffers opened and in a fragile state. Furthermore, you do not want to leave cached writes in volatile RAM before they are written to the hard drive.

Also, many devices may support more RAM than they currently have. Video controllers, caching disk controllers, and printers generally have sockets or slots

---

[1] *Maximizing Memory Under DOS 6.0*, Prosise, Jeff, *PC Magazine*, August, 1993.

for adding memory. Even if these expansion points seem filled, check with the vendor to see if the devices support chips with higher densities. High-resolution and 24-bit true color may not perform well until they have enough memory to support the full image. Older PCs with SVGA cards may have only 256 kB of memory; they do support 1024 x 760—but not well without 1 MB of fast *SRAM* (static RAM) or *VRAM* (virtual RAM). Similarly, printing images to a laser printer with only 500 kB may be slow (if not impossible). Postscript printers, which receive streams of data and instructions and process these within memory, are particularly vulnerable to insufficient memory bottlenecks.

```
+----------------------------------------------------------------------+
|                  Memory utilization by major component               |
+----------------------------------------------------------------------+
|      Component          Length        200kb       400kb       600kb  |
+----------------------------------------------------------------------+
| Memory in use by DOS       12416                                     |
| Memory in use by drivers   51088   ■■                                |
| Memory available for use  496784   ■■■■■■■■■■■■■■■■■■■■■■■            |
| Largest block available   215536   ■■■■■■■■■■■                       |
| QMAP executable size       81248   ■■■                               |
| Largest contiguous avail  296784   ■■■■■■■■■■■■■■                     |
+----------------------------------------------------------------------+
```

Figure 4.3 Portions of memory not returned to DOS after running and completing a DOS-based application.

UART and serial caches

If the Universal Asynchronous Receiver/Transmitter (UART) serial controller port chip in a PC is series 8250, 14550, or 16540 and you experience poor performance with serial communications, replace it with a newer 16550 series chip. This newer chip—it costs approximately $13—includes a 16-kB buffer which improves performance with high-speed modems or communications under multitasking operations. It is not always necessary to replace the serial controller chip on the motherboard; the only time this is necessary is when communications are routed through the standard serial ports. Use the utilities described in Chapter 3 and included on the tools disk.

Alternatively, adapter cards with the same or comparable serial controllers will perform comparable high-speed and multitasking communications. For example, it is possible to install and control up to four modems in a typical PC with a multitasking system and a true multitasking communications package such as DCA Crosstalk. This is possible since each modem has a different port address; it is not possible to maintain multiple connections if only 1 byte of data is buffered with older UART chips. Note, serial boards (without a modem) with a 16550 UARTs are available for about $35. Therefore, if you communicate with a bus-based adapter board and you are experiencing communication bottlenecks and reliability problems, explore the possibility that this card has an outdated UART chip. Replace the card, its chip, or the chip on the motherboard.

Older PCs are not the only systems that may become overloaded due to *normal* serial I/O. UNIX TTY was optimized for terminal support at 9600 bits/s. It is not the best communications server platform. Modem lines, facsimile support, graphics printing, and image scanning support through standard serial ports will create a CPU and bus gridlock because of the TTY port bottleneck. Graphics I/O under UNIX is better supported by SCSI and SCSI-2 devices. You will need to explore fax, voice mail, and E-mail performance under UNIX for each platform, operating system, and peripheral device. There is no set of techniques other than to explore system utilization with system performance measurement tools such as IOSTAT, PS, PROF, NETSTAT, and trace-type tools.

Modem speeds and protocols

Standard voice line WAN connections require modems at each end to establish a digital data connection. Speeds vary from the outmoded low speed of 110 bits/s to about 14,400 bits/s. Most modem links are established at 2400 bits/s, although increasingly, most users and services are switching to 9600 bits/s because it is far more cost effective and much faster. There are also modem protocols that provide for bit error correction and on-the-fly data compression. CCITT defines these protocols; the following are a sampling of ones in common use: V.22 at 2400 bits/s; V.32 at 9600 bits/s; V.32bis at 14,400 bits/s; V.42 supports error correction (prevents losses by requesting retransmissions); V.42bis supports maximum compression to 57,600. Realistically, transfer rates of 24,000 bits/s are realizable. V.32terbo and V.Fast represent emerging standards. V.32terbo provides base speeds to 28,800 bits/s with up to 115,200 bits/s with V.42bis data compression. V.Fast provides base speeds from 14,400 to 19,200 bits/s with up to 76,800 bits/s with V.42bis data compression.

However, when two modems establish a connection, they must negotiate the highest modulation and standard which they both have in common. This is not the fastest speed one modem supports but is based upon the fastest speed and protocol both have in common. Often modems essentially supporting the same protocol and connection speed but from different manufacturers, may communicate only with inferior protocols and speeds. Additionally, line noise and glitches tends to slow transmission with no hope of restoring the speed to higher initial values. As a result, the best methods to optimize modem connections is to acquire the fastest modems available from the same manufacturer and to work with a common carrier to make certain you have reliable and noise-free connections. Also, for WAN connections that are established daily and for long periods of time, monitor the line speed. When connection speeds fall, break that connection and try to reestablish a new one at the highest possible speed again. While not pertinent for most organizations, you might also consider acquiring compatible pairs of modems supporting the Microcom MNP 10 protocol. MNP 10 dynamically adjusts for line noise, will initiate a connection on a noisy line and increases speed accordingly if the line stabilizes. Rural, cellular, or international laptop users benefit most, however. MNP 10 works for both data communications and fax transmission.

If your organization maintains virtually continuous modem connections, consider replacing the analog or voice-based link with a digital connection. Digital connections tend to provide a minimum speed of 9600 bits/s. Most lines are established for 56 kbits/s for the same monthly cost as 9600 bits/s today. ISDN provides two 56 kbits/s for asynchronous data transmission, and frame relay provides speeds in multiples of 56 kbits/s. The equipment is different. You will need CSU/DSU devices in place of modems, but you are trading slow dial-up connection times, busy lines, central offices, varying line speeds, and line noise for instantaneous digital connections.

Add another CPU

Coprocessors and multiple CPUs enhance performance of multiprocessing, concurrent processing, and threaded operations. Since most computer systems will show an average CPU load of around 20 percent, undertake this upgrade only when performance benchmarking shows that the CPU represents the critical path without slack. Also, ascertain that your hardware and operating system can utilize the additional CPUs. When the CPU is heavily utilized, Figure 4.4 shows the effects of incremental CPUs in a networked, multiuser, client/server environment.

Symmetric CPU performance

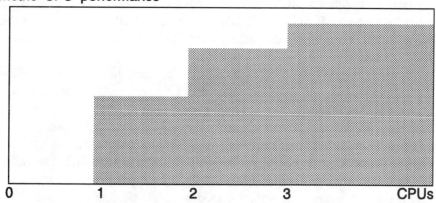

Figure 4.4 Additional multiprocessors increase CPU capacity and incrementally improve overall performance with a declining utility for each added processor.

Note that there are performance differences for asymmetric and symmetric multiprocessing, also for special add-in coprocessing hardware, and you may see performance *degradation* instead of improvements. In some cases, multiple processors yield slower performance because the overhead of dividing and threading the process requires substantially more CPU time than the process itself. This is an example from Windows NT Advanced Server. The built-in utility, Performance Monitor, shows that Symmetric multiprocessing under Windows NT provides about 30 percent performance improvement for about 75 percent of benchmarks, and about 10 to 20 percent performance degradation for 25 percent of benchmark tests. This degradation comprises disk subsystem bottlenecks and the overhead involved in trying to coprocess sequential numerical tasks.[2] Although most benchmarks do not characterize real work loads very well, realize that multiprocessing or coprocessing is not a panacea for improving performance of simple applications and straightforward tasks.

Under *asymmetric processing,* the workload on a system or server is directed to the different CPUs by a prearranged formula that usually has no bearing upon the actual workload. Under *symmetric processing,* the workload is balanced across all the CPUs based upon CPU utilization; ideally, extra workload would be balanced equally among additional processors, as is the case with symmetric coprocessing. The *dual processor* IBM PS/2 295 splits workload under OS/2 and LAN Server such that one CPU handles OS/2 and user applications while the second CPU handles NOS and network traffic. Windows NT and UNIX (depending on variant) support symmetric multitasking and workload balancing.

Some add-in processors may be specialized for background or multitasking modem and fax capabilities, scalar or matrix processing, or numerical floating-point processing. Unless you need these specialized tools—and the software supports them as well—they will not affect performance. Recall, too, that the CPU must be the bottleneck at least some of the time for you to realize a practical benefit from adding another CPU or upgrading to a system that supports dual or multiple CPUs. In many cases, though, two or more processors may have none or even a detrimental effect on overall throughput and process completion speed. The master CPU may spend more CPU cycles determining how to delegate the work than in actually performing the work that it once did alone.

Upgrade the CPU

Newer generations of CPUs tend to outperform prior processors by 30 to 80 percent. Intel is positioning the Pentium chip as 1.3 times faster than the fastest 486 processor, and up to 1.8 times faster when applications have been recompiled and optimized for true 32-bit operation. The installed base of computing hardware tends not to benefit from faster chips; the architecture of many motherboards is ill-suited for CPU replacements or add-in cards. Subsystems, the actual wiring architecture, memory speeds, wait states, bus speeds, and disk performance are not always adequate to support a faster CPU.

Consider carefully the effects of replacing CPUs in older system boards; some of the newer chips require more power and create more resulting waste heat than the infrastructure can support. Under such conditions, power fluctuations will be more destabilizing and excess heat will tend to damage the new CPU and surrounding chips. Added heat sinks or powered muffin fans do not always

---

[2]*First Looks: Microsoft Windows NT Advanced Server,* Gunnerson, Gary, *PC Magazine,* September 28, 1993.

provide sufficient surface cooling; fans may also add decibels of unwanted noise. Also, the Intel Overdrive chip sockets and zero insertion force (ZIF) sockets were designed into systems prior to any availability of chips to fit those sockets; as such, the Overdrive route may not be a viable upgrade option. The clock-doubled or clock-tripled chips generate more heat than some systems can tolerate. These chips may include chip-mounted fans that are taller than a motherboard or case can accommodate. The fan is called a *thermal cooling module* or a *TCM.* They may also generate radio frequencies that exceed FCC Class B or even the less strict Class A requirements.

While AMD, Cyrix, TI, Buffalo Products, and others are providing pin-compatible substitutes with some enhanced performance, the performance gains must be evaluated against your observed bottlenecks. Chips providing Intel 486- and Pentium-type performance in 286 or 386 semiconductor packaging do not necessarily provide full compatibility. Specifically, numerical and floating-point coprocessing may have been excluded so that the chip could fit the smaller preexisting socket. Also, instruction, data, bus, and other I/O channels may be limited to the 8 or 16 bits provided with the smaller footprint. CPU performance will tend to be faster with these newer chips through advanced logic and more frequent clock cycles. As such, CPU-intensive activities such as database and spreadsheet calculations will be enhanced while I/O operations will tend to experience limited improvement.

Many applications, particularly older applications, can run more slowly on a faster processor. While Intel provides a usually consistent upgrade path, there are some pitfalls. Specifically, IBM- and TI-licensed DLC and SLC variants do not include floating-point hardware, run with a slower clock or optionally slow the clock to conserve power, and come on suboptimal motherboards. Also the upgrade path for ASIC and RISC (reduced instruction set chip) is filled with compromises. Some instructions optimized for one-cycle completion can require several clock cycles on newer chips. This can be a function of which instructions are hard-wired on the new generation of chips and which commands are further decomposed into elemental instructions for the new processor. Additionally, the timing requirements when parsing instructions for parallel processing may preclude an application from running faster on new CPUs. In fact, some applications do run slower on the Intel Pentium chip than they do on 486-series chips, as the next chapter explains. The interrelationship between CPUs, bus traffic management and signal arbitration, system hardware components, compilers, and storage subsystems increases the complexity of CPU-based performance optimization. Do not merely assume that because some applications—as well as those which a manufacturer compiles into a benchmark— run faster on a newer CPU or upgraded platform yours will too. That is false logic and incomplete computer performance analysis.

In fact, early systems based upon Pentium chips have not necessarily been optimized for the new processor. Some manufacturers take shortcuts merely in order to get a Pentium-based machine to market before competitors. Some

Pentium systems do not have full 64-bit data paths, a Level 2 (write-back rather than write-through) cache, or a local bus video path. Furthermore, due to a manufacturing defect, Pentium systems utilizing early Intel Mercury PCI chips do not provide the Level 2 cache. Interaction between the PCI and EISA buses on Pentiums with both also decrease overall performance by 50 percent because of the need for wait states and synchronization between the dueling buses. Design defects and shortcuts also slow the performance of other PC-clones and workstations, including Intel-based, RISC, and PowerPC machines.

CPU performance can be increased by merely replacing the clock crystal on the system motherboard. This clock doubling, clock tripling, or crystal timing change approach is not for the faint of heart or those with access to a single computer. Although many vendors sell systems with "pushed" chips, they are not reliable. The alteration voids warrantees of CPUs and motherboards, increases overheating problems, and causes applications with critical driver timing to fail in unexpected ways. Some applications will fail to work at all.

Add-in coprocessor cards that work instead of, or in conjunction with, the motherboard CPU provide substantial performance gains for applications that were formally CPU-bound. While add-in cards with a 486 CPU that utilizes existing 286 or 386 motherboard memory improve performance of complex spreadsheet calculation, AutoCAD, or MathCAD, you may create new bus and memory channel bottlenecks at this higher level of CPU operation.

When CPU upgrade is possible and seems to provide substantial enhancements, consider instead substituting those key systems for turnkey replacements. The net cost in terms of hardware, software, labor, and time is apt to be reduced. Sell the old systems or hand down the hardware *food chain*. Consider the cost versus the benefits. Typically, a new system will cost only 25 percent more than upgrading an existing system—and you now have the benefit of two working systems. If you choose to upgrade an existing system, and do not plan to completely upgrade all aspects of the hardware, consider the cost and benefits of upgrading only the CPU and simply relocating the bottleneck to the bus or disk. A new system may provide better reliability, warrantees, on-site service, and costs only about 25 percent more than a new CPU, more RAM, a faster disk drive and controller, and an energy-saving power supply. Additionally, the added expense for the new system provides at least 100 percent performance improvement by virtue of having *two* working computers instead of one.

Also note that some CPU substitutions are better than others depending upon workload characterization. For example, upgrading the CPU on a 486 33-MHz server to a 50-MHz may provide better service than replacing that chip with the DX66/2 66-MHz chip. The reason for this disparity is that the external communication clock speed for the 66-MHz chip is 20 to 33 MHz, and therefore the *slower* 50-MHz chip with a 50-MHz bus will provide *faster* I/O.

Some vendors refer to coprocessors or CPU-upgrades instead as *accelerators*. There is a lively market for accelerators for PCs and Macintoshes. Specifically,

Kensington, Kingston Memory Products, and Buffalo Products provide CPU upgrades in the form of pin-compatible replacements for the CPU, or as plug circuit boards that replace, bypass, or augment the original CPU in PC-based systems. Radius, Applied Engineering, DayStar Digital produce expansion boards with Motorola 68040 and 68030 chips and RAM to augment Macintosh performance to the Quadra-level. Envisio provides a JPEG compression coprocessor to offload CPU-intensive processing of compression and decompression of graphic files; although this NuBus card is not a CPU substitution, it provides an effective means to better graphic processing performance and creation of QuickTime movies.

Add cache

Either add a hardware cache *or* install caching software. The most effective application is for caching hard disks and CD-ROMs. A Speedcache+ cache (for MS DOS and Windows) turned an "antiquated" Seagate ST4096 with a seek time of 28 ms into a disk with average seek times of 14 ms. Consider that not all caches are equivalent. For example, MS SMARTDRV improved that Seagate disk performance only to 22 ms. Most disk caches provide read buffers; some provide write buffering as well. This *lazy-write* option improves I/O performance by delaying disk writes until the CPU is idle or has free capacity. Consider that the buffered data changes are maintained in volatile memory until they are actually written to the disk; this represents a slight risk of data loss or file corruption.

While cache does not improve actual disk throughput—that is generally constrained by the speed of the disk, heads, disk controller, and system bus—it will at least double the performance of read- and write-intensive seek operations by minimizing the actual disk head movements. It is important to realize that the additions of more RAM for disk cache increase the cache hit in decreasing efficiency. A cache hit may take 100 ns (1 ms). However, the cost of a cache miss may cost 4 ms to search the cache contents and perform an indirect memory and then *another* 40 ms to seek and fetch the item from disk. Cache is very effective at increasing the speed of CPU and data operations.

The cache hit math is interesting. Increasing the cache hit rate from 30 to 69 percent decreases processing time for 100 requests from 806 ms to 29.9 ms. This is a 2,596 percent performance improvement.[3] Realistically, cache hit rates for a stand-alone station can be increased to an average of 70 percent from nothing (without a cache as is often the case for laptops). The math for increases in hit rates yields station performance improvements of about 10,000 percent. Is that realistic? Not really, although overall you can expect to double disk performance. Before assuming that new hardware and faster CPUs are the answer, consider reconfiguring cache, installing a different cache, or testing a caching controller.

---

[3]*Maximizing the Performance of Your Server*, Derfler, Frank J. Jr. and Schireson, Max, *PC Magazine*, October 26, 1993.

CacheAll from C&D Programming Corporation buffers removable drives, local hard disks, CD-ROMs, and network devices too. It buffers both read and written data. However, caching written network data can be very risky since multiple users may access the same data records frequently and thus maintain outdated copies in their local caches. Local caching of network drives is pertinent when the same data is frequently read from the network. For example, this includes loading application .DLLs or overlays from the server, frequently refreshing CAD drawings or images, or rereading a static master database stored on the network database server.

There are other types of cache too, not just disk or network cache. Panacea provides Winspeed, a set of Windows-optimized video drivers and video cache which provides performance almost indistinguishable from that of high-end graphics cards. The secret is with the optimized drivers. Add more memory to increase cache size. Cache can also be used as output buffers. This would be in addition to augmenting memory for the output device on the output device. Although printing time itself cannot generally be improved, RAM can be allocated to buffer the data flow for the print or drafting job. As a result, the access to applications on the computing system will be returned sooner to the user.

Not all buffers are created alike. Hardware buffers built into stand-alone boxes that are installed between the system and the printer are the most trouble-free and demand the least configuration. Hardware buffers built into adapter cards (such as LaserMaster's Winjet adapters) are outstanding enhancements, not only for the speed improvement provided in the construction and transfer of the page image to the printer, but also for the enhanced resolution provided by these cards. For example, LaserMaster provides up to 1200 DPI with *stock* Hewlett-Packard LaserJet series IV printers and 800 DPI with *original* Canon and Hewlett-Packard LaserJet series II printers. Second-party print queues and print buffers tend to perform better than software provided with the operating system; just make certain that such drivers and logical devices will coexist peacefully with other drivers. PC Qwik provides a software-based printer cache that not only works well, it also compresses the print jobs. Expect to see a 50 percent compression for text and up to 85 percent compression for graphical print jobs. This means that you can queue more print jobs or allocate less RAM to the printer buffer itself. Note, too, that PC Qwik adjusts RAM usage between RAM, cache, and print cache on the fly for even better utilization of scarce MS DOS resources.

Install improved device drivers

Check that the currently installed device drivers are not a bottleneck; memory conflicts are more apt to slow performance than better drivers are to improve performance. Nonetheless, it is clear that tuned drivers that are compatible with the devices, motherboards and configuration, operating system, and applications will perform better. Matrox, IBM, and Panacea show how their optimized video drivers increase overall results on graphic-intensive operations by 10 percent or more. As a side note, Matrox produces an Impression video card that provides exceptional 1024 x 760 24-bit Windows performance. However, its 800 x 600 256-color, which is less memory- and time-intensive than the higher resolution and should have run even faster, ran more slowly than 1024 x 760 24-bit true color, ran more slowly than a standard SVGA card, and more slowly than Panacea. Matrox responded that new drivers, tuned for resolutions and colors other than their specialty, true color, were forthcoming to address these shortcomings. Figure 4.5 compares the WinMark output for different device drivers.

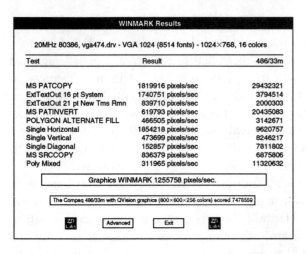

WINMARK Results

20MHz 80386, vga474.drv - VGA 1024 (8514 fonts) - 1024×768, 16 colors

Test	Result	486/33m
MS PATCOPY	1819916 pixels/sec	29432321
ExtTextOut 16 pt System	1740751 pixels/sec	3794514
ExtTextOut 21 pt New Tms Rmn	839710 pixels/sec	2000303
MS PATINVERT	619793 pixels/sec	20435083
POLYGON ALTERNATE FILL	466505 pixels/sec	3142671
Single Horizontal	1854218 pixels/sec	9620757
Single Vertical	473699 pixels/sec	8246217
Single Diagonal	152857 pixels/sec	7811802
MS SRCCOPY	836379 pixels/sec	6875806
Poly Mixed	311965 pixels/sec	11320632

Graphics WINMARK 1255758 pixels/sec.

The Compaq 486/33m with QVision graphics (800×600×256 colors) scored 7478559

| Zb Labs | Advanced | Exit | Zb Labs |

Figure 4.5 Performance variance based upon substitution of different device drivers.

Similarly, OS/2 v2.x provides tuned "seamless" drivers for video that provide a 10 to 35 percent performance boost for graphic-intensive operations (including Windows 3.1 under OS/2). Also of note, running graphic applications under full-screen modes provides up to 33 percent faster completion times than running them under tiled or windowed displays. This is particularly true for OS emulation running under different environments. For example, DOS and Windows run faster under OS/2, SunSoft, and SunOS in full-screen mode. However, this is not always the case. For example, most Sun workstations have a PROM-based terminal emulator that is orders of magnitude slower than a terminal window; use a window instead of full-screen mode.

Also, the Matrox 1024 x 760 256-color drivers had occasional glitches that caused problems with older releases of user applications. Any conflicts between drivers, software or system upgrades, and OS patches will slow I/O, or halt the system. System failures are the ultimate in performance bottlenecks; even one crash can reverse all gains. Such conflicts are difficult to uncover since they occur at such a fundamental level in the operating system. However, occasionally check with device manufacturers, review CompuServe messages and libraries, or call the OS vendor for driver updates. For example, an improved Matrox video driver for MS Windows did address many of the observed application glitches.

Effective device drivers are critical for the new generation of PCs. Epson provided a Progression PC with their Wingine Graphics Accelerator and an Intel 80486 DX 25-MHz CPU for evaluation purposes. The machine did provide outstanding WinMark video results, but average disk scores. Actual work performed on this machine confirmed this discrepancy. However, Epson technical support pointed out the need for a new BIOS chip, better IDE drivers, newer system drivers installed through a flash load process, and some other configuration adjustment. Indeed, overall performance increased 3 percent with this attention.

Old and almost-right drivers

Improved devices drivers do not represent the single performance problem with devices. It is also likely that operating systems are patched or upgraded without thought or action for attached hardware devices. Disk controllers, video display boards, printers, and backup tape devices may not work as well when fundamental software is changed. This is likely to occur with UNIX workstations and PCs particularly, but also other systems and platforms too. For example, you might upgrade MS Windows from version 3.0 to 3.1, or from 3.1 to NT. Did you consider how that might affect the Adaptec SCSI controller and its drivers? How might it affect you if the current devices and drivers are not supported by the new version as frequently happens. Often drivers are hardware platform and operating system dependent. What will work for Sun UNIX will not work or work well for Vines, SCO UNIX, or IBM AIX.

You will want to maintain current drivers for all devices. Old and outdated drivers will usually create compatibility problems, erratic results, and, rarer still, slower than expected performance. Vendor manufacturing may ship new hardware with older drivers. Typically, devices on a system will either work or not work. However, complex devices, such as caching disk controllers and PostScript printers, will provide minor performance benefits with newer drivers. If these devices see substantial service as with disk controller drivers, you may find that even these minor performance benefits are important for you.

PC users should be aware that PC DOS (from IBM) creates hidden system files called IBMBIO.COM and IBMDOS.COM. This differs and is incompatible with the MS DOS files IO.SYS and MSDOS.SYS (from Microsoft). These files end up on floppy disks when you format them as system disks and tend to cause compatibility problems when these disks are used on sneakernets between machines with different versions and releases of DOS. COMMAND.COM also differs in substantial ways.

OS emulation

Although operating system emulation and so-called *compatibility boxes* provide a means to run a different operating system or computer environment, these are not fast. The single exception seems to be PC DOS under OS/2 since it is integrated into the operating system. Otherwise, MS Windows is slower under OS/2 and in

SoftPC or WABI. Insignia's SoftPC is particularly slow since it provides Intel 80286 emulation. SoftWindows, also from Insignia Solutions provides MS Windows compatibility within other UNIX operating systems, but it will still provide 286 emulation. Apple is seeking to provide System 7 operating under PowerOpen on a PowerPC at no more than a 50 percent performance degradation. Disk emulation such as MAC-in-DOS and similar tools do not provide the level of performance as found within the native hardware and environment because you are reading one disk format within the context of another with the tools of another.

Emulators interpret code designed and compiled for one environment and convert it into machine code suitable for a different operating system and CPU. This may not be true for the Apple System 7 port to MS Windows and UNIX. The GUI is built for those environments to run within those operating systems and not emulate the functionality within those environments. Code interpreters tend to run significantly slower than native code. If speed of performance is the issue, run an application in its native environment. When performance is gauged upon interoperability, convenience, and information sharing there may be significant benefits from emulators.

Optimization tools

There are tools available that perform benchmarks *and* then offer suggestions or actually perform configuration changes to the computer system. For the most part, these tools offer simple advice. They may suggest limiting the complexity of the bootstrap files (for example, AUTOEXEC.BAT and CONFIG.SYS) and the number of processes they initiate. When on-line help information is available for these tools, their value increases dramatically. Examples include Skylight, WinSense, and Performance 2.x. When these tools offer general suggestions, the on-line help provides the means to add detail. For example, the suggestion that you optimize the hard disk to improve performance means little until you can associate that concept with the actions of adding a disk cache, increasing free space, and defragmenting files. The more complex the operating system, the more useful the optimization tools are in providing performance documentation and practical help.

Optimize hard disks

Data I/O bottlenecks are common when large amounts of data are created, retrieved, or in some way processed. Yet, the most common cause of client station and server bottlenecks is the data I/O limitation imposed by hard drive seek times, strictly a *mechanical* limitation. In a client system, the disk idles 95 percent of the time and when data is requested, it then begins the head seek thus creating an average 16 millisecond seek time. One millisecond represents controller electronics delay, the remaining 15 milliseconds is head movement. If server disks are busy nearly 100 percent of the time, that represents a queue service bottleneck in and of itself. Disk service even for a server with multiple disks still consists of 95 percent head motion and seeks and only 5 percent data access. This translates into the bottom line that 95 percent of disk bottlenecks are mechanical delays. Anything that can minimize the seek time is a true performance improvement. Furthermore, disk I/O should be reviewed; it is an essential benchmark if only because disk operations are measured in milliseconds while CPU and most operations are measured in micro- or picoseconds and thus represents a delay 100 to 1000 times more significant than most electronic processing delays.

Cache and RAM disks are effectively electronic replacements for hard drives. Any data or instructions retrieved from cache, RAM, or RAM disk can thus increase performance quite dramatically by saving 15 milliseconds. RAM and caches will generally locate and reference data in under 140 microseconds. While a cache does not provide 100 percent replacement—that is, a factor of the cache hit rate—it will nonetheless save 15 milliseconds at the hit rate and add in about 140 microseconds at the miss rate because it must still search RAM first.

Data I/O bottlenecks are common where overcommitment of available RAM causes pages to be swapped to the disk. Also, an inadequate or overloaded data storage architecture becomes a critical path. Improved system configuration and mere maintenance often address this flaw. Other times, improved hardware will boost I/O and optimize system performance. The information you will need to pinpoint the cost of a data I/O bottleneck is a disk cache hit rate report, a data seek and transfer rate for the connected hard drives, and a disk file mapping. Most disk caches—software or hardware—will report hit rates, efficiency, and data throughput levels. Field engineering tools such as DiskPro, WinSense, Check It, QA Plus, and some others included on the tools disk with this book will compute average seek times and average data transfer rates. You really do not want a true sector and track mapping of how data storage is used. That would be just too informative and inscrutable for most of us. Rather, you want a report as provided by MACE, Norton Utilities Speedisk, or DCF/2 showing file fragmentation levels. The next few sections discuss how to improve data I/O performance.

File system performance

OS/2 v2.x HPFS includes two new functions for improving file system performance. Specifically, the *scatter/gather* function provides the ability to read data from discontinuous disk sectors (chained files) in a single I/O operation and also the ability to fetch an entire file into file cache. This provides dramatic gains, particularly on LANs. Disk access can also be improved by increasing the number of tree-structured subdirectories for all operating systems which maintain flat directory hierarchies (OS/2 HPFS maintains names in a double-linked sorted B-tree for faster access). Although some of these operating system enhancements are specific to OS/2 v2.x, the concepts for enhancement can be applied to other platforms. Searching for a file in a flat file space is slowed by access times, file name searches, and conversions into the actual physical address on the disk. Reduce the number of files in any subdirectory. Create logical folders. Similarly, do not allow the operating system to search paths and volumes for applications and data sets. This slows access at load time. Instead, use batch files with full file path names or limit the search to a selected, active, or immediate subdirectory.

Create parallel disk subsystems

Add disk controllers or disks. Single-disk systems or systems with a single disk controller with a data bottleneck can be optimized by splitting data over multiple disks. Performance may be further increased by installing multiple disk controllers. RAID is described in later sections. Figure 4.6 illustrates this method.

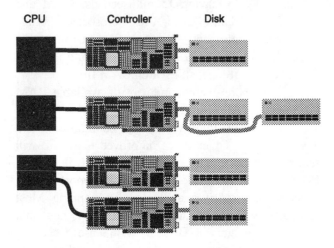

Figure 4.6 Bottlenecked disk performance may be improved by creating more channels for reading and writing data to an actual physical medium.

Performance increases are dramatic for disk-bound systems. Because the CPU is running below its capacity, it can support and coordinate more disk controllers, effectively yielding the data throughput gain. When multiple drives are stacked upon multiple controllers, net achievable disk performance can reach 4-ms access times and 40 Mbits/s throughput by virtue of the parallel channels, even though each disk individually may provide access times of 12 ms and data throughput rates of 3 to 4 Mbits/s.

However, older systems with existing MFM and RLL disk controllers can see a 10 to 40 percent performance boost with ESDI, IDE, SCSI, or SCSI-II disk controllers. Independent disk array (IDA) from Compaq represents an integrated RAID 0, 1, 2, or 4 capability. When these options are provided, realize that RAID 1 is much slower with write-behind disk writes, while RAID 4 provides better disk utilization and improved read and write performance (with the disadvantage of poor performance when an array disk fails). Note that when disk controllers are built into the motherboard, the data paths may already be optimized for the integrated controllers. The performance of the older disk drivers may also be far better than just-released drivers for the newer adapters. In this case, bus adapters may not provide so significant an enhancement. They also may create conflicts and incompatibilities. Assess this technique carefully.

Engineering workstations and other proprietary platforms benefit from this technique as well, even though the bus adapter interface is different from the seemingly more standardized and available PC adapters. Options also exist for SMD, Multibus, VME, SCSI, and proprietary controllers, even though they may be more limited. Some older SMD controllers are actually quite fast because they maintain rotational position sensing information to optimize the disk access sequence and perform speculative pre-fetching to anticipate future disk requests. The most reliable method, however, is to create parallel channels as shown in the prior figure. It is also useful to know that SCSI controllers support two types of communication, namely, asynchronous and synchronous. Surprisingly, asynchronous is slower as the number of devices on the bus increases, but synchronous controllers negotiate a predictable rate regardless of load or number of devices. Furthermore, daisy-chained disk drives as found on VMEBus, Multibus, CMD, and SCSI encourage adding hard drives up to the actual capacity of the controller card. This is inadvisable. Figure 4.7 lists the number of disks (and other I/O devices in the specific case of SCSI) commonly supported on various controllers.

I/O Interface	Number of devices supported	Supplemental devices
ST-506	2	2 floppy drives or tapes
MFM	2	2 floppy drives or tapes
RLL	2	2 floppy drives or tapes
ESDI	2	2 floppy drives or tapes
EDI	2	2 floppy drives or tapes
SCSI	7 I/O devices (total)	
IDA	4 large capacity disks (RAID)	
SCSI-II	7 I/O devices (total)	
CMD	2 to 4	
Multibus	Controller specific	
VMEbus	Controller specific	

Figure 4.7 Number of devices controlled by different controllers.

Optimize disk device support

Although it is economically sound to *chain* drives up to the controller's capacity, this is a common mistake in terms of performance. For example, although an SCSI interface can physically support seven devices, including disks, tape units, CD-ROMs, printers, and other global network devices, the management overhead is tremendous. Furthermore, it is difficult to correctly configure the interrupt and priorities switches even for matched devices, let alone for a hodgepodge of devices. Enhance high-performance stations by providing one controller card per storage device, or reduce the total number of hard drives by installing the largest drive(s) available to provide the required storage capacity. It is also possible to replace slow storage units with those that have more platters; this often provides data transfer speed enhancements through the parallel efforts of the extra heads.

One useful note for those with multiple SCSI controllers for devices that are only used sporadically, such as a tape drive and CD-ROM: a unified device driver such as Corel SCSI can allow you to attach all these devices and hard disks to the same controller. Because the tape drive and CD-ROM are not used often, integrating all these devices saves the power that would be needed for the extra cards and improves bus performance since the bus controller will not have to poll the extra controllers periodically.

Redundant arrays of inexpensive disks (RAID) are an *expensive* alternative for storing large quantities of data; they do provide some significant performance benefits. Disk reads are about five to ten times faster than disk writes, and so writing data partitioned across multiple disks provides faster service. It also provides faster read service, but usually it is the writing that becomes the bottleneck. Generally, you see four or more 500 MB drives in a RAID storage module. These also may be referred to as *disk farms*.

So far, RAID is available in 6 levels. Level 0 provides strictly performance improvements by writing data across several disks at the cost of safety and fault tolerance. RAID level 1 is called *mirroring* because data is written to two mirror-image disks. Read performance improves because both images can be read concurrently, but write performance decreases about 20 percent over a single system because the data must be written twice. RAID level 2 provides data striping with error detection and correction techniques. Level 3 includes error correction technology in the drive controller, but only write/read access is allowed at a time. This may provide suitable performance for large blocks of data. RAID level 4 provides multiple reads across the different disks at the time, an enhancement necessary for database operations. Level 5 provides the highest RAID performance with simultaneous reads and writes; it is a software extension to an operating system. A disk array can dramatically improve sluggish database, graphics processing, and OLTP disk operations. However, an array with a failed unit provides poor performance until removed, replaced, or restored to operation.

Increase local disk speeds and transfer rates

Seek time is not the only performance issue, especially for servers that sustain continuous data requests. Sustained data transfer rates are critical too. Hard drive performance becomes crucial for file-intensive client applications also. Note that all buses are faster than 8-bit and 16-bit disk controllers such as RLL, MFM, and the persistent AT ST-506 standards. Since MFM disk controllers support sustained disk transfer speeds of 512 kbits/s, SCSI supports about 4 Mbits/s, SCSI-II supports between 5 and 8 Mbits/s, and ESDI controllers support about 6 Mbits/s, local disk speeds are very relevant bottlenecks. These transfer speeds are all slower than the bus channel. For example, consider the loading of a 10-MB graphic image or GIS vector data file. Systems bootstrap from disks, applications are loaded from disks, overlays page to disk, temporary files are created on disks, databases are stored on disks and views are built there, and queued network print jobs are temporarily stored in disk files. Disk access speed is measured in milliseconds and is a composite of disk rotational speed, head access speed, sector interleave, alignment error rates, and data bus widths. Faster disks improve performance dramatically. If at all in doubt, substitute a faster disk and test the new configuration.

A second factor in physical disk performance is the disk controller. Wider data buses increase data transfer speeds by increasing the number of bits that can be transferred in parallel. Controllers (with suitable software drivers) supporting a wider data bus might enhance performance. Alternatively, wider buses provide data transfer in parallel with simultaneous disk control commands; this yields a two-way conversation between CPU and disk instead of slower sequential control. Note that all software and hardware timing parameters must support the wider bus in order to achieve performance boosts. Bus-mastering controllers off-load the CPU and move files through memory without CPU resources. Caching disk controllers increase performance for read-intensive operations (database and transaction-processing applications) by buffering most frequently read data or most recently written data in fast RAM.

Establish optimal sector interleave

Hard disk read/write movements often default to factory settings or controller preferences, or are established by operating system parameters. These settings are called the disk interleave factor and establish the order in which the pie-shaped sectors and concentric tracks are accessed. Random interleave values can shortchange a good controller and fast disk. Various utilities measure disk rotation speeds, head access times, disk controller capabilities, and file sizes to calculate an optimal interleave factor. Interleave factors are pertinent to MFM and RLL disks, rarely to SCSI, and *never* to IDE disks; you will damage the IDE disk. Before trying to optimize your hardware, be sure that it can be optimized without physical damage. You might also check that the disk has not already been optimized by the electronics or through prior effort.

Examples of utilities which optimize sector interleaving include Norton Utilities, Optune, and MACE; such utilities are available for MS DOS, OS/2, UNIX, and specific NOSs. Some tools even partition, low-level reformat, and move data on the fly. Performance is rarely degraded, and disk access can be improved up to 15 percent. Similarly, disk block size—the smallest unit stored on a hard disk—influences disk performance. While smaller blocks are more efficient in terms of disk space utilization, larger blocks tend to be more efficient from a disk access speed viewpoint. File block size, read-ahead record buffering, and disk-to-memory transfer block size are usually operating system parameters. Adjust them to match applications, NIC buffer sizes, cache space, and available system memory.

Reformat at a low level

Over time, the strength and differentiation of the magnetic fields on a hard drive decay; bits are lost. The physical recording substrata expand and contract with temperature variances, and they also stretch, sag, and warp under their own weight. The same physical changes affect the drive motor and its rotation speed as well as the disk controller motor and disk heads. The read/write head may no longer align precisely with the format tracks on the disk. Dead spots creep into the media from head strikes, dust, and normal wear. As a result, media errors creep into the drive. These may not cause overt system-level disk errors, but they may initiate frequent data transfer errors and requests by the disk controller to reread the data. Recall that digital on/off bits are represented by analog representations provided by strengths of magnetic fields. Repeated reads clearly degrade disk performance and ensuing system performance. Tools such as SpinRite or QA Plus locate and mark bad spots while moving or recovering data on the fly.

A low-level media format reinitializes and realigns the tracks to the head and motor parameters. Furthermore, a low-level format locates and marks defects as areas best not used. It is important to recognize that a low-level format may differ from a system-level format. A system format may partition the disk into usable structures for that operating system. A low-level format is controller-specific and is often initiated from BIOS calls or special diagnostic routines. The UNIX DIAG is one such program, as is the MS DOS DEBUG call to C800:G5, where many disk controller cards and their diagnostic and initialization routines reside in encoded PROM firmware.

Defragment disks

Most operating systems chain files and recycle space from deleted files on an ad hoc basis for disk space efficiency and performance. As files expand in size, grow smaller through deletions, or are marked as erased on a disk (files are rarely actually erased from the disk, only marked as free space for recycling), they fragment into chains of small blocks. As an example, it is easier to link newly added individual records within a database than to rewrite the entire database to account for the new, revised, or deleted records. It is not practical to rewrite a 10-MB database to account for a single new 20-byte record; instead, records are added to chained file blocks. Figure 4.8 depicts the inefficiency of chained files.

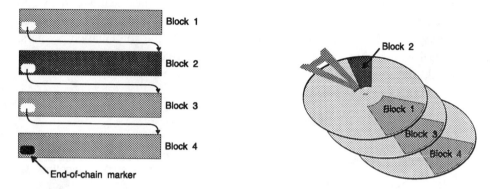

Figure 4.8 Chained files are inefficient to read because they require multiple disk seeks and reads.

Defragment files on your hard drives. Chained files increase file access times dramatically. Stacker-compressed disks and HPFS (OS/2) disks tend not to defragment as frequently as UNIX or DOS filing systems; this represents one approach to maintaining file access speed. When disks fragment and disk performance slows by more than 10 percent, run a defragmentation utility. The alternative for operating systems or environments without such tools is to back up the data volumes, low-level format the drives, and then restore the backup. Make certain that the restoration is not a true volume restoration, but rather the logical directory and file-by-file restoration. Files will no longer be fragmented. Norton Utilities *Speedisk* or the Ziff-Davis *PC Magazine* utility *Defrag* for DOS, Norton Utilities *Speedisk* for UNIX, *DCF/2* for OS/2, and *Public Utilities* from Fifth Generation Systems for the Macintosh are utilities to unchain files. Some such tools also allow you to optimize placement of operating system components and critical applications in areas of the disk that are faster than others.

Unchain files

Utilities for defragmenting chained files and creating continuous, contiguous disk blocks exist for most operating systems. This improves disk access performance anywhere from 5 to 20 percent. It is very relevant for files that are read more often than they are written, such as executable files, configurations, operating system or network software, and databases. It is particularly relevant for database servers.

Some operating systems do not provide this defragmentation facility. UNIX is an example. Nonetheless, disk performance degrades over time as files fragment into chained minimum-sized blocks. The same defragmentation effect can be achieved by backing up the system to a tape (or other medium), reformatting the disk, and restoring the tape to the disk. UNIX system administrators generally avoid this because of the labor.

Contiguous free space speeds the disk writing time. Defragmenting disk space improves not only write times but also read times. Contiguous block reads (and read-ahead disk buffers) improve the access times for files that are read and reread, as records in a database are. When blocks are contiguous, the read heads do not have to seek widely scattered blocks or translate the continuation pointers, as Figure 4.9 illustrates. Contiguous blocks do not have continuation pointers. The next block to read in this case is the next most accessible block.

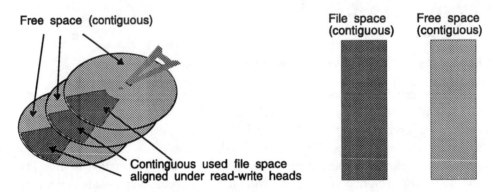

Figure 4.9 Files maintained in contiguous blocks are more efficient to read.

Maintain free disk space

Disks that approach capacity by definition lack contiguous blocks of free space. Block writes, temporary data swapping, and paging to disk create a situation called *thrashing* in which the heads continuously look for enough space to write the data blocks to the disk. This is time-intensive. Disks with less than 10 percent free space impose a significant overhead on the station. Servers with little free space create a bottleneck that can be solved only by adding disk space or by purging files and records.

It is interesting to note that UNIX systems measure disk space with an extra margin. A UNIX volume is not actually full until file space in use reaches 110 percent of capacity. Because UNIX systems recycle free space on the fly, free space tends to fragment into *clusters* of the minimum-sized block (usually 4 kB). UNIX systems without that 10 percent margin thrash while establishing the long connected chains required for most significant files. The search is slow. In any event, the largest available contiguous disk space should be sufficient to contain the largest single file on the system with room to spare. Free up disk space, increase disk size, install a whole disk compression driver (SuperStor, Stuffit, DiskDoubler and AutoDoubler, or Stacker, for example), and defragment files.

Increase free disk space

Provide more available disk space. Performance can be poor even when the disk is half empty. Reduce the number of dead and unused files on the disk. Microhelp provides an interesting MS Windows tool called *Uninstaller* which traces all linked libraries, referenced data files, and executable code. It then lets you remove them. It is also useful for documenting what applications require which files. Archive those that are infrequently used for reference purposes only. Remove any that are unneeded. Many operating systems and applications install a large number of nonessential files when initially set up; if the applications provide installation options, capitalize on setup options in the future. Do not install the complete application. Instead, choose your options. For example, OS/2 PM provides communications options to mainframes, terminal emulation, and a database access tool. These three options require 22 MB of additional disk space. When installing UNIX, consider the need for the Bourne Shell, the C Shell, C compilers, GREP, AUK, LINT, YACC, and CD-ROM drivers. Consider also the need for extra software that may be available with the installation tapes, such as EMACS, X Windows support, and TEX. While disk space may seem inexpensive and readily available with the current large disks, consider the effects on disk seek performance and the extra overhead associated with daily backups.

Delete games, bitmap images, useless utilities, and system commands you rarely use. All operating systems are shipped with games. They are useful for teaching new users system basics and mouse controls, and occasionally as a means of breaking the tension. They do take up space and proliferate unless some control is established. Sound files are space hogs at 17kB/s. This includes verbal document notations, MS Windows .WAV files, and other quasi-compressed sound files. Consider removing sound unless it provides essential services.

One word of advice: never get rid of the editor that comes with the operating system. On DOS, this might be EDLIN or EDIT. It is NOTEPAD in MS Windows, EE in OS/2, and ED or EMACS in UNIX. You never know when the system might break and someone will come to help fix the system. That editor may be the only tool to repair bootstrap files. If you can quickly identify existing dead files, do so, and delete them. A software monitoring program called FILESTAT from Solid Oak Software is another effective option. It is a terminate and stay resident (TSR) utility that runs only under DOS and MS Windows and tracks all disk access. It will show what files are accessed, and consequently those which are not. You will be surprised to find that perhaps only 5 percent of your disk is ever really used. Figure 4.10 illustrates a shortened list (12 of the 321 active files) as reported by FILESTAT over two days. A separate report listed 4089 files that were not accessed in two days, and an older list showed 3780 files that were not accessed in three months.

The Windows help files are at least 100 kB apiece. Wallpaper and bitmap images users want to store can require as much as 200 MB. If you need .BMP images, consider converting them into .RLE encoded files (with WinGIF or a tool like it), since MS Windows considers these two formats identical. This will yield from 50 to 90 percent in disk space savings. Another program, called HOG.EXE, shows which directories use the most space, as Figure 4.11 shows.

```
    StatRept v1.05 - Copyright (c) Solid Oak Software, Inc. 1992

                                 Total    Last
    Full file name              Accesses  Access
    ------------------------------------------------------
    D:\PCS_LOGS\LOCAL\04231993.SOS      11  05-05-93
    D:\VENTURA\ENVIRON.WID              11  05-05-93
    D:\VENTURA\SPLDICT.PD               1  05-05-93
    D:\VENTURA\STANDBY.DLL              1  05-05-93
    D:\VENTURA\USER.WFT              2076  05-05-93
    D:\WINDOWS\SYSTEM\8514SYS.FON       2  05-05-93
    D:\WINDOWS\SYSTEM\ANTQUA.TTF        2  05-05-93
    D:\WINDOWS\SYSTEM\ARIALBD.FOT       1  05-05-93
    D:\WINDOWS\SYSTEM\ARIALBD.TTF       5  05-05-93
    D:\WINDOWS\SYSTEM\ARIALBI.TTF       5  05-05-93
    D:\WINPRINT\FONTS\VRBL____.TTF      2  05-05-93
    D:\WINPRINT\FONTS\WDB_____.TTF      4  05-05-93

    321 files are active.
    File created on 05-05-1993 at 12:42:22

    StatRept v1.05 - Copyright (c) Solid Oak Software, Inc. 1992
```

Figure 4.10 FILESTAT report shows filing access and some unused files.

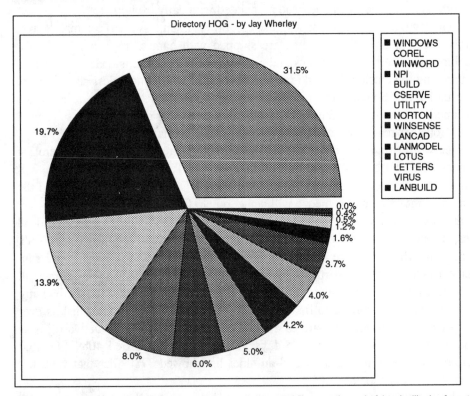

Figure 4.11 HOG.EXE (for DOS FAT tables only) shows directory and file usage in a colorful and utilitarian format.

This should not imply that current tasks cannot be optimized as is; this aspect is addressed next. Temporary swap files are frequently created to buffer file-intensive operations. When an operating system crashes, these temporary files may remain. They may contain partial views of the application which crashed. While these files may provide a means of recovering lost work, consider deleting them when they are no longer needed. These files have names such as `98479847.TMP`, `'8393.TMP`, `document.TMP`, `document.$$$`, or date and time stamps for names and file names with just numbers. MS Windows also creates large temporary files for images and clipboard objects.

Directory and file nodes

Hard disks also become full because they run out of space to contain directory and file path names. If the file system runs out of the specialized space to contain file names, it does not matter how much free space exists on the file system. There simply is no more room to store new files. However, existing files can be expanded. A hard disk contains more than just the actual data. It also contains a file directory which references the actual locations of the data. These structures may be optimized (as part of the operating system design) for speed of access and continuity, or not at all, as is the case with DOS FAT (file allocation table).

Limits usually appear when a user attempts to create more than 256 file names in a DOS floppy disk or under a subdirectory. UNIX, OS/2, NetWare have higher limits, while Banyan Vines 4.x will support a maximum of 64 k directory entries (65536 i-nodes) per server. This becomes a performance issue when the disk thrashes, or even crashes, for lack of directory space. These problem are prevalent on networks with E-mail, image scanning and retrieval systems, and servers supporting MS Windows for clients without permanent swap files. Specifically, most E-mail messages are generally 40 words or less but each one represents a directory entry; these are often saved for posterity. Every scanned image (compressed to 76 kB) is a file entry. MS Windows creates many .TMP files and these often persist beyond the end of a session.

Performance solutions range from applying patches to correct these shortcomings in an operating system or network operating system, creating logical disk partitions, or adding new hard drives specifically for these directory entry—intensive applications. Adding new drives tends to be a better solution, and these need not be large drives either; a hard drive as small as 30 MB could easily store 65536 40-word mail messages. MS Windows benefits dramatically with a permanent swap file (rather than a temporary one allocated for each session), created on a contiguous area of a single hard disk; this file should be twice the size of RAM plus 4 MB. Paging usually requires between one and two times RAM.

Data compression

Another method of increasing disk space is to use data compression. This exists in two main categories. The first and older technology is file compression. Individual files are compacted by removing repeating sequences with a run-length code or by replacing repeating entities with a code. Typical file compression methods include ARC, ZIP, Stuffit, DLR, Compress, and special techniques for images which are discussed later. The second technology is to compress entire disks, including the file allocation tables, and compress and retrieve files on the fly. There are many programs available, including DoubleDisk, AddStor, and Stacker for DOS and MS Windows 3.x, DCF/2 for OS/2, Times Two for the Macintosh, and others for just about every other operating system. This includes mainframes, minicomputers, and many proprietary platforms.

The disk compression programs work by either compressing individual files on the disk or creating a single file encompassing the entire disk which includes your files already in a compressed format. The method used for data compression is generally run-length encoding (RLE) or a common string substitution from a lookup table, and it is a *lossless* compression method. The actual rate of file compression varies. Executable code might compress 10 to 20 percent, text files tend to compress by half, and graphic images will compress to as little as 10 percent of the original size. This yields an average doubling of disk capacity. ZIP files, as they are already compressed, will not compress more on a compressed disk.

Text and files generally can be compressed to half-size, executable programs are compressed to 80 percent of original size, and graphics are compressed from 15 to 25 percent of original size. Graphic images, such as photographic scans, bitmap images, and other such data files tend to consist of 75 percent blank space or repeated information. While it is possible to compress a 30-MB bitmap to 7.5 MB, the resulting file still represents a substantial use of disk space. Lead Technologies, as one example, provides JPEG (Joint Photographers Expert Group) standard image compression software that will infinitely compress images. You determine how small you want the file. As this is a *lossful* or *lossy* technique, you must determine how much information loss you are willing to accept. The resolution of the image does not change, it is merely the information variety and content that changes; colors tend to mute and objects tend to blur with increased compression.

Theoretically, disk compression should increase effective data transfer speeds since more actual data can be read from the disk. In reality, performance varies substantially by product, CPU, and platform. Generally, file decompression is performed on the fly by the CPU or a coprocessor (built into the disk controller). Some products increase performance, others provide parity, and some decrease disk speed performance by 30 percent. In general, read operations from a compressed drive tend to be marginally faster because the compressed data is read in clusters of 8 kB instead of 1 kB or 2 kB as is normal for DOS or 4 kB in OS/2. On the other hand, write performance is generally worse because the files must be tokenized, compressed, and stuffed into the master compressed file.

Disk space performance can more than double, and this can include RAM disks as well. Disk compression applications are not without cost in terms of disk space, CPU overhead, and RAM. The programs themselves require disk space that is not compressed, RAM to contain the compression driver, and CPU overhead to expand and compress files. Data compression imposes extra complexity but is a viable optimization opportunity. One risk is the extra attention required to reactivate a system and recover data in the event that a partition or disk fails.

While you save significant amounts of disk space with image compression, secondary performance results include faster image loading time from disk, faster processing time, and reduced overheads for creating image output. Lossless compression techniques tend to have a minimal effect (or a detrimental performance slowdown) on loading and processing times since the objects must be restored to original before normal processing can occur. Additionally, since lossy image compressing is a permanent adjustment in the size of the object, network transfer times are significantly reduced as well, since a smaller file must be transferred over the network channel. Lossless compression will have no effect (or a detrimental result) on network delivery (latency) times since the objects must be restored to original before normal processing can occur.

Data compression is not limited to only text and images. Data files and entire database spaces can be compressed manually with compression utilities or compressed on the fly with operating systems, auxiliary systems. Lotus 1-2-3 files can be compressed. Database workspaces with tables, reports, masks, rules, permissions, and views are candidates for lossless compression techniques. Automatic data compression is particularly effective for operating systems which support multitasking, concurrency, or threading. For example, AS/400 DB2 databases can be compressed on a record-by-record basis to provide a nearly two-fold disk space improvement and a 47 percent speed improvement since disk access time is reduced. Some UNIX-based client/server DBMSs can be compressed for similar disk and performance improvements; DTFS for UNIX is an example.

Speech and continuous motion video represent enormous bandwidth and data storage requirements. Compression techniques for continuous voice can condense voice by a factor of 20 times. The sound quality may suffer because the compression is usually lossful—ranges of frequencies are typically dropped—but bandwidth and performance is increased. Since full motion video represents about 24 frames of duplicate information per second with only minor frame-to-frame changes, some effective compression techniques retain only a few master frames and the sequential changes between frames. Also, the master frames themselves can be optimized with JPEG techniques. Since each master frame can represent 30 MB of information, this optimizes the utilization of disk space enormously, but also improves the display performance of the video. As few storage media can support such high data transfer rates and fewer LAN protocols can tolerate the bandwidth monopolization, both speech and video compression are the staples for computerized dubbing and editing.

Reorganize file placement

Physical file placement on disks also affects disk transfer rate performance. The read/write heads normally return to a rest position. Additionally, certain sequences of tracks are faster to access than others—usually the inner tracks. Placing key files there will improve system operation about 2 to 3 percent. The best files to place in this area are files that are frequently read and never written.

The files most frequently read are operating system overlays, network software overlays, and application overlays. The operating system itself is read and loaded into memory only once; in some cases, the operating system is loaded into memory only once a month or so after the system crashes. UNIX and OS/2 operating systems and network file servers are rarely rebooted; the general consensus is that this leads to the least file system damage and wear and tear on station components.

The operating system kernel is low-priority; the overlays and library files are high-priority. However, extended support files are loaded or called frequently. Examples include dynamic link libraries (.DLLs), code overlays, and subroutines for large applications. This is true for .DLL files (MS Windows and OS/2), .OVR files (UNIX and DOS), and the nonresident portion of DOS TSRs and NetWare NLM routines. Even simple MS DOS benefits from positioning MSDOS.SYS and IO.SYS as the first entries on the hard drive. Position data reference files, databases, and other files that are more frequently read than written in outer tracks. Dead files and infrequently invoked executable code should be placed on the edges of the drive. Although any performance gain is slight, this technique is a one-time event with no cost except for some maintenance time. Utilities, such as Norton Utilities Speeddisk, MACE, and DCF/2, help optimize file access.

Solid state disks

RAM access times range from 11 microseconds for static RAM (SRAM), typically used in CPU hardware caches, to 70 microseconds for the standard memory in fast PCs and high-performance workstations. This is at least 100 times faster than the fastest hard disk or disk array. While it would be desirable to create massive disk caches to improve this fundamental performance bottleneck, few systems are robust enough to support a RAM cache larger than 2 MB. Furthermore, the overhead and the hit rate for such caches usually do not show benefits with caches larger than 256 kB for PCs, 2 MB for PC-based servers, and 2 MB for UNIX and VMS systems.

However, imagine the performance gains possible with a solid state disk! This is increasingly feasible as the price for large memory chips decreases. IBM and Hewlett-Packard sell laptop computers with 20-MB solid state disks on PCMCIA adapter cards. Also, these and similar laptop computers provide the operating system or the MS Windows shell in PROM. The performance improvements are startling. For example, MS Windows on the Hewlett-Packard subnotebook is instantly available. Data access times from the solid state disk are best measured in microseconds. This technology is applicable to other platforms as well.

Disk Emulation Systems is one of a growing number of niche manufacturers providing solid state replacements for mechanical hard disks. Target platforms include UNIX file servers, PC-based superservers, VAX systems, and Intel 80486 network servers. A disk with 256 MB currently costs about $40,000. However, the performance is such that the solid state disk I/O can average 1 millisecond, rather than the standard 15 or 16 milliseconds typically seen. This lower limit seems to be a function of the disk controller, since few engineers have seen it necessary to optimize controller performance when controller response time represents just 6 percent of mechanical disk seek and access times. Because controller performance represents 99 percent of solid state disk seek and access times, the issue is different. In time, vendors will optimize controllers.

Since more than 95 percent of the I/O delay is caused by disk head times, a typical hard disk is limited to about 40 to 60 I/O events/s. This is a fundamental measurement used by most DBMS and application developers. However, this can be increased to about 1000 I/O events/s with a solid state disk. If you want to minimize a disk I/O bottleneck, consider a solid state disk, or even a disk farm with multiple solid state disks. Just as a disk farm of mechanical disks or a single volume spanning multiple drives provide access times about four times faster than a single hard disk, you could expect to see access times in the 0.25 millisecond range with a solid state disk subsystem.

While a solid state disk represents the cutting edge for disk I/O optimization, it still represents a fairly expensive proposition for most organizations. Another alternative, already alluded to, is feasible for many operating and network operating systems. Consider creating a RAM disk as large as possible or as large as needed to contain master database tables, work in progress, or other data that is accessed repeatedly in an on-line transaction processing environment. The effect should be the same, although the scope is not as large.

Increase I/O channel speed

Most computer systems become bottlenecks when the input/output channel is saturated with requests to devices including memory, data storage, video, and network interfaces. Since the bus is literally a part of the motherboard and may actually be etched into the Fiberglas, bus upgrades usually mean acquisition of a new motherboard or a new base system. A system is rarely CPU-bound. Rather, the internal communication channel, or bus, is the bottleneck As computer systems have become more complicated and faster, designers have widened the system bus and increased its transmission speed. VME has replaced Multibus, MCA (IBM Microchannel Architecture) and EISA (enhanced industry standard architecture) have replaced ISA (industry standard bus), and VESA (video enhanced system architecture) represents the newest design. The VESA VL-bus with 36 MHz supplants the 1.8-MHz bus of the original PC XT. Basically, the bus is no longer a singular backplane communications channel. Instead, there is a direct connection from the CPU to memory, a second specialized bus for video and other devices, a direct connection for data storage, and a fourth bus for other device adapters. A controller synchronizes and maintains these distinct data communication pathways for a substantial increase in system component performance.

Channel upgrade

You might ask how you would bypass bus bottlenecks. The most obvious answer is by upgrading the local computer system to a machine with a more substantial bus architecture. You may notice that the newer systems tout a new bus architecture. The reason is that problems with CPU and data storage capacities are not as significant or as solvable as those solved by building a system with a wider bus. Most computer systems consist of product lines with increasingly more sophisticated buses.

Sun Microsystems workstations have different performance characteristics; faster systems tend to have faster buses. Even superserver manufacturers have increased their products' bus transmission speeds from 30 Mbits/s to over 250 Mbits/s. Similarly, computer systems based upon Intel chips (i.e., 80386, 80486, and Pentium) are upgraded by replacing them with more extensive systems. The secondary effect is that the other system components are probably more substantial as well, thereby providing other optimization effects. A 386-based system with an EISA bus will provide better data throughput to disk, video, and network than a comparable system with an ISA bus. However, note the expansion of the bus bandwidth may only move the bottleneck to the disk controller or disk—if any of these components cannot sustain the increased data traffic, as Figure 4.12 illustrates.

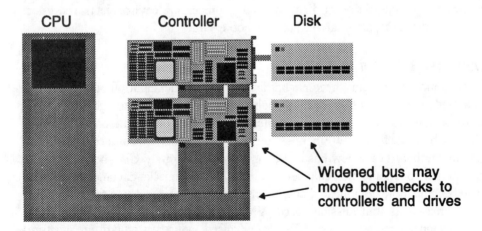

Figure 4.12 System-wide bottlenecks are not easily resolved.

Improve channel flow

Special bus adapters improve performance by taking control of the bus and managing traffic. These devices are called *bus-mastering controllers*. They are primarily available for video, network interfaces, and disk storage. These devices do two things. First, they off-load overhead from the CPU and the bus controller. Second, they manage access to the bus for more efficient throughput.

Parallel and serial channels also represent a channel bottleneck. Although this is not really the bus, these pathways represent fundamental performance bottlenecks for many tasks. Printing through a parallel or serial port is generally limited to about 120,000 char/s in widths up to 8 bits. While many manufacturers have agreed to provide enhanced parallel and serial ports under the PCMCIA slot format, many existing systems and printers are not certain to benefit from this technology. Instead, current technology such as the LaserMaster WinJet bus adapters can bypass slow ports and substantially enhance text and graphic printing. These adapters also provide enhanced printing resolution from existing laser printers.

Also, modem access is limited by older universal asynchronous receive/transmit (UART) chips, which may buffer only a single character at a time. Therefore, it is easy to overrun this buffer and thus require retransmission. Most PC systems with this older chip are easily upgraded by replacing the chip with the newer UART 16550 from Intel. The substitution not only improves performance, it also provides the ability to multitask applications in the foreground while downloads and uploads occur invisibly in the background. This is possible because modems operate in the 120- to 14,400-char/s range and the slowest PC provides processing of at least 500,000 char/s. As such, simultaneous tasks on a windowed computer system do represent a performance gain. Digiboard even provides a dual-port serial card with two buffered UART chips; one is for reception and the other is for transmission. However, you should also note that successful communication under multitasking operating systems or GUIs generally requires that communication software directly own the port rather than share it with system drivers. This is pertinent for MS Windows, OS/2, and Windows NT.

Increase CPU speed

Let us face it. Most of us think that the fastest way to increase performance is to replace a CPU with a faster CPU. This is not always practical, financially possible, or technically feasible. Chips have different numbers of pins, may be soldered to boards, may have different communication pins, voltages, refresh rates, signals, and have different requirements. Sometimes, a 386/SX 12-MHz chip can be replaced with a 386/SX 16-MHz chip for a 33 percent improvement in speed. Intel also provides 486 DX/2 chip sets running internally at 66 MHz and the so-called Overdrive chips for replacement of slower ones. Furthermore, companies such as Kingston provide small circuit boards with faster CPUs to replace a slower CPU, and there is incipient market for pin-compatible chip upgrades. Similarly, other vendors provide bus adapters with newer and faster CPUs to off-load the preexisting CPU. Effectively, these are coprocessors, which are described later in this chapter.

The Intel iComp chart, as previously shown in Chapter 3, exhibits the performance characteristics of Intel chip sets. The naming conventions confuse the issue somewhat. Nonetheless, this is useful information for making performance assessments. However, substituting a faster chip for a slower one does not necessarily mean that your goal of faster application performance will be achieved. In fact, you could also experience performance degradation.

The infrastructure to support the faster processor must be in place. Static RAM, crystal clock speeds, refresh rates, wait states, and other technical details affect the feasibility of direct CPU substitutions. Furthermore, when you simply substitute a faster CPU, you may only reposition the bottleneck from the motherboard to the backplane bus.

It is important to realize that performance improvements of newer-generation chips show less than one order of magnitude change over prior generations, that is, they are about 10 times faster. In fact, the Pentium may provide about a 1.4 times speed improvement over a 486 chip, or about a 1.8 times improvement when the application is recompiled specifically for the Pentium. Some of these same compilers improve 486 performance about 60 to 180 percent. Keep these performance metrics in perspective when assessing the possible improvements.

Performance improvements may vary depending upon your applications. Integer and floating-point operations will improve with faster processors or upgrades to processors with internal math capabilities. In other words, Lotus 1-2-3 or AutoCAD might improve substantially, whereas database or graphics applications may show little effect. You need to understand where your performance constraint is and what component has no slack time.

Memory allocation and management

Adding and reallocating system memory is the most viable means of improving the performance of an existing system—that is, without replacing the system. Computers typically have at least three types of electronic memory. The CPU has memory built into it to contain data and instructions. This RAM may be as little as 2 kB or as large as 64 kB. The Pentium chip has two different caches and paths for more efficient performance. The second type of RAM is called static RAM, which is memory as fast as the CPU that is wired directly to the CPU. Static RAM is generally 16 kB to 1024 kB in size. This memory is used as a cache for intermediate results and for storing data and code until the built-in memory has room for more information. The third type of memory is the slower RAM, the banks of chips which house applications, images, and user work. PCs map this main memory from 640 kB to 64 MB (or more), as do most systems intended for UNIX and other proprietary operating systems. A system with sufficient memory will run faster. Even when adding memory is no longer feasible—for whatever reason—how that memory is allocated can have substantial effects.

Minimize configurations

Minimize the environment and system configuration. The most effective means of improving performance is to reduce the workload on the system. Decrease the number of system drivers, background processes, and extra support tools and gimmicks. Do not load terminate and stay resident (TSR) programs, background mail requesters, images or wallpaper, iconized applications, or on-line calendars, calculators, and enhanced file management tools. Remove tools that automatically load at startup or login. Replace images with wallpaper, or wallpaper and patterns with single-color backgrounds. Reduce the number of similar fonts on the system; for example, Bookman and Garamond are serif faces similar to Times Roman. Remove all performance measuring tools; these require system resources and slow performance. SPF/2 for OS/2 takes resources in spite of its feature to account for its own percentage of CPU cycles and subtract it.

Fonts are an incredible "deal"; sets of several hundred are available in Postscript type 1, type 2, and type 3, True Type, ATM, Bitstream, and other formats for $50. However, they are no bargain for your system, since that can represent 70 MB of disk space and the overhead to reference all of them within a type manager. Instead, minimize the number of active fonts on the system. Not only do they require disk space, reference to them is retained in memory at all times. Disable font shadowing under OS/2. If speed of performance is more important than RAM and disk space, create bitmapped fonts at standard resolutions for faster display. (Note that bitmapped font support is being replaced by better algorithms and native integration of uniform fonts for display and output.) Run only one on-the-fly font-scaling program. Do not run True Type, ATM, Monotype, Agfa, and Bitstream at the same time. The differences between a True Type representation of Garamond and a Bitstream version are minimal. Furthermore, the need to mask Helvetica by other names, such as Swiss, Chalet, and Zurich, merely provides the opportunity to have multiple copies of the same information on your system. It is unimportant for most users; those creating art work, advertising, or precision typesetting may need all these type libraries for the nuances, but most systems are better without retaining the disk and configuration overhead.

However, consider converting font formats to one standard to consolidate type libraries. If applications require different type libraries, consider creating different boot files and initialization procedures to minimize font overhead. Also, consider the approach of moving the disparate applications to different machines.

Simplify. Shorten search paths, limit environment variables, and assess the effects of memory management and task switching software. As most operating systems now support some form of task switching, time sharing, background processing, or multithreading, remember that these come with a performance hit.

IBM reports a 5 percent decrease in work throughput for each added OS/2 v2.1 multitasked background application. Run benchmarks for multitasking on your operating system to assess performance effects. If you need access to multiple processes concurrently—as with inbound fax or mail—consider running these on a separate computer instead. Adding minimally configured PCs may cost less than the time spent trying to optimize the performance of concurrent operations on one system. There are likely to be conflicts, sudden failures, and capability problems, too, with concurrent processes. Performance is generally better when configuration is simplified. This is true for most situations and most platforms.

To reduce the time required to reboot a system or initialize a GUI front end like MS Windows, minimize the number of applications and processes invoked at startup. This includes RUN=, LOAD=, and icons placed in the startup folder in Windows; commands placed in the UNIX bootstrap; and commands and devices loaded by CONFIG.SYS, AUTOEXEC in DOS and OS/2; and RESTARTOBJECTS= in OS/2.

Instantanenous power-on options, as provided by the Hewlett-Packard Omnibook computer, added to any MS Windows computer with Instant Recall UPS from PowerCard, or emulated by software, such as PC Resume also from PowerCard, speed up desktop loading. These PowerCard tools provide an immediate means to create a full image of memory and store it on disk; the memory image is recalled from disk with all processes intact and the user can begin working again. This feature represents a tradeoff of initial computer speed for disk space; if your PC has 12 MB of RAM, you will need that disk space. (Both PowerCard products also provide a safety feature for saving intermediate work.) The instantaneous power-on option is likely to be added to many types of platforms, not just PCs, as vendors standardize software distribution on flash ROM, PCMCIA cards, or PROM chips.

In the larger sense, system configuration is extraordinarily important. When the boot files, startup parameters, swap files, WIN.INI, and SYSTEM.INI were tuned on the Epson Progression, it performed near the top of its class, yielding 17 percent overall Windows performance enhancement. The addition of a specialty WinStore caching IDE controller in place of the motherboard IDE controller enhanced disk operations about 125 percent, on par with a fast 486 disk subsystem. However, WinStore performance with a software cache in RAM (in various sizes) was not as efficient or effective as either the software cache or the caching controller alone.

Add RAM

When computers have insufficient memory, tasks and processing operations are not completed as quickly as is otherwise possible. Segments of random access memory (RAM) are copied to some slower storage medium. When there is insufficient memory in the system, information is moved to the next memory structure in the hierarchy. Each memory type is about 10 times slower than its predecessor. When the main memory is exhausted, data are moved to disk, which is generally at least 100 times slower. As you might guess at this point, it is very reasonable to increase the main memory size; this will increase system performance dramatically for disk-bound operations. You are trading off faster memory for slower disks.

Buffers

Buffers are memory structures for containing information about the data file: its placement, size, access time, and access rights. Because the structure stores actual data records and blocks for transfer to and from disk storage, it is called a "buffer." Generally, you need as many buffers as file operations. Buffers are generally required for reading operating system or network operating system overlays, for dynamic link libraries, for main memory RAM to disk operations, and for every file opened for user applications. A single database record could require the data file, a main index, a secondary index, and links to a text-based memo field. The record can reference another 6, 10, or 15 slave database records.

When there is an insufficient number of buffers, these structures are recycled. This means that the CPU will spend time recreating the buffer for the next disk access and effectively finding the file on the disk again. This can be slow because it entails multiple disk accesses to reestablish the buffer. However, while it may be desirable to set the number of available file buffers very high, they do subtract from available RAM.

Cache

A *cache* is also a buffer, but in the traditional meaning of the word. It provides temporary storage for data between memory and other devices—primarily disks, but also tapes and CD-ROM as well. Caches can buffer both reads and writes, and sometimes caches are established separately for each. Caches vary in size. Static RAM for the CPU is a data and code cache. Caches contain the last accessed data or the most frequently accessed data. These represent a performance enhancement because the cache is checked for the required information before a slower memory, disk, tape, or CD-ROM is searched.

The percentage of times these data are found in the cache is called the hit rate, and the miss rate represents the percentage of times the slower memory is searched. Surprisingly, hit rates of even small caches (256 kB) are about 50 percent. Increasing the cache size to 1 MB may increase the hit rate to 78 percent. Some database operations where the same records are continually requested, word processor paging where the same file is scrolled from top to bottom, and other such operations can yield a cache hit rate approaching 100 percent.

Creating overly large caches subtracts from available RAM; this may affect system performance. Large caches can increase the cache search times. Because cache searches occur at the speed of the RAM, extensive caches rarely in themselves become performance hits. What tends to happen is that the cache hit rate, and hence the effectiveness, increases at a decreasing rate, as shown by Figure 4.13. Ultimately, increasing the amount of RAM devoted to the cache provides negligible effects.

```
+--------------------------------------------------------------------------+
| SPEEDCACHE PLUS version 4.05                    CONDENSED STATUS          |
| (C) Copyright 1986-1992 Future Systems Solutions, Inc. All Rights Reserved. |
+--------------------------------------------------------------------------+
|       %Of cache    Reads:Writes  %Read Hits  %Write Hits  (%Request Hits) |
+--------------------------------------------------------------------------+
| Drive A:    0.0%         0:0        0.0%        0.0%       (  0.0% )       |
| Drive B:    0.0%         0:0        0.0%        0.0%       (  0.0% )       |
| Drive C:   62.4%        80:1       94.6%       44.5%       ( 63.6% )       |
+--------------------------------------------------------------------------+
| Cache Allocated:   2280.0K of 2280.0K  (100.0%)     Slack:   855.5K (37.5%) |
+--------------------------------------------------------------------------+
```

Figure 4.13 Cache hit rate statistics.

This cache usage report shows only the effectiveness of your cache at its current size allocation. Sometimes you will want to know what happens when you increase or decrease the size of the cache or change the allocation of your RAM. It is certainly reasonable to optimize performance of your system by moving system RAM between buffers, threads, file spaces, RAM disks, spoolers, system resource blocks, and caches. In general, a cache of at least 256 kB is useful for text-based system caching. Database applications and GUI-based systems should have at least 512 kB. More cache merely increases the hit rate. Note that it takes about one CPU cycle to find an item in the cache. It takes about 15 CPU cycles when the cache misses, but it also takes between another 20 and 100 milliseconds to locate the item on disk. As a result, a cache miss is disproportionately expensive, and if the cache hit ratio becomes too low (that is, the number of cache misses becomes too high), performance suffers. Figure 4.14 shows the effects of adding more cache and the decreasing utility of each additional allocation. This does not mean that you should not add more cache; you may find that this extra memory for applications and swap space provides more speed improvement than disk cache.

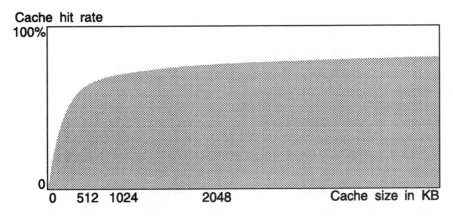

Figure 4.14 The effectiveness of cache as cache size is increased (MS Windows 3.1 and Speedcache+).

Not all caches are the same. Microsoft provides SMARTDRV for the MS DOS and Windows environments. However, better caches are available that provide faster performance, higher hit rates, and caching for removable disks and CD-ROMs. Examples include PC-Quik and SpeedCache+. SpeedCache+ from Future Systems is easier to configure and provides extensive information on cache performance. Note that while AMIDIAG showed the effective disk seek and transfer speeds of a Seagate drive cached by SMARTDRV to be 18 ms and 864,000 bits/s, Speed Cache+ showed 14.6 ms and 1.5 Mbits/s. Although the actual differences with real work may be minor, installation, configuration, and information provided may help you make better decisions and tune performance more accurately to your needs.

Configuration

System configuration refers to the hardware and software components of the system. This has substantial effects on computer performance. While this chapter has shown that faster CPUs and faster and wider buses tend to increase performance, the composition of components, the priority of those components, and the quantity of components also affect performance. Clashing DMA, interrupt addresses, and primary/secondary priority access rights can add 25 to 50 percent overhead to ordinary operations. Running a computer in a 100 degree room can increase overhead even though the computer equipment is rated to 130 degrees in a non-condensing environment; chips are not always reliable in a hot environment. Too many bus adapters creates a bottleneck of determining who gets access to the bus channel, adds demands for power, and increases the internal heat, with long-term system reliability effects, too. These are all performance issues, but not all are speed of processing performance issues.

Specifically, a SCSI (small computer system interface) adapter can support up to seven devices. These are usually storage disks, but also could be printers, CD-ROMs, scanners, or tape drives. A fully populated SCSI "daisy chain" tends to be difficult to correctly configure for the best performance of all attached devices, and it also represents a narrow communication channel (much like the system bus) for so many devices. Although improved SCSI device drivers, such as Corel SCSI, may simplify configuration and reduce conflicts between attached devices, SCSI-II provides a wider communication channel. You may find you get better disk performance if you add no more than two devices to a SCSI chain. When data or logical disk volumes "span" two or more such disks, you also may see improved disk access times because multiple disks are searched for the data simultaneously.

Substitution of bus-mastering controllers for dumb adapters, VESA adapters, or special hardware devices tends to increase performance by 10 percent or more. Note that the VESA VL-bus specification precludes the use of the FIFO buffer above 33-MHz speeds and fewer than three devices. The buffering and wait states degrade performance. Additionally, how the bootstrap files are designed, how large they are, and how many screen and printer fonts they reference affects performance. While these later issues are configuration issues, they are called environment settings. As such, they are discussed in the next few paragraphs.

Compaq Computer SystemPro Server provides an interesting configurable performance feature. Specifically, adapter boards can be assigned as *locked* to increase their relative priority for bus management and contention. Locked boards receive more polling attention than standard unlocked ISA or EISA boards, and thus slightly better performance.

Preinstalled configurations

Never assume that a computer has been appropriately optimized. Many PCs from different vendors were evaluated for this book; many gained 10 to 20 percent in performance with some simple optimization. One machine even gained 140 percent. All came with MS DOS 5.0 or 6.0 and MS Windows 3.1 already installed and other preinstalled software. Perhaps the most surprising finding was that most of the machines were poorly configured to support the anticipated performance loads. Specifically, all of the machines lacked a permanent MS Windows swap file of the correct size. One machine with 8 MB of RAM had an insufficient 2 MB temporary swap file. Many systems did not load SMARTDRV or had the minimal default of 512 kB despite 16 MB of RAM. Few loaded DOS or drivers into high memory areas. Several vendors provided AUTOEXEC.BAT files with references to nonexistent subdirectories and quality assurance software. DOS 6.00 machines were configured for the disk file compression drivers, but any floppies formatted with these machines contained the extraneous 51 kB file called DBLSPACE.BIN. Most of the device drivers provided were at least two revisions out of date; recent driver bug fixes, patches, and performance enhancements were missing.

Even though most of these machines supported higher VGA resolutions, all were configured for 640 x 480. The methods for selecting the higher resolutions were poorly documented since these machines had special video buses and non-standard drivers. One motherboard and matching monitor even supported a stunning non-interlaced 1600 x 1420 resolution in 24-bit color, but the possibility or method to reach this was not adequately documented. Perhaps even more interesting was that many of these machines were configured in CMOS so that the CPU cache was disabled or only partially enabled to buffer CPU and bus I/O. One machine based upon an Intel 80486 50 MHz chip and bus was configured in CMOS to run *slow* and emulate IBM PC AT chip and bus speeds. Why? Even computers that could support the faster 32-bit disk I/O were not configured for this in the 386 Enhanced options in MS Windows control panel. Again, why indeed? Excellent machines were configured for manufacturing convenience and simplicity. It was not the case that default values were chosen; they were configured *badly*. Perhaps, marketing and manufacturing wanted these machines to appear to be docile, plain vanilla, defect-free, and totally compatible with standard office software. Nonetheless, it is clear that better configuration can provide many degrees of performance optimization.

Environment

The environment in a computer system involves how RAM is allocated to buffers, caches, and main memory. It also involves where device drivers load into memory, how special memory areas and their names are allocated, how multitasking is supported, what disk and directory paths different types of commands search, how data and applications are swapped to disk from memory, and where applications look for their data. The more complicated the operating system, the more complicated the environment becomes. MS DOS is a fairly minimal operating system with few environment settings. On the other hand, the Macintosh environment, which borrows heavily from HP Smalltalk and UNIX, has a complex environment. OS/2, as a multitasking system, also has a complex environment.

The environment is represented by initialization and configuration files. Examples include CONFIG.SYS and AUTOEXEC.BAT for MS DOS and PC DOS, the bootstrap files in UNIX; COMMAND.CMD, AUTOEXEC.CMD, CONFIG.SYS, and many other referenced .INI files for OS/2; and WIN.INI and SYSTEM.INI, to name but two, for Microsoft Windows. Novell NetWare contains similar information in its startup file and .man INI files. With each revision and update of these complex general-purpose applications, the environment has become more complex. In fact, MS Windows has become so complex and such a widely used system that many vendors have created applications to interpret the environment, and provide optimization tips. Skylight represents such a tool. Figure 4.15 shows some hints from Skylight.

Furthermore, MicroHelp has created a product called the UnInstaller for MS Windows to untangle the effects of the many available Windows applications which affect the environment through new variables, configuration sections, directory structures, and private environment information. Specifically, most computer systems will run faster when these files are smaller. The fewer devices, keyboard remappings, and macros that are loaded into memory, the faster the system will run. The shorter the search paths are, the faster the system will run.

Overall, however, setting the environment is an art that yields relatively minor performance gains. For example, maintaining fewer true type fonts in WIN.INI minimizes Windows loading time; that is really it. Likewise, having fewer items in these files minimizes memory reserved for their use and also search time through the files for information contained within. That sounds like a major advantage, but realistically, the benefits are derived mostly when loading Windows itself or other applications into memory. Loading times are one-time events, not ongoing operations with consistent effects.

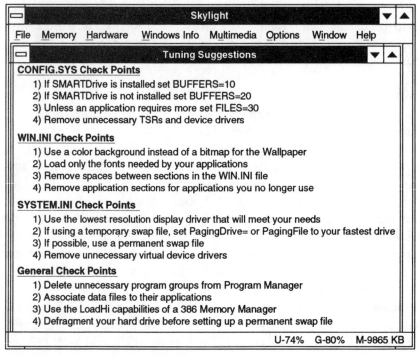

Figure 4.15 Optimization hints from Skylight for MS Windows.

Simplifying the configuration is probably more useful because it will minimize the potential for conflicts when adding new applications or devices. Use an uninstall routine to remove the dead wood, comment (if possible) on the purposes of each section and remove those without purpose. Realize that simple configurations as a matter of course will not only tend to be faster but also require less effort over time. If nothing else, that simplicity itself will optimize your time.

Install specialty hardware

Examples include hardware caching disk controllers and bus-mastering disk and video controllers. Hardware solutions tend to be faster than software solutions. Specialized memory on adapter boards tends to be faster than the general-purpose main memory. Furthermore, memory management and processing algorithms for these devices tend to be tuned for the specific tasks. As a result, many—not all—adapters improve performance dramatically. One note: software disk caches often outperform caches on controllers. The software algorithm is better, and because it requires fewer steps to access a cache, it improves overall performance.

Beware stacking disk caches. If a hardware cache improves performance and a software cache improves performance, the assumption that more is better is wrong. This is particularly the case when the software cache is larger than the hardware cache. Multiple caches working together tend to produce increased seek times and worse performance as caches clash, with duplicate information and duplicated attempts to bypass mechanical disk and device accesses. You will find it better to choose one approach; if you must try both, benchmark performance.

The WinJet printer controller, for example, provides the full 6-page/s print speed for desktop publishing on a 386 system instead of 1 page/min with MS Windows True Type in RAM. CorelDraw files that require 12 min in native mode take 5 min on the WinJet. However, realize that such times are critically dependent upon the system, RAM, print spool space on a hard drive, disk swap partition space, and CPU speed. The improvements were not so dramatic for a 486 machine, but were very appealing nonetheless.

Replace applications

Consider replacing GUI-intensive word processors with text-based applications. Lower the workload. Replace color drawing programs with hand-drawn art. Reduce the time spent searching CompuServe for the new time-saving shareware. Cut down on the effort spent looking through threaded E-mail for techniques on optimizing system performance. Reduce the time spent in computerized activities. Assess the effort and expense spent on activities that are constrained by computer performance. There may be better solutions for the organization.

Replace slow 8-bit applications with 16-bit or 32-bit applications. Examples include video drivers, caches, disk controller drivers, and the operating system. Much of the performance boost available under UNIX and OS/2 (rather than DOS or Windows) is provided by optimizing the operating system for the 32-bit hardware. Windows NT will be faster than Windows 3.x because it is designed for at least 32-bit CPUs and system buses.

Not only will enhanced performance be achieved by substituting operating systems supporting 32 bits, but end-user applications are enhanced when they are redesigned and recompiled for 32-bit operation. In some cases, applications are already built for 32-bit operation and bypass Window bottlenecks with enhanced drivers and internal routines. AutoCAD and CorelDraw are examples of applications that bypass standard Windows drivers.

Improve work methods

The most effective method of improving computer system performance is through assessing how you or another user performs a task to find a better way to do it. Optimization means improving the quality of the results as well as the more visible goal of improving the speed of results. As such, consider that a text-mode word processor may provide better service than a GUI-based one.

Similarly, fast typists may provide faster data entry with a text-based form than with fancier, more colorful scrolling GUI screens. Word for Windows is a resource hog and needs a faster machine. On the other hand, DOS-mode Wordstar is fast on almost any platform (although spell checking, search and replace, formatting, and other such CPU- and storage-intensive processes are dependent upon processor and disk speed). Furthermore, content is not obscured by the form and presentation errors of WYSIWYG GUI display. As such, you may find you write better with a simpler word processor than with a complex desktop publishing tool.

On the other hand, more complicated tools are apt to provide better results. For example, Wordstar may be adequate and more efficient than Word for Windows, but Doc-to-Help macros in WinWord make the trying task of creating camera-ready manuals and on-line hypertext help possible for the average person. Similarly, it may be easier to train people to use the pulldown menus and help bars in AutoCAD for Windows than to use the obscure keystrokes in the DOS version.

Reduce computerized tasks

The Luddites, who tried to destroy machines in England in the 1700s, would like this next optimization suggestion. Consider the importance of each task. Those that are not important should not be performed—even if you have been performing them for years. Some are just time wasters. Other have little utility. Get rid of the computers. Consider the costs, benefits, and scope of these tasks.

E-mail, network fax, EDI, and mailroom activities may be tasks that should not be computerized. Someone has to route incoming network facsimiles. Someone has to delete old faxes; delete misdelivered, unread, and aged E-mail messages; and deal with undelivered EDI information. Consider how easy it is to send a fax on a standard fax machine—not much harder than making copies. It is one of the simplest tasks in an office. And you want to automate it? Stuffing and sending a letter or an overnight document is not much more difficult.

Downloading that new utility from a Bulletin Board Service (BBS) takes time. In addition, extracting the files, reading the attached information, searching for viruses, and actually trying it out and learning how to use it represent a substantial investment. Time and money may be better served by buying an application with a known quality. Responding to and creating new mail for Internet and CompuServe could be all-consuming with minimal reward, and thus just a waste of time. Even the effort to computerize fax transmissions, particularly when documents and images must be scanned and reformatted as a presentable composite before transmission, represents an investment of time. The result is that some tasks are best optimized by not even doing them.

Consider these few examples as you read through the rest of the chapter. Maintain a perspective on your optimization goals. While most of the optimization methods discussed are effective and have been proven effective, consider that each may provide only one or two percentage points improvement.

Create object associations

For example, link DOC=WINWORD.EXE, LAN=LANMODEL.EXE, and TXT=NOTEPAD.EXE so that double clicking on a file object will automatically invoke the application with the pinpointed file.

Multitask

If your computer system and operating system can sustain the load, run operations in the background. The effect may represent no more than a 5 percent reduction of foreground resources. This is an effective technique for OS/2 and UNIX. MS Windows 3.x does not multitask well; background operations tend to stop when minimized or pushed behind a foreground window. Some data communications programs will continue satisfactorily if the system supports the UART 14550. MS and PC DOS do not support multitasking, but DOS operations can be run as true multiple tasks under OS/2 or Quarterdeck.

Multitasking is not effective for tasks requiring thinking, intermittent user input, or continuous monitoring. Batch spelling checks have given way to interactive tools; as such, the metaphors have changed. Multitasking is effective when the background operation requires no intermediate control, while the foreground task is pushed no faster than a person can think. Spreadsheets and word processing are good foreground operations. Graphics and presentation design are usually too resource-intensive to allow background operations to complete.

Integrate activities

TyIn 2000 and the Intel SatisFAXtion modems provide methods of integrating E-mail, voice mail, faxing, and remote connections through a single board. These represent an effective advancement of technology. A single supplier provides all the components in a unified package that requires less bus space and less energy than two or more components. The software tends to be more important than the quality of the hardware, so choose the package carefully. Replacing the total package or just the software and then learning the new version is not an optimization of your time. Figure 4.16 illustrates a multifunction product.

Figure 4.16 A single-board adapter that provides modem, fax, voice mail, and multimedia sound.

Similarly, consider how a task is accomplished. An 800-based mail order organization must generate billing, a pick list, a shipping label, and other collateral material as well for each order. It may be cost-effective to install side-by-side printers to generate the billing at one printer, a pick at the next printer, and a self-adhesive mailing label on another unit. Organizations with a small volume may consider a specialized label printer such as the CoStar or Seiko; it is an improvement over cutting and taping or gluing.

Better tools may speed up results, or they may provide higher-quality results but with a compromise in speed. For example, a printer dedicated just to forms may improve speed and simplify the work process. Or a specialized printer designed strictly for envelopes or labels, such as the CoStar Address Express or the CoStar Labeler provides the means to create package shipping labels and separate billing, without the need for paper changes, printer setups, or special envelopes with glassine windows and preprinted forms.

Laser-printed spreadsheets clearly look better than dot matrix output, but take longer. Similarly, full-color graphs of the same data take longer to print and are more expensive to produce, yet provide more satisfying results at board meetings and customer presentations. Some applications are processing-bound when they print—meaning that the printer is not the bottleneck, the CPU is. For example, it may take 10 minutes for CorelDraw to construct the image layers of an illustration regardless of the output device. Will a color image provide more effective proofs than a gray-scale composite sample or the four printed separations? Probably. That is one form of process optimization.

Stand-alone facsimile machines are easy to operate: stick the paper in the feeder, dial a number, and press the start button. It may not get more efficient than that. However, you may be wasting paper printing out the fax masters for transmission. You are likely to be losing valuable information and transmitting at peak phone rates. Computer-based faxing may provide the following advantages. First, it eliminates the intermediate printing step, lost pages, and delayed output. Second, the process of faxing from a computerized phone book provides a significant log of outgoing (and incoming) faxes. Not only are faxes tracked by a phone number, but also sender, recipient, company, and notes are maintained in a database. Third, faxes can be sent off-peak. This not only frees up the phone line during normal business hours, but also minimizes the phone bill.

Network fax technology is improved with stored graphic signature blocks. These are images—created by scanning a person's signature—and stored on the network for document inclusion. The signature images solves the problem of sending legally binding documents, an important concern for law firms. However, note that maintaining a signature on the network is a security risk that some organizations will find too risky.

Cost and labor savings

Computer technology can decrease costs and workloads. You merely have to analyze what is computerized and what is manual, and the priorities and costs for these tasks. For example, you might automate the printing, faxing, addressing, and envelope stuffing with price lists based upon formulas in spreadsheets. It does not matter that the information is individualized for each recipient. While the most obvious solution is to hire a programmer to build a database to solve this problem, it could also be automated with some clever spreadsheet macros. These mechanical sequences of keystrokes or mouse movements could look up information, including delivery information and actual price quotes, move it into cells reserved for printing, perform the calculations, and then send the print area to a fax, or even to a unit such as the TyIn or the SatisFAXtion.

EDI

Alternatively, for those customers who maintain a modem and the facilities for electronic data interchange (EDI) or who demand it, this information could be uploaded to their system for integration into their pricing and inventory systems. EDI is very effective for improving job turnaround times. Some organizations, GTE subsidiaries among them, require EDI for all vendors because other methods are too expensive for their operations. Data conversions are generally cost-effective and far more accurate than transcriptions.

It is also possible for the spreadsheet macros to send the information to two different printers at the same time—one for the price report, and one for individual mailing labels—or even to send some reports in one format to a printer, other reports to the fax, some by modem, and some by E-mail so that a person subsequently can make a phone call and discuss the new pricing with the customer. Object linking and embedding (OLE), dynamic data exchange (DDE), and drag-and-drop also provide many other possibilities for automating and enhancing user activities. These examples were specifically chosen because they are simple and common activities. While many organizations might view these approaches as using expensive technology for something that can be done manually, a cost-benefit analysis may show that some repetitive and time-consuming tasks can be accomplished with better accuracy in fewer hours.

Specialty printers

Assess so-called *simple* tasks within the context of optimizing organization efficiency. Another cost-saving alternative is an inexpensive envelope printer. The per-unit amortized cost for an ink jet unit tends to be cheaper than the marginal cost for windowed envelopes. It is also easier to fold an invoice or addressed bulk mail without concern for how the piece must fit relative to a window. Mass mailing is also optimized with an envelope printer, if only because it saves the step of applying the label to each envelope. There are several vendors providing medium-speed units, including CoStar.

Other specialty printers can solve different types of problems and cut costs. A bar code label printer can improve inventory tracking, material handling, and product losses. This POSTNET bar coding unit could provide appropriate mailing tags for Federal Express or the ZIP+4 postal codes for the USPS. Likewise, a magnetic ink character recognition (MICR) printer prints the specialized Federal Reserve bank codes, standard check information, individual check amounts, and logos—on blank safety paper at a cost of a penny per check rather than at a cost of 10 cents per check provided from banks and service bureaus. Furthermore, such units can integrate without any programming into common accounting software, including Quicken, Macola, Platinum, and Real World.

Organizations that create hundreds or thousands of checks—payroll checks or small refunds—may find it convenient to augment MICR check creation with stored graphic signature blocks. These are images—created by scanning a person's signature—generated and stored on the network for document inclusion. The signature image solves the problem of mechanically stamping or laboriously signing every check. However, note that maintaining a signature on the network is a security risk that some organizations will find too risky.

Some vendors have begun providing laser cartridge refills, remanufactured cartridges, or new cartridges suitable for standard laser printers with MICR toner. This may present a more cost-efficient test of in-house check printing with existing equipment. You might question such issues of check durability, type and code durability, and adverse affects, if any, on your laser printer and its service warrantee. You should probably dedicate at least one such unit solely to MICR toner since it will not only be inconvenient to change toner cartridges, but perhaps abrasive to the fuser drum and corona wire assembly.

The entire check is printed and numbered as needed, with various collateral stubs or secondary pages on standard sheet paper. Checks no longer have to be specially printed on pin-fed form paper and limited to once a week. The software does not need to be informed that checks were voided because they were misaligned. Errors or voided checks can be reprinted correctly with the *same* check numbers. Checks also could be written from multiple bank accounts without changing stock and realigning the printer. Create-a-Check from Create-a-Check, Inc. and BlankCheck from Magnetic Software work with standard laser printers with special MICR toner cartridges. Of note, you can change toner cartridges on a single printer if the toner and drum are contained in the same unit. High-volume check writers should know that laser MICR printers from ACOM print 32 pages per minute on safety stock. This avoids the need for signature stamps, preprinted checks, mechanical paper bursters, and refanners.

Color output

Inasmuch as it is possible to optimize many GUIs by reducing the screen resolution and setting the display to monochrome or a minimal gray scale—in fact, the Macintosh for years was monochrome only—the color and resolution limitations seriously hamper the display of information. Color is important for setting tone, importance, and contrast, while higher resolutions can increase the density of the information presented. Color output has become less expensive, and resolution has increased as well. Color is useful for providing more effective graphs and images that represent an organization, improving the perceived quality of the workmanship and of the individuals performing that work.

Low-end color dot matrix printers (from Citizen and Seiko) are available for several hundred dollars and provide resolutions (260 x 200) several times better than the best video displays. For triple that amount, you can have a Lexmark PostScript printer with 360 x 360 ink jet and thermal wax printers with three primary colors and black for highlights. While color printing is not necessary in every office, and perhaps not even in every organization, an accurate and inexpensive proofing capacity represents a good optimization time and reduces errors when creating four-color desktop separations for desktop publishing, images, graphic designs, and CAD blueprints.

Optical character recognition

Keying information into systems by hand is tedious, slow, and prone to error. Instead, when data cannot be converted from one electronic format to another, they can be read by machine through optical character recognition (OCR). While vendors claim 99 percent accuracy, the reality is that one error per 10 words is expensive to correct. However, these accuracy rates are generally for ordinary photocopied text.

Accuracy rates and utility can be substantially improved by selecting clear copy and good typefaces, and also by training the application to recognize the typefaces you commonly see. Also, applications such as Caere OmniPage Professional include spelling dictionaries attuned to character misinterpretation. "I" can look like "l," and "i" or "t" or "|"or even "!" can become confused with "1." Within the context of a word and position within the word or sentence, the meaning can be clarified. Accuracy and utility can be improved in other ways, too.

Text can be masked so that only certain portions are read. Bulk editing with a graphic view of the original can also be more cost-effective than keystrokes.

Some tips for improving the accuracy and speed of scanning include setting the scanning resolution as low as possible, turning the color mode off and using line or gray-scale mode only, installing the latest scanner driver, and providing copy with the greatest contrast between the background and the characters. Such simple steps will speed the actual scanning time and raise the probability of 100 percent text recognition accuracy.

If for nothing else, OmniPage and a flatbed are useful in an organization to recover all those computerized documents that have been lost, misplaced, or corrupted. Scan them in from hard-copy originals and you have them again in an editable format. Text recognition software also provides a new use for B/W scanners that have become outdated by color scanners. The quality of the scan—resolution and color—is not really pertinent for OCR.

Optical character recognition is available with many fax packages. Typically, recognition accuracy is lower than with hard-copy printouts because the line noise and lower resolution of most facsimile transmissions limit the quality of the source document. Nonetheless, a typical fax converted to text may require 4 kB per page versus the 70 kB typically required per image page *with compression*. If you can tolerate the error rate, savings in terms of disk storage can be substantial, as you can well imagine.

Bar code readers are not as general-purpose as flatbed scanners and OmniPage Professional software. They do not read text. They cannot recover lost documents. They do, however, read one of a dozen or so previously specified bar codes with 100 percent accuracy and can cut keying time and errors in production environments.

Delay new software

Software upgrades and new releases do not make for optimum performance. In general, software gets more complex, includes more functionality, and requires more disk space. Upgrades may resolve substantial performance issues, as with the dBASE 4.1 version released to resolve basic functionality and speed of performance issues. The new version at least worked. But new releases provide other less than optimal results. Consider Corel Corporation, which is not singled out for any reason other than that its stunning success with their graphics illustration package has empowered the company to add many new features to each revision. For example, CorelDraw 2.1 requires about 7 MB of disk space. CorelDraw 3.0 requires 33 MB of disk space. CorelDraw 4.0 may well necessitate a CD-ROM device for code, overlays, bitmap images, clip art, and other goodies. Although, many important functions in CorelDraw have been improved both from the speed of performance vantage point and in terms of user utility and functionality, consider the impact of such software upgrades.

Also, upgrades that install over older preexisting versions often leave debris in the form of support files, configuration files, and overlays or .DLL files not needed by the upgrade. In order words, the upgrade has been tested to see how it actually performs, but not tested in terms of how well the upgrade installation removes traces of the earlier release. You might consider either installing the upgrade to a new and empty subdirectory or installing it over a duplicate of the older version. Compare the files in the two directories and remove the deadwood. Tools, such as MicroHelp Uninstaller described earlier in this chapter, track down related disk files and mark them for removal.

When there is a fundamental upgrade in the operating system or graphics shell, the effects may ripple throughout all software applications. You may need more memory, more CPU horsepower, and new releases of device drivers, and nonetheless see some new system compatibility problems. Once these operating issues have been resolved, there are the secondary problems of spreading the upgrades throughout an entire organization. If only a few people upgrade—by their own choice—data file compatibility problems may soon force them to abandon their upgrades or compel the MIS organization to make a fundamental decision to either support only one release or upgrade the entire organization. Such choices are costly. Change brings new costs. This tends to be suboptimal for some time after the change.

Upgrades also bring about new training and support costs. All those new features raise questions about how to use them. Sometimes the new features replace existing functionality, with the result that old work must be converted to account for the loss of functionality and the shift to the new. Consider all those Lotus 1-2-3 versions 2.0, 2.1, 2.2, 2.3, 2.4, 3.0, and 3.1 and the effects on macros written by users when an organization shifts to the newest releases and decides to support only one DOS-based and one MS Windows-based version. Suppose the organization decides that the upgrade costs are so high that it is worthwhile to shift all 450 users to Quattro Pro or Excel. What will happen to all those macros? How compatible will they be? Who will convert them? So what if Lotus Improv will "improve your view"? Sometimes, you must balance user performance gains against the fully burdened costs of installing upgrades, retraining users, or making fundamental software changes.

Modem connections

In general, establish remote connections at the highest possible transmission rate. Modem speeds vary from 300 to 14,400 bits/s. Anything under 2400 bits/s is slow and generally expensive in terms of time. Most BBS services which charge for connect time have a premium for 9600 bits/s that is double the standard 2400-bit/s rate. Assess your time, phone connection charges, and the actual connection time costs. You will probably find that the faster speed is actually cheaper unless you have substantial thinking time during the connection. If high-speed modem connections are PC-based, check that the serial I/O buffer is based upon the 16550

UART rather than older and defective versions with a measly 1 byte buffer, as explained earlier in this chapter.

Modems which include on-the-fly data compression can achieve a four-for-one data compression; the normal compression generally achievable is a two-for-one compression. This will increase throughput by two times. On-the-fly compression is usually performed with only a minor lag in transmission because the stream of data is compressed in parallel with the transmission. Note, however, that the modem on the other end must support the same compression method. Generally, this means that the modem on the other end must be of the same type or from the same manufacturer. Furthermore, on-the-fly data compression of already compressed files—these include ARC, LZH, and ZIP files—merely increases transmission time because it takes longer for the modem to realize that the data stream cannot be compressed further than it already is.

If you share a phone line for voice, fax, and modem, disable call waiting before initiating connection. The call waiting beep will corrupt fax transmissions, cause connections to fail, or add noise to the data transfer. The usual method is to type *70 before making the call. This sequence could be added to dialing string or provided as part of the initialization string for each phone call or for the modem setup. Most communication software and terminal emulators support this feature.

Video refresh

Some graphic-intensive operations are bottlenecked by the speed of repainting the screen. This includes graphic design, desktop publishing, CAD, image processing, and almost all processing within a GUI environment. If performance is an issue and video is a bottleneck, there are two possible courses of action, as the next sections explain.

Reduce video workloads

The first is to simplify the computing environment and reduce the overhead. For example, take a GUI-based data entry operation and run it in a text-based environment. If the environment cannot be replaced, minimize that environment. Reduce the number of processes running simultaneously, reduce the font overhead, simplify the layers of resolution, or use fewer colors. Run full-screen rather than in windowed modes. It is far easier to improve video performance by lightening the load than by increasing the horsepower. This will also have the secondary benefit of improving overall system performance.

Add video horsepower

The second possible action is to add horsepower. Install a video coprocessor with a Weitek or S-3 chip. Replace an existing video controller with a bus-mastering video board. Upgrade the system to one supporting local bus video, a method in which a bus is added strictly to support the higher-information bandwidths required by GUI environments and image-intensive applications. Gains vary from milliseconds to 20 s.

You will not notice gains of milliseconds except when you run benchmarks designed to stress the display over 30 s; only then will 44 million pixels per second seem much different from 9 million pixels per second. The reason is that few applications paint more than 1 million pixels at any one time. Even a full 1024 x 768 MS Windows display in 16 colors only represents 389,120 pixels—not even a million pixels. Generally, the split seconds gained become think time, suspension of activity, or even process time if the application designers realize that video will be a bottleneck and construct parallel processes.

Video resolution and modes

Although video resolution as a factor in video speed was previously mentioned, it is repeated here for clarity. The amount of information repainted on the screen can be minimized by reducing the video resolution—the number of pixels displayed and the number of colors in use. Monochrome requires only 1 bit, whereas monochrome VGA may require 4 or more bits. Note that monochrome 4-bit VGA requires the same overhead as 16 colors—also 4 bits. The information content of 16 colors is very useful, and you will do yourself a disservice if you shift to 4-bit monochrome mode. Understand the implications of your attempts to optimize performance. Big speed changes are evident when the screen requires more than a million pixels, as with 24-bit true color.

Video displays

Video displays vary in color size, resolution, dot pitch, scan rates, video speed, and technology used. A couple of issues are important in terms of system performance. If you plan to function in a gray-scale or B/W mode and configure the system that way, resolution will be superior if you drive a monochrome or gray-scale display screen. A single-color phosphor provides greater sharpness than that provided by multiple electron beams or multiple scans. Additionally, from a safety viewpoint, the single-color displays tend to produce lower EMS and RF pollution, pollution which has been linked to miscarriages, leukemia, cataracts, brain lesions or cancers, and other maladies without confirmed scientific proof.

Resolution and dot pitch are factors of how much information can be displayed on the screen at any one time. Performance-wise, a larger screen with more information means that more overhead and time are typically required to paint the screen. However, higher scan rates and *smaller* dot pitch increase the sharpness and clarity of the image for better display fidelity. Higher scan rates and a noninterlaced display also minimize flicker; some say flicker causes eye strain. Flicker is also a factor of electric cycle rates in the displays, of background electric lighting, and of moire or strobe effects.

Laptop displays typically use either LCD (liquid crystal display) or gas plasma technology in order to minimize weight and display thickness. Gas plasma tends to provide monochrome orange images against a black or dark background. LCD displays are either a reflective silver on a black background or the reverse. Some LCD displays provide color. Active LCD displays provide better performance than passive LCD displays. First, active displays create light for brighter images rather than relying upon reflective ambient lighting. Basically, this means that active displays are easier to see. Second, the viewing angle for active displays is considerably wider, which means that you will not have to adjust your viewing angle to see the image and that people sharing the screen with you will be able to see the screen images directly from the sides, as Figure 4.17 illustrates.

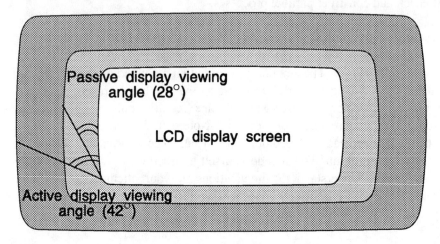

Figure 4.17 Active LCD displays provide greater latitude in viewing the screen.

Memory
Many video systems and accelerator cards support more than the minimum amount of memory. Insufficient memory will hobble these cards and affect performance, or prevent use of higher screen resolutions. You might check whether older systems have empty memory sockets. This is particularly pertinent for PC systems sold for Windows when the VGA resolution was 640 x 480. These video subsystems may support higher resolutions, but do so well only when fully populated with memory—memory which may cost as little as $9.

Power consumption
Performance for many notebooks and laptops can be measured in how long the computer will run on a single battery charge. Active color matrix screens use three or more times as much power as passive monochrome. Disk drives that continue to spin even when there is no need for disk access waste power as well. Portable computer users must make choices between speed, overall CPU performance, and battery longevity. These performance goals usually represent tradeoffs. Here are some methods for extending portable computer battery usage and usable life:

- Charge battery when not in use (nickel hydride batteries do not retain a discharge level memory)
- Drain Nickel-Cadmium batteries fully before recharging to avoid the discharge level memory
- Set lower values for screen brightness and contrast; select a monochrome display
- Use all power conservation features
- Minimize the number of disk writes
- Minimize temperature changes
- Do not use in a frigid environment
- Use the AC adapter whenever possible
- Power off facsimile and data modems when not in use since they use a lot of energy

Power consumption is not only a laptop issue. Many buildings do not have the infrastructure to support the desktop computers as needed by the organization. Who really wants to pay the money to rewire and add the necessary cooling capacity to support a 420 watt computer on every person's desk? Computers that turn off the monitor, stop the disks, and reduce the power level to the CPU reduce electrical loads, energy costs, and heat output. These "green" computers conforming to the Environmental Protection Agency (EPA) *Energy Star* program represent certifiably energy-efficient systems and a means to optimize performance within the imposed limitations. Energy Star computers consume 30 watts or less when unattended. This also has the effect of increasing the lifespan for electronics, mechanical drives, and monitors.

Consolidate functionality provided by multiple adapter cards into single cards. As mentioned earlier in this chapter, replace modem, fax, and voice mail cards with single units supporting all these features. A single NIC with ODI or NDIS drivers can replace multiple ones for gateway or routing functionality. Multiple modem cards can be replaced by units with multiline support. Not only will this reduce energy usage, it will also lower the internal operating temperature of the computer and increase the usable lifespan of the computer.

Artificial bottlenecks

Most operating systems contain built-in bottlenecks caused by fundamental design choices. Specifically, MS DOS was designed as a single-user 8-bit operating system when 8 kB represented an expensive investment in memory chips. As a result, a large program space was seen as 64 kB while a far-sighted individual granted two 8-bit address spaces in case someone saw a need for 128 or 256 kB in data space. What seemed a reasonable design decision has created the 640 kB DOS memory address limitation, the EMS, HMA, and LIM memory management extensions, and many complex attempts to stuff more operating system in high memory to free space for actual applications. Other DOS limitations include the

A-Z disk partition space, the limit to 256 items per directory, the longest path length of 250 characters, the longest single path in the environment variable at 67 characters, and the 99 files that can be opened at any one time. These limits are artificial, but nonetheless very real impediments for performance, and thus very real limitations.

MS DOS is not alone; other operating systems and network operating systems have artificial boundaries too. MS Windows 3.x is limited to two 64 kB segments of system resources, a problem for some users who want or need to run multiple applications concurrently. The overhead required for each window or form limits it to about 50 applications. Banyan Vines, of course, has just expanded support for more *inodes* to support more complex file systems. Vines also sets limits on the size of a swap space (to 8 MB) and the number of swap spaces per disk (maximum 8) and file server (maximum 16). But Banyan was built upon UNIX and it has limitations also. When swap space and RAM become limited, the system *thrashes* in that memory is juggled between RAM and disk without productive results.

File spaces were limited to 2 GB and were only recently expanded to support file systems several magnitudes larger. Support for concurrent or asynchronous operations is limited by the hardware architecture, the limits of RAM and RAM addresses, and the ability of the OS to share CPU time and swap segments. Artificial limits include limits on the number of messages supported, the number of simultaneous connections which a server will maintain, or the number of sockets assigned for communications.

Likewise, NFS and other NOSs are typically constrained by preset allocations for simultaneous sessions, stacks, or I/O buffers. Some may dynamically allocate these pathways; yet most do not. More complex message-oriented and object-oriented network operating systems and GUIs are limited by the number of pipes, named pipes, NFS daemons, streams, or other connectivity channels. When the limit is reached, no amount of tweaking, performance tuning, head scratching, and hoping will alter these walls. Only when these walls can be moved, torn down, or expanded can these fundamental bottlenecks be resolved.

Feature exploitation

Many GUIs, operating systems, network operating systems, BIOS versions, and applications have hidden features, unexploited configurations, functions not completed or fully implemented at the initial product release. MS Windows 3.x, WFW, and NT have many of these. MS DOS and PC DOS has some. The Apple Macintosh exhibits a few in both System 6.x and System 7.x. As attractive as these opportunities may seem, exploit them with care. Some only work under very specialized circumstances as the next three examples show. The 32-bit disk access option in MS Windows only works with specific Western Digital controllers and clones which are exactly 100 percent compatible. Similarly, while IDE disks can support 512 byte data transfers, most PC ROM BIOSs limit data activity to the

128 byte sectors. While a newer BIOS version could fix this problem, it is not yet forthcoming. Meanwhile, Ontrack Computer Systems Drive Rocket bypasses this limitation. Likewise, Sun Microsystems provides a performance enhancement called the *Database Excelerator,* which is described in Chapter 6. These utilities or features capitalize upon performance tradeoffs or not-quite-complete implementation. These features should be part of the product, but are not yet.

If these exploitations are actually useful they will be fully implemented or included as standard functions in future product releases; otherwise, they are relegated to the scrap heap of clever ideas that are never completely resolved. The window of opportunity is about one half of a generation between sequential product releases. It takes about half a generation for the opportunity to be noticed and commercially exploited—and also be noticed by the primary vendor. Anti-virus, disk data compression, and file undelete or deleted file recovery—what were OS enhancements provided by third-party utility software—are now generally part of an operating system or the basic support library.

Although the three enhancements described above actually provide about 30 percent speed of performance improvement for disk access operations, implementation is risky. Technical risks abound—you could corrupt your data and database files. Configuration and compatibility shortfalls provide some more of the risk. The rest is financial; it takes resources to implement these opportunities, train people to use them, provide documentation for these complex options, time to fully test and install them, and the likely possibility that these exploitations will be formally included, disabled, or even excluded with the next primary vendor release. You are well advised to perform a cost-benefit analysis—or at least carefully scrutinize the results and eventualities from a less-traveled path—before committing yourself or an entire organization to this risk.

Truthful optimization cost

In addition to the financial costs for buying new equipment, upgrades, and spending money for outside consultants or diverting in-house specialists for performance optimization, there are other subtle costs and serious risks too. There are significant risks to optimizing operations. MIS, computerized accounting operations, and data processing have become assembly line activities. Anything, just about anything, can upset the smoothly running balance that has developed in the computer-driven and computer-controlled paper mill. Performance optimization is one of the risks. New hardware, new software, particularly upgrades and enhancements, and the sudden tweaks to configuration files and parameters can disable local and networked operations. Certainly, that is the wrong result. That is not the only cost.

Consider the expense for training people to labor with a different system, network, or software. This cost is not only seen with the direct training costs, but also in terms of lowered efficiency during a transition period and subsequent personal help support. This transition period could last as long as a year for some operations. Such chaos could destabilize the work environment and cause some people to work elsewhere. That increases the pressure to contribute and produce results. Furthermore, sudden changes or too many changes impede results simply because too much has occurred; often people cannot assimilate all the new changes. The MICR printer and the label printer and the new word processing software can easily represent too much for the users. It can also represent too much for the managers to implement. You might consider the scope of optimization and the potential effects on an organization before undertaking a daunting optimization process.

Conclusion

The most effective means of improving system performance is to lower the workload. If you decrease the system load by half, you increase effective performance by 100 percent. You will have doubled performance. One caveat is that you accurately assess the cause of performance bottlenecks. Typically, stand-alone (non-networked) single-user systems experience bottlenecks first on hard disk I/O, then in bus capacity, then in CPU capacity, and then at graphic video display. This load is always caused by a software application. Thus, the most effective method for improving performance is to see how the application's performance can be improved, whether by replacement, substitution, or code enhancement. There might be better software available.

You can also reassess how a system is used. There are always better ways to accomplish goals and get work done. To merely assume that performance can be improved by running the work on a faster machine misses easier methods of enhancing it. You can scan text or codes instead of keying them in. You can send E-mail instead of a facsimile. You can send broadcast, personalized messages instead of individual letters. You can address letters and packages automatically with a label or envelope printer instead of with cut-out windows. You can stop doing a task that has no value to the organization.

On the other hand, you can address the bottlenecks and resolve them. Disk-based bottlenecks can be circumvented by caching software or better caching software and by replacing slow units with faster drives, replacing single drives with two such units, or replacing two drives with separate controllers. Achievable performance gains are in the range of seek time reductions of 14 ms to 10 ms and transfer speeds of 1 Mbits/s to 4 Mbits/s, or 60 Mbits/s on superserver computers. Since disk activity represents from 5 to 40 percent of a typical application's time, gains range from 2 to 230 percent overall performance improvements. The issue is whether peak disk activity bottlenecks can be optimized.

Likewise, you can substitute a faster CPU or replace the system as an entity. The difference between 386 and 486 systems or between 486 and Pentium systems is about 20 to 40 percent in added power, the same as for other platforms. Since CPU activity represents from 5 to 30 percent of a typical application's time, gains range from 1 to 10 percent net overall processing speed improvements. The issue is that peak activity bottlenecks will be optimized for CPU-bound processes, and actual performance gains will rarely be as high as 100 percent. The same math is applicable for bus and video bottlenecks. You can possibly achieve a 10 percent performance improvement. A new platform and CPU with a better architecture may yield a doubling in overall performance, about the same performance change that can be achieved by improving the performance of an application or lessening the system load.

Operating system optimization hints

This last section in this chapter includes optimization techniques and hints for some common operating systems that are represented in *Computer Performance Optimization*. Before trying any or all of these ideas, benchmark performance. You will want to know if they work, how well they work, and if they work on different platforms. Second, if these ideas necessitate that you remove or modify files on the system, make certain that you can restore them in case of errors. Take precautions. Some files are sensitive to minor changes and will prevent the system from starting or booting. Please make sure that you have a boot diskette (or tape) that *works* (test it first) so that you can restore the system to its pristine and original working condition.

Even when deleted files are available on original distribution diskettes or tapes, individual files may not be easily restored. Replacing these few missing files may entail a full application installation over the original file space. Files are often packed into sectors without file names for differentiation, or the files may be compressed into bundles or individually compressed. Special optimization, customization, and user files may be removed by this process. Make certain you can get those files back; copy or move the files to a dead file directory or to a separate floppy disk or backup tape. Also, check that the backup is usuable. Too many people make backups that are not functional and recoverable.

General hints

Free up dead disk space
Remove unneeded applications
Remove old temporary files
Remove installation routines
Remove bitmaps for backgound displays
Remove games, sounds, and color images
Remove on-line help (primarily from networked clients)
Remove languages, compilers, interpreters if not used
Remove PCMCIA support files (for desktop machines)
Remove power management features (unless used)
Remove applications you do not need
Remove pirated applications (if you did not pay for it, you probably do not need it)
Check for and remove file chains
Unchain fragmented files
Low-level format disks (on-the-fly is best)
Relocate key applications and software to optimum disk positions
Add memory to system
Use a faster disk subsystem
Install a solid state disk or disk subsystem
Use a faster CPU
Use a faster modem (i.e. replace a 2400 baud unit with a 9600 baud unit)
Test clarity of voice grade lines for modem-based communication
Disable swap files or virtual memory when using using a modem
Make more subdirectories with fewer files in each
Shorten search paths and the number of possible search paths
Optimize configuration of static cache to cache the entire RAM space
Check the PC bus speed and set it to the fastest speed the software will accept
Install applications with a minimal configuration; avoid the extra file baggage
Delete reinstallation or reconfiguration programs from the hard drive
Do not display graphic images when a placeholder can be used instead, or an image hide command that will show pictures as boxes
Download system bitmap fonts to printer for faster printing
Lower the graphics resolution required
Disable animation
Lower priority of printers, spoolers, and accessory tasks
Recompile applications to take advantage of optimizing compiler features, 32-bit memory spaces, and new instructions on chip sets

DOS

Use a faster disk subsystem

Use a faster CPU

Minimize CONFIG.SYS

Minimize AUTOEXEC.BAT

Minimize the environment, including paths and named variables

Do not install duplicated drivers

Load a disk cache

Enable disk cache lazy-write or write-behind option

Load a RAM disk and stock it with often-used data and applications

Load DOS into high memory

Load drivers into high memory

Use extended rather than expanded memory

Use disk compression to increase disk capacity

Run a task switcher for multitasking and memory containment

Use FastOpen drive:=xxx, where xxx is the number of disk file locations to
retain in memory, to improve initial file access, and enable FASTOPEN to
increase access to often used files

Find recently used files with DIR %1/P/O:-D

Use XCOPY when copying multiple files

Install DOSKEY to recover last commands

Delete ANSIS.SYS, DRIVER.SYS, KEYBOARD.SYS, PRINTER.SYS, and
DISPLAY.SYS from \DOS if they do not appear in your CONFIG.SYS

Remove SHARE.EXE from \DOS and CONFIG.SYS or AUTOEXEC.BAT if it
is not needed (it may be needed in multitasking shells and MS Windows)

Minimize STACKS, FILES, BUFFERS, and LASTDRIVE

Use UMBFILES option

Disable the EMS driver if not needed

Load memory management drivers in high memory

Macintosh

Add more RAM

Use a faster disk subsystem

Use a faster CPU (replace or upgrade machine)

Replace logic board (through Apple)

Install a larger disk

Install a software-based caching disk driver

Install a software-based caching CD-ROM driver

Disable System 7 file sharing

Replace Finder with a faster, more efficient application

Do not upgrade to System 7

Install the System 6.x patch for faster SCSI transfers

Use a paged memory management unit (PMMU) chip for virtual memory with
System 7

Virtual memory (swap file space) should not exceed twice available RAM

Avoid the use of NuBus slots for intrinsically busy attachments

Upgrade the processor (chip replacement)

Install a static RAM cache

Add a cache card

Install a coprocessor or accelerator card

Run a file defragmenting tool

Install a disk compression tool

Upgrade to a MAC supporting 32-bit data paths

Install a 24-bit graphic accelerator card (verify effectiveness first)

OS/2

Use a faster disk subsystem

Use a faster CPU

Add more memory

Add more static cache

Increase I/O buffer size

Increase disk cache size (for FAT and HPFS)

Enable disk cache lazy-write option

Minimize CONFIG.SYS

Minimize AUTOEXEC.CMD

Minimize COMMAND.CMD

Minimize the environment, including paths and named variables

Optimize IOPL, PRIORITY_DISK_IO, PRIORITY, THREADS, MAXWAIT,
and TIMESLICE

Do not install HPFS unless disk volume is greater than 100 MB

Do not load the IFS driver unless running HPFS

Optimize the IFS HPFS settings for your RAM availability

Do not install duplicate drivers

Remove unneeded device drivers from CONFIG.SYS

Close applications upon exit

Create a large swapper file; keep swapper file unfragmented

Load a disk cache
Do not allow the \TEMP disk to be full or nearly full
Do not load a RAM disk
Use disk compression to increase disk capacity
Use an optimized screen driver
Minimize the number of active fonts
Minimize the number of tasks initiated at startup
Minimize the number of separate sessions
Set idle sensitivity to a lower value
Use G4 or TIFF compression with IBM 40x9 graphics printers
Minimize the number of background tasks
Reduce task switching
Run applications in full-screen mode
Minimize the number of icons in visible folders
End applications before shutdown
Turn off lazy write for critical applications
Do not use DOS defragmentation utilities even on DOS FAT partitions
Run multiple MS Windows applications in single Win-OS/2 session
Use 32-bit applications
Disable the MS Windows spooler in Win-OS/2
Reduce EMS and XMS memory allocations to 64 kB
Tune the WIN-OS/2 and DOS-OS/2 settings for COM Port direct access and
    exclusive use if needed for emulation performance
Do not load DOS drivers globally unless all sessions require most of same
    drivers
Load DOS high and provide sufficient DOS FILES
Maximum or limit RAM available to a DOS sessions

SunOS

Use a faster disk subsystem
Add more disks rather than larger disks
Use a faster CPU
Add more memory
Add more static cache
Increase the size of the inode cache
Remove unneeded compilers, shells, etc.
Minimize the number of background tasks (kill)
Disable read after write verification
Install RAM or the Database Excelerator drivers
Lower process priorities (nice)
Pipe output to next application (rather than creating a file)
Serialize processes (asynchronously rather than synchronously)
Install a keyboard history or SET HISTORY=40 to keep the last issued
    commands
Optimize serial I/O with special hardware processors
Optimize serial I/O with special software
Use raw disk partitions rather than logical partitions
Stripe objects across multiple disks

UNIX

Use a faster disk subsystem
Add more disks rather than larger disks
Use a faster CPU
Add more memory
Add more static cache
Remove unneeded compilers, shells, etc.
Minimize the number of background tasks (kill)
Disable read after write verification
Lower process priorities (nice)
Pipe output to next application (rather than creating a temporary file)
Serialize processes (asynchronously rather than synchronously)
Install a keyboard history or SET HISTORY=40 to keep the last issued
    commands
Optimize serial I/O with special hardware processors
Optimize serial I/O with special software
Use raw disk partitions rather than logical partitions
Stripe objects across multiple disks

VMS

Create separate directories for E-mail files
Increase Wsextent to 2048 (dafault=512) and Wsmax ≥ Wsextent
Use a faster disk subsystem
Use a faster CPU
Add more memory
Add more static cache
Minimize the environment
Do not disable security
Do not install duplicate drivers
Create separate directories for E-mail files
Increase Wsextent to 2048 (default = 512) with Msmax ≥ Wsextent
Build a stand-alone (no applications) backup tape
Speed boot time; mount volumes with the /NoRebuild command
Copy new software to disk first for installation
Do not allow directories to contain more than 127 blocks of file names

MS Windows

Use a faster disk subsystem
Use a faster CPU
Add more memory
Add more static cache
Check for proper manufacturer preinstallation
Minimize CONFIG.SYS
Minimize AUTOEXEC.BAT
Load DOS into high memory
Load drivers into high memory

Run DOS sessions in high memory with LocalLoadHigh=True in the
   SYSTEM.INI file under the [386ENH] section

Minimize the environment, including paths and named variables

Do not install DOSKEY and other utilities not needed by Windows

Do not load a mouse driver for Windows (if it is built in)

Do not install duplicate drivers

Defragment the drive before creating a swap file

Create a large swap file (about twice the size of RAM plus 4 MB)

Increase the swap file size

Close applications upon exit

Load a disk cache

Enable disk cache lazy-write or write-behind option

Enable FASTOPEN to increase access to often used files

Do not allow the \TEMP disk to be full or nearly full

Do not load a RAM disk (cache and swap files are faster)

Disable Print Manager, or install a faster third-party replacement

Print direct to a port

If system has more than 12 MB of RAM, disable swap file

Use disk compression to increase disk capacity

Minimize WIN.INI and SYSTEM.INI (remove blank lines and unneeded lines)

Use the minimum acceptable screen resolution

Run Uninstall (Micro Help) to remove old software

Do not load multiple font managers

Minimize the number of active fonts

Turn off scalable fonts (the rasterizer) for display purposes

Do not load desktop bitmap image

Do not load patterned wallpaper

Minimize the number of tasks initiated at startup

Minimize the number of background tasks

Run applications in full-screen mode

Minimize the number of icons in visible group folders (icons) and the number
   of folders in Program Manager

Decrease the icon spacing so that more icons will fit within a group

Check the 32-bit Disk Access box in Virtual Memory Dialog form if your bus
   and controller will support the FastDisk option

Add MouseInDOSBox=0 for faster cut and paste

Set Ctrl-Alt-key combinations (hot buttons) to launch favorite applications

Do not use multimedia

Remove .WAV, images, and other extras from the system

Delete the unneeded WAV drivers from SYSTEM.INI and the hard drive

Delete .HLP files (on-line help)

Move .HLP files (on-line help) to server or secondary storage

Remove .DLL files that are not (no longer) needed

Change (increase/decrease) the SYSTEM.INI setting PageOverCommit=x,
   where x is a number between 1 and 20, to change the amount of virtual
   memory for multitasking applications that are swapped to the hard disk

Change the virtual memory setting to match the PostScript or other printer's
   actually installed RAM quantity

Print in PDL rather than PostScript mode

Change DOS applications to exclusive execution in the advanced PIF settings

Give DOS applications 100 percent foreground priority so that they will run faster

Use DOS FastOpen drive:=xxx, where xxx is the number of disk file locations to retain in memory, to improve initial file access

Reclaim the DOS page frame if you do not run DOS programs that need expanded memory by adding this option to DEVICE=EMM386.EXE and FRAME=NONE to CONFIG.SYS, and add NOEMMDRIVER=TRUE under the [386ENH] section in SYSTEM.INI

Use the DOS translation buffers, if unused, by adding the option DEVICE=EMM386.EXE I=x000-x7ff to CONFIG.SYS, where x represents the hexadecimal address of the free high memory area, and add EMMINCLUDE=x000-x7ff under the [386ENH] section in SYSTEM.INI

Set stacks=xx,yyy to larger values to overcome hardware conflicts or to address unreliable and erratic application or system performance, where xx equals the number of interrupts dynamically handled and yyy is the size of each interrupt buffer in bytes

Use 32-bit applications or the 32-bit MS Windows 3.x extensions

Minimize the number of groups in Program Manager

Minimize the number of items in a group in Program Manager

Allocate direct communication port access and bypass standard com port drivers when employing high-speed communication

Provide faster DOS session switching by setting INT28Critical=False in the SYSTEM.INI file under the [386ENH] section; (note that this will crash or hang stations on a network because it needs the interrupt set to True)

Establish a shared Windows group with read-only properties within a shared directory; use the [Restrictions] section in PROGMAN.INI with NoRun, NoClose, NoSaveSettings, NoFileMenu, and EditLevel to prevent access to Control Panel changes and the personalization of the desktop

X Windows

Use a faster CPU

Add much more memory

Remove frivolous X programs

Minimize the requirement for bitmaps and iconsp

Do not load the X logo

Replace background bitmaps with color background (xsetroot -solid cyan)

Minimize the number of initiated processes in your environment

Minimize the number of active widgets (and icons)

Replace applications that do not use shared libraries

Recompile applications having static links to use dynamic ones

Move processes from overloaded X servers to other servers

Run the X terminal manager locally rather than from the server

Design multiple window applications rather than applications that require multiple instances of the same application

Employ a faster malloc() library

Manage and resuse dialogs rather than creating and destroying new ones for
each instance

Upgrade the version of UNIX to one with fewer memory leaks

Restart the X server when memory leaks become large

Minimize the number of paths searched for system-wide, user-account-wide,
and class-wide for resource commands and properties

Eliminate optional environmental variable settings

Check for class names in capital letters that may load program binaries and
allocate memory based upon non-existent resource commands

Replace 8- and 16-bit PC graphics adapters with faster 32-bit cards

Replace older X releases with newer versions that convert floating-point code to
faster integer calculations

Close applications upon exit

Minimize number of active fonts

Minimize the number of background tasks

Run applications in full-screen mode

5

Application
Enhancement

Introduction

Applications are represented by utilities, single-user applications, networked applications, client/server applications, and distributed computing applications. This chapter covers optimizing the performance for different types of applications. Applications are also either text-based or run within a graphical environment. Text-based applications will inherently run faster than their graphical counterparts because there is less overhead in painting 24 lines of 80 characters than in converting those characters into kerned images and then painting 333,000 bytes (or even more) of image data. AutoCAD for DOS runs faster than AutoCAD for Windows. A text-based SQL query tool runs faster than a similar X Windows request for SQL information. A directory listing is faster than a tree construction in a graphical file manager.

Since applications represent the most substantial performance bottleneck, it is important to recognize the difference between a computer bottleneck and a process bottleneck. In the first case, the computer is slow. In the second case, the computer is used badly, or certainly not with full effect. There may be alternatives to solve the same process with better tools or methods. This chapter shows you how to be attuned to these nuances and tune applications appropriately. Some applications apply asynchronous processing to overcome the otherwise linear delays in data processing. Software design tricks can overcome the inherent bottlenecks in performance; some applications are better than others. For example, applications may also support user interrupts so that mouse movements and keystrokes take precedence over computation. This makes the computer system more responsive to the person than to the task; the computer seems quicker and always available to the user. The tasks can be completed when the system or component utilization levels provide free resources.

If performance is a problem just with the operating system and network access, there are fundamental problems that must be addressed before you even consider the user applications. If you see performance bottlenecks at the hardware, configuration, installation, or network levels, run benchmarks or invoke diagnostic tools to ascertain the source of these limiting problems. (However, if you perceive network bottlenecks are to blame, see Chapter 7.)

The heart of any computer operation is in effect the applications as the user sees them. These applications may be layered upon priority and task control managers, network operating systems, or server operating systems, but in any case they will be on an operating system, such as a DOS, OS/2, UNIX, or GUI shell (including Macintosh, Solaris, X Windows, and MS Windows). The user applications typically use 75 to 99 percent of the processing capability of stand-alone and server systems in bursts. If you are seeking to optimize performance, consider applying 75 to 99 percent of your tuning effort to the applications, rather than the architecture, CPU, platform, or disk subsystems.

This chapter will show you how to benchmark and optimize the performance of both text-based and graphical applications. It will also show you how to configure computers in order to optimally address the requirements of different applications in different operating environments, and suggests methods of recoding and optimizing applications for which you have the source code. The major topics include the items enumerated in the following list:

- General optimization tips
- GUI-based applications
- TSRs
- Background processes (multitasking)
- Local and remote processing
- Memory management
- Garbage collection
- Calculations and force reductions
- Platform selection

- Character-based applications
- Overhead minimization
- Multitasking
- Swapping
- Heap space
- Duplicate resources
- Table lookups
- Search techniques
- Partitioning the workload

General optimization tips

This section provides some general information on making a computer run faster. It provides quick information on what you can do to increase application performance. This chapter also shows the rationale for evaluating performance and choosing from the options that you have. Computer performance does not become an issue until actual user applications are run on the system. Run benchmarks. Upgrade components that are slow. If you have reached the capacity of the platform or limits of the operating system, you will have to optimize performance in other ways. You will want to discover that before you seek to optimize the applications that run on top of the operating system.

Typically, applications run faster with more RAM, larger CPU caches, larger disk caches, storage disks supporting faster seek and transfer times, faster disk controller interfaces, multiple disks, a wider or faster bus, a faster CPU, and a faster video display. The order of that listing is important; the components are listed in decreasing order of importance. If you see performance bottlenecks at more than a few components, the computer is too sensitive. Avoid the trap of upgrading a system in small pieces; the time can be better spent evaluating and entirely replacing the bottlenecked system with a faster platform.

Applications tend to run faster with more memory because they can load more application code or data into memory at one time. Since RAM is faster than disk by a factor of at least 100, this provides the greatest enhancement. Exceptions to this rule include DOS-based applications that do not use expanded or extended memory, as well as any application that is small and in no way stresses the limits of available memory. Increasing the CPU cache, which is usually static RAM, to its limit improves the coordination of getting instructions and data to the CPU for processing; this improves the overall efficiency of the CPU. Most CPUs tend to process only 10 percent of the time or less, as Figure 5.1 shows, with the MS Windows utility CPUUSE.EXE, which is provided on the tools disk.

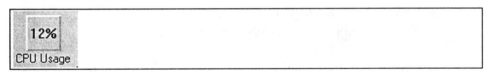

Figure 5.1 CPU Use shows CPU utilization with a minor time delay.

As stated in the last chapter, cache and RAM disks are effectively electronic replacements for hard drives. Any data or instructions retrieved from cache, RAM, or RAM disk can thus increase performance quite dramatically by saving 15 milliseconds. If you can code a lookup table so that it stays in RAM, or preload a master index or customer list, for example, into a RAM disk, you will save those milliseconds each time a request is repeated for that information. Function code that is frequently referenced should be easily found and not swapped as segment, overlay, or dynamic link library. Code such that key components are RAM-based rather than disk-based.

The typical CPU—this includes stand-alone systems, network clients, and network servers—spends 90 percent of its time waiting for instructions or data from RAM or hard disk. Run MEM, SPM/2, PSTAT, and other utilities to see CPU and RAM utilization; however, RAM utilization values may not be accurate for operating systems that frequently page to disk, since the system will write RAM to disk in the form of a swap or temporary file in order to make more *virtual* RAM available to your applications. Figure 5.2 illustrates CPU utilization also, but notice that the disk appears to be a bottleneck when an autosave file operation is executed. SysUse is also an MS Windows utility on the tools disk.

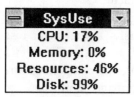

Figure 5.2 SysUse shows CPU, memory, system resources, and disk utilization.

Note that it is unwise to rely upon only one benchmark or utility to generate performance information. As you can see in Figures 5.1 and 5.2, CPU results are rarely shown in real time and may lag behind operations. While both of these utilities show approximate loads, the values at a single instance are not as exact as a graphical timeline, which these utilities provide. Also, it is possible that the load levels are wrong; you would not want to base an expensive upgrade and buying spree on limited, inadequate, or inaccurate information.

Because the RAM is 100 times faster than the hard disk, anything that can create a closer link between these two improves performance. As such, larger disk caches raise the hit rate for locating data in cache rather than on the disk. As illustrated in the prior chapter, the hit rate, or effectiveness of the cache, increases to a point, after which adding more cache is functionally irrelevant. At that point, only faster disk subsystems improve performance. Since the difference between last year's fast disks with 14-ms seek times and this year's units with seek times of 10 ms represents a 29 percent improvement, it is worthwhile to replace disk subsystems when disk I/O is the bottleneck. Note that this rarely results in a 29 percent systems performance boost even if the disks are the active system constraint; disk activity represents no more than 60 percent of CPU cycles even in the most demanding graphic applications. You may boost overall performance by 18 percent. Even with faster disk drives, the difference between RAM and disk is still roughly a factor of 100, so there is substantial room for improving system performance by increasing the disk throughput and access speed.

One way this can be achieved is with faster controllers. Install 16-bit controllers in systems that will support them and are currently constrained by 8-bit adapters. The same holds true for systems that have 32-bit or wider buses, but adapters with smaller data widths. Avoid controllers with built-in cache. While this is a great idea, recall from Chapter 3 that you are stacking caches, and the hardware one may not have as effective a caching algorithm, or one tuned as well to the operating system. Benchmark caching controllers before committing to them. As mentioned in Chapter 4, some specialty caching and data compressing controllers worked better than the native motherboard controller did, while some were not even as fast as old and well-optimized RLL or MFM drivers, and others worked well only when system configuration did not include software for caching. It is important to realize that there are substantial differences between controllers with wider data paths, controllers with faster components, controllers with specialty features (such as hardware caching), and controller drivers; test before assuming better performance and compatibility with your operations.

By the same reasoning, more disks provide a wider bandwidth for accessing data. Similarly, multiple disks with multiple controllers increase the amount of data that can be accessed simultaneously. The only limitation is how much data the bus can support at any one time and how much communication among multiple disks and multiple disk controllers the CPU can manage; it is usually a timing bottleneck and queue service limitation, rather than a strictly capacity-limited bus or CPU issue. As such, when the CPU or bus control is the limitation, advanced bus mastering controllers are pertinent for off loading the CPU and coordinating concurrent tasks. Bus width limitations can be overcome only by wider data buses or data buses that are specialized and separated by function. Effectively, a bus change means replacing the entire system with a faster one.

The CPU is rarely saturated in single-user environments; recall it usually averages 10 percent loading. Exceptions include CAD, complex spreadsheets, mathematical modeling, threading and multitasking, extensive floating-point processing, and processes that are CPU-intensive, such as image conversions and vector or matrix processing. In such cases, the applications will benefit from a numerical coprocessor, array processor, scalar processor, or floating-point accelerator. These are secondary CPUs that perform the complex math in fewer clock cycles than the general-purpose system CPU. For a secondary CPU or coprocessor to yield performance benefits, the application must be aware of the chip and be compiled *specifically* to take advantage of its special processing capabilities. This also is true for many Intel and RISC chips. The same holds true for applications initially developed for earlier revisions of chips. Typically code compiled for use on an Intel 80386 will run faster on the 80486 chip (250 percent faster) or Pentium (350 percent faster), but not as fast as when that code is recompiled specifically for the newer generation chips. This is partially due to better compilers, compilers that take advantage of new features in the chips, such as dual pipe-lining, and compilers that optimize code. Some compilers also remove inefficient duplicate code or code that serves the same purpose as built-in system calls and functions.

Check with the application vendor for relevance, or see the Intel publication that describes PC and MS Windows applications which benefit from Intel math coprocessors. Benchmark carefully before you make an upgrade with Cyrix, AMD, IBM, Buffalo, Intel, or TI chip sets; some do not support floating-point processing, instruction or data caching, or pipe-lining. These chips may provide better generalized performance and be plug-compatible with existing sockets, or they may provide only specialized performance increases that may not pertain to your applications' specific bottlenecks. Also, recall from Chapter 4 that some systems will not physically accommodate the waste heat from upgrades or provide sufficient head room for the 80486 upgrades or Intel Overdrive chips with chip-mounted heat sinks or thermal cooling units.

If you are running on an Intel 386-based platform, consider replacing that system with a 486 system; most 486 chips include a built-in math coprocessor while some reengineered and Intel-licensed chips do not. Choose the new system with care. Since the system is engineered for better overall throughput, you may realize more substantial performance gains than just a CPU upgrade. However, some tasks are so infrequently performed that benefits are not material. While a floating-point processor will increase the speed of bitmapped font generation from vectored formats such as Bitstream or Adobe, this is usually a one-time event. Fonts which are scaled on the fly are scaled by integers and then bit-specific hints are applied; they do not benefit from a coprocessor on most operating systems.

Lastly, graphic display coprocessors or enhancement boards are generally insignificant except when they provide special resolutions, increased image density, or true color display. In those cases, they provide a *function* otherwise unavailable. While these cards do increase display performance—the WinMark benchmark shows performance ranges from 2 million to 60 million pixels per second—this corresponds to one-sixth of a second time saving on a typical screen redraw. It becomes pertinent only for graphic applications, and only those graphic applications that intensively redraw the screen or continuously refresh the screen.

Application redundancy

A key killer of disk space, training costs, configuration, and technical support is redundant applications. While this could mean duplicate copies of software on client systems and servers, it is more likely to mean that WordPerfect for Windows and MS WinWord are loaded for the same user. It could also mean that one group uses WordPerfect and another group uses Lotus AmiPro. Redundant applications are more likely to occur with customized software built from dBase, Foxpro, Paradox, or other user and programmer tools. An organization is likely to employ more than one development tool for essentially the same purpose. While there may be valid reasons, this suggests an inefficiency.

Optimizing character-based applications

Character-based applications are by far the most numerous. While many organizations are moving to X Windows, PowerOpen, Macintoshes, Sun Sparcstations, MS Windows, or UNIX-based GUIs, most organizations depend upon financial applications which are 10 years old or more and character-based. Similarly, most database applications that may have started life as host-based CICS applications and were rewritten in a DBMS or 4GL are character-based as well. Even applications ported to a PC are typically dBASE or Paradox applications built with a standard 80-character wide by 24-line text screen. The technique and the tools for building applications within a GUI are only beginning to be funneled down to mainstream organizations.

The first step in optimizing a character-based application is to determine what it is that you (or the target users) want to optimize. It is important to understand what your true goals are before souping up equipment under the impression that the "program runs too slow." Instead, data entry may run too slow or be too time-consuming. It is also possible that printing or actually getting reports is the bottleneck. The difference here is that the computer system itself is not the bottleneck, but some other aspect of the process is. It is too easy to miss the problem or make mistaken assumptions.

Find out in explicit detail what is slow. If it is your own machine that is slow, explore the problem. Specify exactly what is slow. Is it data input, sorting, disk activity, processing, or getting printed output? Is it waiting time for the system to respond to a keystroke or redraw the screen? Consider the underlying cause of the problem, not merely its manifestation. For example, if printing is slow, underlying possibilities include that a printer is connected in a serial fashion rather than the faster parallel link. It is also possible that the printer or logical link between queue service and physical connection is not configured correctly, or a network queue is disabled. The computer system may expect a confirmation from the printer that it is ready for the next chunk to print, but the system times out waiting for a go-ahead signal that never comes; it finally sends another chunk in desperation. The printer could have 2.5 MB of memory, but the application may think it has a value of 0.5 MB, the value which the MS Windows HP PCL driver defaults to when initially selected and installed.

Network printing can create bottlenecks for other reasons too. Typically, a printing bottleneck results from an overloaded printer. The printer could be off-line without paper, without toner or ribbons, with a page jam, or an illegal character sequence. The print queue could be full. A large print job could delay results and subsequently create a print backlog.

Imaging complex graphics or PostScript is process-intensive. Even character-based applications, such as Lotus 1-2-3, could create an image in PostScript mode that creates a printer bottleneck. Other page description languages (PDLs) tend to be more compact and efficient of network bandwidth and printer processing time. A PostScript or standard PDL file sent to a printer with the wrong PDL enabled also represents a configuration bottleneck; you will likely get many pages with some sparse characters or pages with streams of garbage characters forcing you to re-create and reprint the job. Even printers that recognize and automatically switch between PostScript and other PDLs may fail occasionally with networkwide ramifications. Consider multiple network printers with a specific PDL and special paper-handling trays to alleviate these types of bottlenecks.

On the other hand, the user may be complaining about how time consuming it is to enter the same information repetitively, or to perform the same task each week in the same way. You need to account for the fact that people do not always communicate clearly and explain the underlying issues. Typically, a person might say "the computer is slow" when the person means "the task is slow to perform on the computer." Recognize the difference. If the task is slow, assess what tools might improve performance. Consider how to better accomplish the task.

Recall the example from the last chapter in which a price list is faxed weekly to customers. Prices were retyped each week into WordPerfect from a Lotus spreadsheet, then printed, and eventually faxed. The process was split across two applications and two platforms. Instead, the process could be integrated after rethinking how it should be completed. WordPerfect merge mail supports some mathematical capability and could complete the task. Lotus also provides extensive macro capability for providing numerical processes and merging output. Consider that databases lend themselves to creating processed reports and control how and what data is entered. Perhaps a masked-entry database represents a better means for accomplishing the same task than data entry and macro automation in Lotus or transcription and mail merging in WordPerfect.

It is important to be able to make this jump from a specific request or user-analysis in order to make a more fundamental assessment of performance and operations. The alternative is that you will satisfy the requests for more horsepower without finding better solutions or addressing the underlying problems. You do not want to merely speed up WinWord for a user with more memory, faster video display, and an upgraded CPU when the user is complaining about the screen performance for typing when in *preview* mode.

The issue could well be that the user is not typing in the normal mode or does not have the view enabled to show picture place holders rather than the full bitmap. It is possible that *autosave* is enabled for time periods as short as 5 s, an unreasonably short interval which could artificially boost disk and CPU loads on any system to capacity. It is also possible that bitmaps are not shown as smaller monochrome thumbnails but rather as full four-color monsters. Figure 5.3 shows that the Picture Placeholders option for WinWord display is enabled.

As a result, a user scrolling through a document will experience substantial delays while bitmapped images are displayed. This example is not meant to pertain exclusively to GUI-based word processing applications, or even WinWord specifically. In fact, most applications provide user-configurable settings and options to bypass preview displays, online help, pulldown menu displays, reindexing, recalculation, or screen refresh. These facilities were provided by application developers because they recognized the inherent delays in these resource-intensive operations and have provided a method of bypassing them to improve user response time.

Picture placeholders speed up how the application paints the screen and how pictures are added to an application. The format affects the speed of loading a data set (or document) and the disk space required to contain that file. File size is not only a function of image format (vector images tend to use much less than bitmapped images—and there are many different formats of bitmapped images as Chapter 4 explained) but also of how an image is inserted into the file.

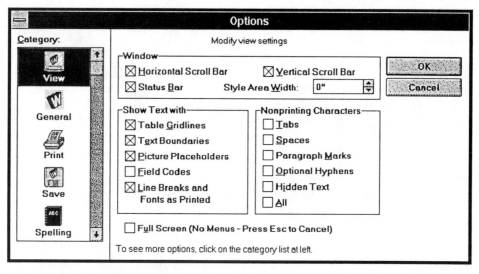

Figure 5.3 Displaying bitmaps in WinWord increases CPU and disk utilization. This degrades response time as the user experiences it. It also increases file sizes. Check the picture placeholders option as shown.

Dynamic data exchange (DDE) and object linking and embedding (OLE) are primary culprits under MS Windows, although the method for image insert does matter. An image embedded from another MS Windows application requires about three times as much memory (and disk space) as an image inserted as a permanent part of the file. Images that are linked maintain only the setup information for the linked object and retain significantly less RAM or disk space since multiple copies of the same image are not retained in different applications. However, the graphic image is only as reliable as the strength of that DDE or OLE link. Similarly, when Apple, IBM, Novell, and OSF complete their OpenDoc specifications for network integration of objects and compound documents, similar tradeoffs will apply.

Consider also that better tools are already available within the environment, or that the user is misusing the applications. You may not know all the features and functionality of an application. Consider the problem of a Lotus 1-2-3 user who has constructed a spreadsheet that no longer fits in memory because there is a mistaken cell entry at location AZ4096. This increases overall spreadsheet size. As a result of this unwanted padding, RAM requirements are also increased. The 420-kB worksheet with the empty-cell bloat may require only 80 kB when it is exported with only the active cells included, as Figure 5.4 shows.

A user could also have developed a series of cells to calculate loan returns and spread valuations when built-in PV or NPV formulas would provide exactly the same results in fewer cells with less overhead. Built-in functions usually would provide results faster than formulas because they are optimized for Lotus. This same point can be made for applications created by programmers in Basic, C, or a database language. Use the built-in tools in the compiler, in source libraries, or call functions available in the target operating system. This is more efficient in terms of resource utilization. Built-in functions are also debugged and less likely to have defects, and often are optimized with versions of the system.

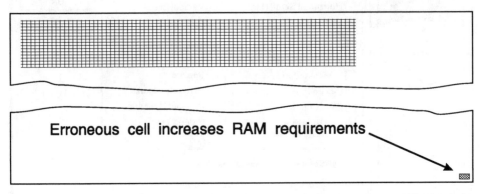

Figure 5.4 A spreadsheet with a cell entry beyond the normal range dramatically increases RAM and disk requirements (for some applications and some releases).

Even a spreadsheet that is larger than memory can be partitioned into smaller linked multidimensional spreadsheets, or results can be extracted from multiple spreadsheets and automatically imported into a master spreadsheet with macros that run when that master spreadsheet is loaded. With UNIX, System 7, MS Windows, or OS/2, large spreadsheets can be linked from smaller parts with dynamic exchange of data; most of you may know this as OLE (object linking and embedding) or DDE (dynamic data exchange). While you may have explored it as a means to increase efficiency and accuracy in complex and compound documents, you may not have considered it as a method to increase performance and minimize disk space. OLE, DDE, and drag-and-drop operations also provide many other possibilities for automating and enhancing user activities. The performance problems created by massive spreadsheets are red herrings; they are misuses solved by proper application of the tools.

When application performance suffers, consider software-based alternatives first. If the software is the bottleneck, consider what software may be better. For example, if compilation and object linking are slow, consider better compilers. If the system is slow in processing a full-color image, consider converting the image to an RLE representation first. Consider compressing an image with a Joint Photography Experts Group (JPEG) algorithm to remove extraneous details and reduce the size of the file. If data entry is slow, consider a faster application. Consider also if keyboard macros will help. A single key sequence with a function key can invoke an entire name, address, and telephone number. For example, "F9a" could mean "World Trade Center, Battery Park, New York, NY 10003 (212) 421-" and this sequence could be inserted into the keyboard buffer. This would minimize typographical or data entry errors and speed up the process. Repetitive operations invoked by key sequences can be automated with a macro containing those same key sequences.

Sometimes, of course, text-based applications are slow simply because they do a lot and just stress the hardware. Many times, substituting (or building an application from scratch) is too costly and too risky to consider; you are committed to the existing application. Lotus 1-2-3 may be slow because the manual recalculation must go through complex numerical formulas. Similarly, removing the image of back and internal layers in a CAD application when viewing the model as a three-dimensional object (rather than as a wire-frame design) is process-intensive. A presentation application, such as CorelDraw, that is generating the output rendering has to convert all the layers and all the line figures into solids. Run benchmarks. Do timings on different hardware. See how these are affected by different platforms and configurations. Will the process actually complete faster on a 486? If this is a significant application in that 30 people perform the same task, acquire a hardware trace, such as the Dekko Systrace adapter for OS/2. This will show where CPU, bus, communications, disk, and other subsystems are performing relative to capacity.

Optimizing GUI-based applications

The importance of graphical applications is increasing. X Windows, Macintoshes, MS Windows, UNIX-based GUIs, and client/server OS/2 applications represent a desirable transformation from the legacy of mainframe applications for many organizations. Unfortunately, graphical applications and visual shells require significant computing capacity. They require more RAM, more disk space, faster disks, and faster CPUs. Graphic accelerators may improve performance. You may also take the view that the faster hardware has provided the means to make some concepts possible in software. Either way, most GUI applications require more resources, and optimization usually means providing sufficient resources so that these applications will work well. You are up against the overhead required to display multiple windows, convert character information into graphic representations, and display more information at higher resolutions. The display that was once 1280 bytes large is now upwards of one-third of a megabyte. You will need from 3 to 5 MB for 24-bit true color displays.

Just as the first step in optimizing a character-based application is to determine what it is that you (or the target users) want to optimize, you should perform the same analysis for GUI applications and environments. Understand the goals before souping up equipment under the impression that the "program runs too slow." The distinction to recognize is that the computer system itself may not be the bottleneck. It is too easy to miss the problem or make mistaken assumptions.

Find out in explicit detail what is slow. If it is your own machine that is slow, explore the problem. Specify exactly what is slow. Is it window management, task management, disk activity, processing, or getting printed output? Is it waiting time for the system to respond to a keystroke or redraw the screen? Can you run multiple applications in the background and switch between them to improve your performance? Consider the underlying cause of the problem, not merely its manifestation.

When performance is a problem for an application, consider software-based alternatives first. If the software is the bottleneck, consider what software may be better, or whether the vendor can provide intermediate releases which fix the observed slowdowns. Given the typical complexity of GUI applications, most performance problems are more likely to be resolved in software than in hardware. Consider that the next iteration of a major hardware component may be only 1.4 times faster than its predecessor, as the Pentium is relative to the Intel 80486 DX/2. Balance this against creating a better algorithm that reduces CPU requirements on critical portions of code by one-third. The change is equivalent, although it is far more likely that the code can be optimized than that the CPU performance can be increased so substantially.

Because GUIs generally support multiple operations at the same time—unlike most text-based environments—consider how you might lower the overhead and CPU for critically slow applications. Kill unneeded tasks. Try to pipe results concurrently from one process into the next process to utilize the power of multiprocessing or threading. This reduces the effective time that may be required to complete an application by maintaining a high load on the CPU while reducing the load on the disk subsystems. If you can concurrently perform CPU-intensive and disk-intensive activities, you may provide very noticeable performance improvements. For example, piping a UNIX stream process reduces the need to create temporary files. This keeps more of the immediate process within RAM rather than paging out to the disk. Piping also reduces the disk overhead for creating these files.

One last point on this topic is that the raw performance comparison between the Intel Pentium chip and the Intel 80486 DX/2 is not necessarily a relevant comparison, or between other chips or platforms. Usability and the mix of processing demands are important concerns too. Furthermore, direct system replacements are usually a better use of money than hardware upgrades; a partial upgrade is likely to cost fully burdened nearly the cost of outright replacement. Plus, a replacement provides two working machines with the capacity to do about twice as much work, whereas the upgrade provides only one machine.

It is likely that users have stand-alone stations or are network clients, which represents a significantly older generation of CPU *and* system architecture. For example, replacing a 80386 SX 16-MHz system with a Pentium or RISC-based Sun Microsystems workstation for a single CAD user represents a substantial increase in CPU and subsystem performance. Similarly, replacing the 80386 with a pin-compatible 80486, inserting an Overdrive CPU in a ZIF socket, or adding a Pentium on a daughterboard may provide more cost-effective results. Just make certain that these hardware upgrades do not exceed the capacity of the PC power supply or overheat the system. Revisit the iCOMP index comparing different CPUs and subsystems. These newer, expensive systems will typically support a specialized graphic and disk DMA channel for outstanding performance. Upgrading hardware can provide significant enhancements for GUI-based applications when it is a financially possible option. For both financial or performance reasons, consider complete platform replacement before making incremental hardware enhancements and upgrades.

Chip and compiler changes

Although manufacturers try to make newer generations of chips compatible with older generation operating systems and application code, better performance is not always possible just by making something ten times faster. Chips with faster clocks, while desirable, push the limits of chip-making technology. Until RAM, board design, network speeds, and long-term storage media begin to match the efficiency of microprocessor chips, better performance results from chips with better algorithms and better traffic and congestion control, from compilers tuned to the idiosyncrasies of each chip generation, and from process multiplexing. In fact, the Intel Pentium and IBM/Apple PowerPC chips represent technological improvements in traffic and congestion control at the electron level. Specifically, the Pentium has a dual pipeline for instruction processing and an onboard cache designed to maintain the speed of instruction processing. However, by reordering the instructions in a program to keep both pipelines full, by keeping chip registers full, and by minimizing memory transfers between the chip and main memory performance is optimized. In general, the most effective method to increase performance is by decreasing the software load; one significant approach is by matching compiler technology with the chip sets, thus optimizing the compiler.

Improvements in optimizing compilers include command line switches that will convert existing code into faster programs with potentially no recoding. For example, Microsoft's C/C++ compiler provides enhancement specific to 286, 386, 486, or Pentium chip sets. Effectively, a preexisting program can be recompiled specifically for each chip set to provide a smaller executable file and an executable which will run faster on the target platform. The compiler converts conditional branches with 16-bit displacements for better performance than 8-bit jumps. It tries to identify double word instructions and convert them into faster ones. Double-word pushes, pops, moves, or comparisons with memory locations reduce multiple instructions into single instruction CPU operations. However, this is not the perfect solution to recycling and enhancing preexisting applications. Some compilers, Microsoft and Borland included, try to convert semifixed variables into labels with values fixed at compilation or into volatile (local) variables. Code conversion is not always perfect in that the resulting optimized, compiled code could perform erratically and overwrite memory, run slowly, or work unexpectedly; the optimized code could perform something completely different. When this happens, designate portions of code that should not be optimized.

Similarly, it is beneficial to avoid an address generation interlock (AGI), which is a processor gridlock. It may also be termed the *extra-clock-cycle penalty*. This problem occurs because a memory address or register referenced by an instruction is unavailable as it is being affected by a previous instruction that has already begun but has not yet finished processing. It also occurs when both pipelines reference the same memory locations or chip registers. A processor is waiting for a data request that is slowed because of a synchronous messaging requirement. The processor stalls. This bottleneck is not a resource limitation, rather an artificial one, as explained in Chapter 4.

AGIs are a problem for the Intel 80486 because of its advanced architecture. Adjacent instructions could stall. However, this is more of a problem with the Pentium chips, RISC, ASIC, and other superscale architectures because instructions separated by four intermediate instructions could create an AGI, and not just once, either. It is possible to experience a rolling bottleneck, where an instruction, such as a move and add, that should execute in two clock cycles may require four clock cycles due to the intermediate instruction stall.

Compilers can correct or accentuate these limitations. For example, a smart compiler will realize that by inserting an innocuous instruction between adjacent AGIs, the overlap can be avoided. The result is executed in three clock cycles; the two original instructions complete in two clock cycles but the extra instruction padding requires the third clock cycle. An even better compiler will realize that the two instructions can be separated into different pipelines so long as each does not reference the same memory locations or registers. As a result, these two instructions complete in a single clock cycle. Performance improvements range from 25 percent to 400 percent. While avoiding AGIs is relevant to only a small subset of instructions, some critical code that executes nearly continuously—such as device drivers—might provide such substantial improvements. A compiler can also optimize far memory calls. An indexed displacement address (far memory) requires an extra operation to build the long address; compilers and programmers try to avoid this technique on a 80486. However, the Pentium requires no such operation and adds no penalty for addressing a displacement address. Compilers that optimize memory management and the dual pipeline provide substantial improvements.

Object-oriented applications

Object-oriented applications, created with object-oriented programming technology (OOP), represent a special case of graphical programming. While it is possible to create a text-based OOP-based application, the development and programming technology is more apt to be found within GUI-based environment-developing tools for a GUI-based environment. The reason OOP technology is discussed as part of the topic of optimization applications is that OOP alone or OOP with GUIs tend to create larger and more complex applications. There tends to be a significant performance impact with object-oriented code.

Specifically, objects represent data fields, scroll bars, icons, command buttons, and windows. All these objects refer to an underlying table describing properties as well as events that occur when certain properties or other events occur. Events include value changes, drag-and-drop operations, clicking a mouse and selecting an object, gaining or losing object focus, and timed or background operations. Selecting objects typically creates a cascading effect of object value changes and cascading events. The cascading events themselves create more object value changes. OOP applies and enforces the concepts of code modularity and reusability. This tends to create modules that work as expected. There is an OOP joke that some objects do nothing until you tell them to do something and then they can do anything unless you tell them not to. This also creates the unanticipated side effects of vague module purposes, code bloat, cascades, and value changes.

Cascading events represent additional workload. The workload requires more system resources, including disk access, CPU time, bus throughput, and video updates. An object change in sequential code-oriented programming usually does not reflect a data entry change nor does it initiate a process until a command is specifically initiated. Sequential code-oriented applications tend to be more efficient with computer resources. An analogy is in order here. Sequential code is best represented by the numbers, with the operators entered into a paper tape calculator. Only one event happens at a time, and it happens only between the operator and a limited number of operands. OOP applications can be likened to a spreadsheet (with recalculation enabled) where cell changes are instantly reflected throughout the formulas in the spreadsheet. The most active object-oriented programming can be compared to a spreadsheet with a circular set of equations. For example, A1=Assets, B1= Liabilities, C1 = Equity. A1 + B1 should equal C1, but C1 is comprised of a component called *Shortfall*, which is equal to B1 + C1 - A1. When Equity is balanced with a Shortfall or capital borrowing requirements, the end result is a circular calculation. This represents unstable code and a significant performance hit.

Lotus 1-2-3 and other spreadsheet applications know enough not to continuously recalculate. Instead, they will show a circularity flag. On the other hand, OOP applications are not that smart or as well optimized. While it is unlikely that an object-oriented application will have a true circularity, it tends to have the recalculate option permanently activated. The cascading effects of object changes create a severe performance hit. Screens are repainted, graphical presentations are updated to reflect wire frame or sizing aspect changes, and data ranges and base values are updated to reflect the current state. Now, all OOP applications are not that processing-intensive. Some are optimized. However, many more represent the state of the art—the learning edge of the technology—and do not confine the scope of the cascading values. In fact, some manufacturers of mainstream applications that are building updates of their products have delayed releasing them until the products are stable and optimized for performance.

While this is important for software application design (and also for operating systems and networks) when you choose which applications to run on your computer system or network, it is controllable if your organization is considering downsizing or reengineering mission-critical applications. The effects of cascading OOP code can result in unacceptable performance levels. While more CPU horsepower represents one solution, understanding the implications of OOP and design possibilities represents a more important issue.

Overhead minimization

Applications can be made to run faster by reducing the amount of work needed to support their activities and by reducing the load on the system. This is best explained by the following list:

- Break large projects into smaller parts.
- Run GUI applications at lower screen resolutions.
- Disable server or system write mirroring for write-intensive applications.
- Stop all system or network monitoring operations.
- Close applications such as clocks, calculators, and E-mail notification.
- Disable drivers for devices that are not required.
- Disable the network drivers and do not attach them to the network.

A common method of minimizing system overhead is to vary the bootstrap process. Rather than redo the setup files each time a special configuration is required, some users create multiple boot files so that the sequence of events for computer system initialization and the loading drivers and user configurations can be varied. In fact, there are utilities for every operating system which provide a means of selecting from two or more boot sequences. In this way, system configuration can substantially vary the allocation of memory among RAM and RAM disks, caches, and other system memory structures; the number of device drivers loading; and even the type or release of operating system initiated. OS/2 provides software to pick between DOS and OS/2. However, more complicated configurations are possible with BOOTSYS, REBOOT, RECONFIG, and other commercial, shareware, or freeware applications.

This process increases the complexity of the operating system. Adding new applications generally creates a need to make modifications to all the various configurations. The alternative is that some procedures and applications will not find the parameters they expect in some of the configurations. However, with some care, this can be an effective method of providing specialized environments on the same computer.

TSRs

Terminate and stay resident (TSR) applications are DOS applications that run in the background and are activated by interrupts. Interrupts are either user-initiated keystroke sequences—called *hotkeys*—which initiate events within the system. FILESTAT, which tracks all file activity, is a TSR that is initiated by disk I/O events. The overhead associated with the TSR is not limited to the memory it maintains in RAM, but also includes the time it saps from other processes when the operating system checks to see if the interrupts have been activated. Generally, do not install TSR applications unless you need them.

If you are running MS Windows, consider loading that before running the TSRs. Create DOS sessions and run the TSRs as you need them within the DOS sessions; they will be removed from memory as each virtual DOS session is closed. Also, consider loading TSRs after exiting from Windows. You do not need the DOSKEY keyboard macro command interpreter and history while in Windows; you need it only within DOS sessions or after exiting from Windows.

Not all TSRs represent a loss in performance. Some TSRs will improve overall performance by providing specialized functions, such as keyboard macros, quick access to information and notes, and E-mail tracking or important messages. Just because they will slow application performance does not imply that they will adversely affect user output. Maintain the perspective between the performance problem and the perception of the problem.

Background processes (multitasking)

Every background task—and that includes DOS TSRs and multiple tasks running in the background—reduces the available system resources. This loss is different from the sum of RAM, CPU, and disk resources required for all these tasks running at the same time. Prioritization and page swapping may provide more than 150 percent effective utilization of the total system resources by utilizing the free resources when available. This is called *time slicing*. While a user is typing a memo and using no disk resources and very little CPU time, a background process could be sorting a database and extracting requested records. The best use of background processes and multitasking is complementary applications. The active task—the foreground task—usually must be one that needs frequent user interaction or user thinking time; the background task should run with little or no interaction once initiated, and coexist without requiring too many resources so that it doesn't affect the user's perception of the computing system's performance.

Memory and task management

Memory management is the reuse and reallocation of RAM pages. RAM is shared from a giant pool and allocated as needed by applications. You must manually manage memory for primitive operating systems, such as DOS. Macintosh System

7 provides better memory management than do prior releases. Windows NT, OS/2, UNIX, AIX, and most mini- and mainframe operating systems have sophisticated memory management functionality. One caveat, though. When too many applications vie for insufficient RAM, the system is said to *thrash*, and pages are constantly moved between RAM and temporary disk files. The I/O and disk bandwidth appear saturated. The problem is not that the bus or the disk facilities are slow. The problem, instead, is that there is either insufficient RAM, too many tasks, or improper task management. No amount of memory management will address this bottleneck.

What does this mean for applications? First, multiuser and large applications should be provided with sufficient resources for optimal response. Of course, you can add RAM—up to the limits of the computer architecture. You can also limit the number of simultaneous or background tasks which are active and assign priorities to prevent tasks from causing other applications to thrash. UNIX provides a NICE command for allocating fewer time slices to background or foreground processes. Note that too many barely active tasks do require task manager overhead and occasional time slices. Furthermore, these tasks may exclusively lock files and records and thus prevent other tasks from accessing them until they complete.

Duplicate resources

Duplicate resources are usually a result of multiple instances of the same application. Many OS/2 and MS Windows applications will first check the task manager to see if a copy is already running. Since these GUI applications generally support a multiple document interface (MDI) or multiple work sessions at the same time, there are few valid reasons to run multiple instances. Similarly, a DBMS should be invoked as a single engine even for multiple users; the alternative is to support duplicate copies of the same code in server and client RAM. This is wasteful of resources and increases the potential for paging to disk and even substituting the same code between disk and RAM again and again. Critical applications that somehow propagate in memory can be compared to the Internet virus. They should be removed and the application itself should be replaced with a more efficient tool.

Heap space

Many applications demand pages of RAM to build index tables, data pointers, and retain the full data set in memory. These tend to hog RAM, but not necessarily the CPU. As a result, the system thrashes as applications try to share the CPU, bus, and disk. This is not an issue for MS DOS unless a multitasking shell such as Quarterdeck Deskview is enabled. It is an issue for Macintosh System 7, UNIX, MS Windows, OS/400, OS/2, and all server or client/server processes. If an application can be revised to allocate less RAM during its execution and instead use RAM as dynamically required, the system will run more efficiently.

Heap space is RAM dynamically used by all processes and programs simultaneously. This memory area must be carefully allocated so that two or more processes do not access overlapping memory space; the alternative usually appears as either an application crash or a system crash. Applications use this space because it is more efficient than allocating a block or page of RAM and holding on to it until process completion.

By the way, MS Windows calls this public data area, *system resources.* Only two 64-kB units, the GDI and USER heaps, are allocated for all icons, program manager groups, and graphic controls and objects. When an application or multiple processes use all these available resources, Windows becomes unstable. It does not matter how much RAM the computer has; this somewhat artificial limitation overrides other paths and becomes a critical one. The only solution is to monitor free system resources for applications that hog it. You might also note that many Windows applications do not always release resources upon completion or abnormal termination. Eventually, the only solution is to exit the GUI gracefully and restart Windows. MS Windows NT does provide more robust access to system resources; however, to date, it only provides 4 MB of RAM per application created for earlier releases.

Garbage collection

One of the problems of dynamically allocating RAM is that it fragments in small blocks just as files on a hard disk fragment into noncontiguous clusters. This creates unusable pockets and impedes performance as applications try to acquire sufficient blocks to meet requirements. Some operating systems try to coalesce this RAM into contiguous pages in a process called *garbage collection* because the areas of RAM are collected together and recycled. The effectiveness is a feature of the operating system. It is not a feature or a function of most well-behaved applications. If the operating system does not recycle used RAM well, there is not much you can do except exit and restart it.

Code linking

Applications that reference function libraries (as in system overlays, system function calls, or dynamic link library) can link to these libraries *statically* or *dynamically.* A static link assumes that the library becomes bound into the application so that calls to that library are made to permanent memory addresses. The application performs faster, but the RAM requirements increase particularly when the library is already in memory for other applications or other instances of the same application. A dynamic link assumes the library is somewhere in memory—at no particular fixed point—and calls to it must be made by an indirect reference. This is less efficient than normal code in terms of overall speed of performance. It also yields benchmark variance from test to test depending on whether the library is in memory or not. If a tool, such as Quantity, shows that calls to a particular library function are expensive in terms of performance or that these calls represent a substantial portion of the performance time, static linkage to an internal library will improve performance. When memory is the limitation, the rare calls to functions are better provided by dynamically linking to a system or added library so as to free RAM.

Code design, compiler, and linker tricks

Many inefficiencies result from application code design, simple configuration selections, and misuse of the compiler technology. While many such flaws create wasted space in the executable and link libraries, they also add labels and dead filler code and increase file loading times. These all contribute to application performance degradation. Functions that run repeatedly represent areas for performance optimization. Offset block sizes for code libraries, sometimes called *alignments*, when set to values larger than 16 bytes waste disk and RAM and increase loading times. It very likely that link libraries with alignments set to 512 bytes—a Microsoft compiler option—could easily have more space wasted than filled with code.

Compiler options are complex and frequently are optimized for the greatest simplicity and for the most likely success in code compilation. Additionally, most compilers generate prologue code as a default unless instructed otherwise. This increases the size of function calls by several bytes and typically increases the number of parameters that must be passed. On UNIX systems, the compiler typically generates 32-bit addresses as default even when 8-bit or 16-bit schemes will shrink the executable code and optimize performance. Shipping product or putting an application into production environments with debug code results from compiler batch or MAKE files that have unrealistic compiler settings. Modules are likely to contain 50 percent debug code. Even when the MAKE files do not contain specific instructions for compiling an application with the debugging options, the link module sources without date changes are not always forced to recompile the object code without the debugging statements.

Do not support functions, modes, and features for which you have no use. For example, there is little need to support MS Windows Real Mode on Intel architecture; standard and enhanced mode are usually sufficient. If you do not need to reference FAR CALLs from one segment to another, disable the compiler options. You can save about 1000 bytes of code overhead and cut the typical memory references from 6 bytes to 3 bytes.

The final stage of application compilation is actually called *linking*. Separate objects are pushed together into a single file and references between objects are generally resolved from named offset addresses to relative memory jumps. The linker provides a number of benefits when optimized for code packing. It eliminates header code for the separate objects. It pushes the objects together and remove the dead padding space otherwise used to separate objects on alignment boundaries. Also, the single resulting segment minimizes the kernel overhead since only a single compound object is loaded rather than multiple ones. These three improvements save disk space and RAM. Furthermore, the FAR CALLs are reduced to jumps or NEAR CALLs; this and the creation of a compound object improves the speed of performance.

The use of existing libraries built into the operating system kernels or libraries normally used for application programming saves disk space, RAM, and loading time and tends to improve performance. Novice programmers or programmers new to an environment tend to duplicate existing resources because they do not know they already exist. As such, they re-create what seems like specialized code. Another flaw is to embed large sections of defined memory variables within a code segment. It is usually better and often possible to allocate memory outside of the code space of the application. This minimizes the size of executable with all its attendant benefits, but it also defers memory allocation and management to built-in system functions and resources. Performance is likely to be much improved, particularly within the context of a multitasking, threaded, or multiprocessor environment.

Application enhancements

New releases of software are larger, require more resources, and often run more slowly than prior ones. You rarely hear of a new release that is smaller and does less; it is hard to sell a new product that does less. As a result, bug fixes, enhancements, and new functionality represent a performance bottleneck. If nothing less, they will degrade performance below the prior level. Unfortunately, you may have no control over the new release if it is commercial shrink-wrapped software. In-house applications or applications which you are designing can be enhanced with an eye toward how to improve performance or at least mitigate CPU- and disk-intensive enhancements. The next few sections detail performance enhancement possibilities.

Elegance before functionality

Performance is not seen as a critical item until an application cannot complete within a reasonable time. Usually, when an application represents a performance problem but has other functional flaws, the approach is to add features and fix functional problems first. What typically results is an application that will function as intended but now has critical performance bottlenecks. At that point, and only then, will management attention change.

Look at functions and at how different processes complete operations. See where the majority of the time is spent processing the application. Pareto's theory is useful here, that 10 percent of the code uses 90 percent of the resources. Use the source code profiler. Ascertain what is slow and apply attention there. Ignore one time events and small modules. Since initial application loading occurs once, it is not really relevant if it is slow. On the other hand, if the application (or module) is loaded again and again to eat I/O and CPU time, see how to retain the code permanently in memory. Files that are constantly opened and referenced—a master index, for example—should be loaded into memory and retained if they fit. More often, applications are optimized by improving data handling, using better algorithms, or changing complex code into simpler or shorter statements. The following three sections discuss these three options.

Data lookup and indexes

Data is usually organized into a repetitive record structure maintained within a file separate from the application. A database engine is not always the most efficient method to access and retrieve this information. The engine itself requires disk space to store, RAM to run, and CPU cycles. Although it is typically faster to locate information through an index than searching sequentially for a match, this is not always the case. Small data sets may be best handled by simple structures and without the overhead of the DBMS engine. The use of the wrong index or the design of a suboptimal query will cause excessive thrashing. Understand the complexity of the data requirements. Match simple needs with simple solutions. Use a code profiler to explore the complexity of indexes, lookups, and simple sequential searches.

Better algorithms

It may take longer to actually create the code, but improved methods may speed the execution of the application. Also, code changes may speed portions of an application with an upfront time delay or with a penalty during other portions of the application. For example, an application could rescale and build an image only after sizing activity and a check to see if the scale has actually been changed. There may be no need to save a file if nothing has changed.

An example in which operations are shifted to speed user-observed processing is the disabling of active indexing during database record entry. Records are added sequentially, not included as part of any keyed record structure. When all new records have been added, the indexes can be rebuilt. This tends to be efficient for data entry by lowering CPU and cache overhead. However, rebuilding the indexes is no longer just an issue of inserting the new records into the index structure, but of rebuilding the entire indexes; that takes far more net time.

Calculation and force reduction

Some CPU-intensive operations are optimized by changing the code and applying different commands that require less CPU or system resources. This is pertinent for DBMS processes, SQL in particular, and for some complex numerical processing. When tabulating totals in a database table, it is possible to extract all relevant records to create a logical view and then calculate the total. The alternative is to keep a running total as records are compared for inclusion. This second approach is faster because included records are not handled twice and disk space is not used to construct the view subset. Another common example of inefficiency occurs when a programmer searches sequentially for a field match when that field is already included as (part of) an indexed key field. When the programmer is searching for all matches, the lookup requires a complete search of every possible record, which is even more inefficient.

Assembly language programmers learn that multiplication by 8 is merely 3 bit shifts. Floating-point processing may require 16 CPU operations of which 6 of those operations require 3 or more CPU clock cycles. For this example, it may be possible to condense 40 CPU cycles into a 1 CPU cycle bit shift. Similarly, programmers may use a complicated CASE structure when a binary branch or IF...ELSE...THEN compiles into simpler code. Also, a programmer may set up a bank of repetitive IF comparisons that must be completely processed when it is unnecessary to continue the stepwise comparison after a match has been made. Also, subscript lookups are faster than complex branching logic. One last note; make sure you have the true bottleneck—one that represents a substantial portion of the overall delay or process time—before rewriting code to speed up performance.

Partitioning the workload

One of the most effective methods for improving the performance of an application is to partition the workload. Having two or more computers working on the same problem at the same time constitutes a parallel-tasking solution with the potential to speed up solution. This technique is not always practical when the same files must be accessed at the same time. It may be feasible when the applications and data sets reside on a network-accessible server (or peer-to-peer work environment). This usually implies that more people will work at the same task at the same time, too. Using the same mode of thought, it is also possible for one person to work on the same task on different machines on the same time. For example, image scanning operations are very slow—up to 10 minutes for four-color images at typesetter resolution. Although it may be desirable to scan many images automatically with a sheet feeder, this is not always possible. First, the originals may reflect different paper sizes and weights, and taken together they may jam a sheet feeder. Second, the sheet feeder may lack the accuracy necessary to feed glossy paper, or it may damage the originals. Furthermore, disk space may be limited, so that originals are scanned to exact size and the image is then compressed; it may not be possible to scan all the images first.

When applications are run across a wide area network, the performance limitation is usually that communication channel. Loading applications and data sets remotely creates a significant delay. Because the applications and the file servers are not the bottlenecks, increasing the horsepower of the computers will not affect performance. Increasing the channel bandwidth is not always economically viable. It is possible that an application runs infrequently—once per week, for example—so that channel bandwidth becomes a bottleneck only for that application. Other activities, such as E-mail, file transfers, and occasional reference to remote server-based applications, do not cause significant delays.

When processing is split between local and remote processors, it may be possible to enhance performance by shifting the balance between local and remote processing. This is not always possible when you do not have access to application source code. If it is feasible, compare the workloads of the client and the server, the size of the loads that need to be imposed, and any limitations to rebalancing the workload. Consider, for example, a crosstab calculation—a report and summation of all accounts receivable for a select list of sales personnel selling to a particular territory during a specified time period. This is basically an ad hoc search through a database for records fitting the limitations. While the simplicity of the search and calculations does not overtax the server, transferring the original data over the network would add additional channel load. Even when a remote user dials in to a local machine and takes control of that machine for local processing, the resulting report may be large enough that there are no significant time savings. As you can see, only those calculations overtaxing the server should be shifted to the remote or remote-controlled CPU.

However, that is neither the problem that needs a solution here nor the right solution. The channel remains the limitation. The question to ask is, how do you get the results or the data to the remote station? The solution might begin by copying the entire database to the remote site. This can be performed as necessary. The data could be copied automatically each night to maintain the timeliness of the remote data. Alternatively, only changes could be shipped across the network to update the remote data. Distributed databases provide a feasible solution. Maintaining the synchronization is an issue only when remote real-time accuracy is important.

While many other solutions to the WAN bottleneck certainly exist, another solution is quite elegant. Simply stated, assess the remote processing requirements. What seems like an ad hoc report because it is created by a user apparently infrequently may in fact be a repeating and standard requirement. Automate the process. Process the report locally. Either ship the printed report by courier or overnight mail, or print the report to a file, compress that file, and ship *that* to the user. Because the user is really interested only in the results, not the process itself, optimize by partitioning the workload where the resources exist to complete the project. Bypass the bottlenecks.

The important requirements for partitioning the workload among other people and machines are that the work can be partitioned and that this process can be coordinated. Duplicate effort is wasteful and inefficient. Oversights and work that is forgotten represent a process flaw. Balance the resource requirements for maintaining control of operations against the cost of changing applications to something more appropriate to the tasks and increasing the horsepower to speed completion on a single system. This example is useful to show that there are many methods of resolving an application bottleneck without directly attacking the bottleneck itself.

Conclusion

To improve performance you have to understand the bottleneck. A computer system and its applications represent a complex system of events, data routing operations, and component performance capacities. Single events or single components can create a gridlock that isn't easily perceived. Furthermore, it is possible to misrepresent the application and how it works, what it does, and the options it provides. Sometimes the bottleneck is how an application is used. The wrong modes, commands, and techniques can spawn an excessive load when other methods will yield the same results faster. And sometimes the results are not even the correct results. Make certain, first, that you understand the process and the different paths you could take to achieve your results. You will achieve better optimization when you understand the interactions and have more options.

When it is clear that the options are limited, the performance of applications is best enhanced by either improving the application itself or switching applications. Move from resource-intensive GUI environments to text-based applications. Critical applications and ones that are not easily replaced present a more complex problem. If possible, optimize performance by throwing hardware at the bottleneck. Know the bottleneck. Understand the effects of increased RAM. Add more RAM for larger CPU caches. Increase the size of disk caches. Defragment hard disks and increase the amount of free storage disks. Add hard disks or long-term storage media supporting faster seek and transfer times. Replace simple disk controllers with faster interfaces or add multiple disks. Replace a slow system with one with a wider or faster bus, a faster CPU, and a faster video display. When it seems that multiple components are creating overlapping bottlenecks, avoid the trap of upgrading a computer system in small pieces and small steps; the time can be better spent evaluating the bottlenecked system and entirely replacing it with a faster platform or application.

Chapter

6

Client/Server Optimization

Introduction

Client/server optimization will not always mean improving server, network, or client speed of performance. That is just one aspect, although perhaps the most obvious one. Client/server computing is about improving organizational productivity, accuracy, user productivity or efficiency, or the return on financial investment. If speed is the issue, then look at optimization that way. If quality or reliability is the issue, establish appropriate criteria. As you consider optimizing a client/server environment, establish clear objectives.

The shift from mainframe and host-based processing toward LAN-based computing is increasing the need to optimize client/server operations. Most LANs and WANs operate with centralized servers and client workstations. It is important to realize that client/server computing actually refers to very little more than computing hardware architecture. It does not refer to quality, performance characteristics, or exactly how processing is divided between the servers and their clients. Functionally, *client/server* processing means only that at least one computer acts as a centralized processor and provides applications, network services, database access, and file access without providing the totality of end-user computing. The client processors perform much of the work. Client/server processing is different from host-based processing in that data-field edit masks, keystrokes, mouse movements, and calculations tend to occur at the client station. Organizations seeking to move from host-based processing or to resolve host-based on-line transaction processing (OLTP) bottlenecks caused by clogged mainframe databases may benefit from client/server computing because the centralized horsepower can be split between servers and clients more cost-effectively than between expensive mainframes and terminals.

The alternative distributed processing architecture to client/server is called *peer-to-peer;* in this architecture all computers share services and files but do not provide significant processing services to other computers. While peer-to-peer bottlenecks tend to be station-based and sometimes network channel-based when the network grows large or busy enough, client/server bottlenecks represent more complex processing environments because a complex workload is distributed among machines.

When bottlenecks clog a client/server network, it would seem appropriate to improve the infrastructure. However, typically only a handful of tasks or processes become bottlenecks. Usually, a client/server operation becomes a bottleneck because the application is processing-intensive. In other words, there is too much work, and the process is slow simply because the operational infrastructure is overwhelmed. There is too much code supporting too much functionality. Applications tend not to be simple or elegant. In fact, applications tend to be Swiss Army knives of utility. The goal of improving environments and enhancing productivity is viewed in terms of providing more functionality and more utility at the cost of more code, more CPU power, more disk space, and longer processing times. Often, these applications are critical to the mission of the organization and cannot be optimized. They represent packaged products, database applications, or high-volume on-line transaction processing. As such, their performance—or lack of it—is beyond control or management. Although other applications may exist to replace or augment the environment, these client/server applications are a given. You will need to investigate the hardware and the networks.

When you measure client/server performance and search for application bottlenecks, you will typically see that the server is overwhelmed. The conclusion to draw is that the server is doing too much work relative to its capacity. Disk, CPU, and memory are the likeliest culprits. The LAN channel bandwidth is not often a problem unless there is something wrong with it. However, LAN channel latency can become a problem for large, distributed, or interconnected enterprises. WAN connections typically are established at 9600 bits/s, at 56 kbits/s, or at T-1 speeds. These speeds represent a bandwidth limitation because they are significantly less than LAN speeds and far less than most applications desire. When WAN connections support multiple users, even T-1 bandwidth can create a performance bottleneck.

There are exceptions. The network bandwidth does become a bottleneck when the client/server applications distribute large blocks of data, as in image processing or CAD, or when the network is simply too large and overloaded. When data use significant bandwidth, more bandwidth must be allocated. When the network is large or overloaded, it must be simplified and partitioned or more bandwidth must be allocated.

General optimization techniques

The most effective method for improving client/server performance is to lower the workload. If that is not possible, split the workload between servers. The network server for file access does not have to be the same server that provides user login and E-mail. Neither of those needs to be the same server that provides the critical database processing. Bottlenecks will rarely occur at clients, but rather at the servers or at the connection between the servers and the clients.

When it is impossible to lower the workload, address the bottleneck. If the server is overloaded, try to distribute that workload elsewhere. Add a server coprocessor or add servers. Push workload to the client. If the network is the bottleneck, reduce the traffic between client and server. Typically, diskless clients or clients that perform a remote program load (RPL) are a network paging nightmare. Clients with disks and enough RAM certainly do not always have to load executable code over the network. Move applications to the client. If data are nonessential and not shared, they too can reside at the client. When the client represents the bottleneck—and this is rare—explore how a faster client computer will improve performance. When a WAN is a bottleneck, increase the connection bandwidth. Recall from Chapter 2 that you must address the active performance constraint to achieve any performance improvement.

Another technique for improving client performance across WAN links is to run the application locally on the LAN, the server, or a special server called a *communication server*. The remote client dials into or attaches through preexisting connections to the local service. The local service is either a LAN, a server, or a communication machine. The remote client initiates a task not on that remote machine but rather on a local resource. Because the application actually runs at the local site on a communication server, performance is the same as if the user were on the LAN. However, information that is transferred by a wide area network—screen updates, keystrokes, and mouse movements—tends to be jerky as a result of the WAN connection time delay.

In the case of client/server computing, only the data really need to be transmitted. Local copies of applications will obviate the need for loading applications and overlays across the network. Alternatively, consider establishing banks of centralized computers running the applications and accessing the data centrally as well. Remote access is provided via a remote control program such as Carbon Copy, PC Anywhere, Novell Communication Server, or Reach Out. The benefit of this approach is that processing is centralized and data transmission occurs at central LAN speed; only actual screen changes are transmitted over the WAN. This is not limited only to text-based applications; GUI screens also can be sent across the LAN at useful speeds.

Essential workloads

Not all client/server applications are essential or critical. If you want to lower the workload, know what the environment is required to do and what it actually does. One of the first steps in optimizing client/server operations is to understand what actually influences performance and how. The best way to improve performance is to excise all applications that are redundant, immaterial, or wasteful. Those games users play during lulls, the planning reports, the spreadsheets, the work processing, or other voice and icon enhancements may well represent nonessential client/server loads. Sound files such as .WAV files not only require at least 17 Kbits/s of disk space, they also have a tendency to demand 100 percent of CPU resources during playback. This is certainly true for MS Windows. This is not to say that you will want to remove games from the system; you may just want to get them off the server. Keep a reasonable perspective as you begin this process.

Processing configuration

Peer-to-peer networks tend toward low-volume utilization of global resources, such as the LAN transmission channel. Any perceived slowdowns are usually caused by station-level bottlenecks. Performance bottlenecks tend to be isolated, and local problems are best solved by optimizing the performance of the local resources. In other words, tune each peer-to-peer station in turn to best meet the requirements of individual users. Later sections in this chapter address the process of tuning individual stations.

Client/server and distributed processing networks represent more complex LAN configurations. Performance is influenced by server loads, workstation loads, channel capacity, and loading—including traffic burst loads, where the intensive CPU work is processed. File servers exporting entire database files for remote processing may not only clog the transmission channel but create backlogs when many stations request files simultaneously. Additionally, the overhead for fetching the files and creating intermediate views may overwhelm the local workstation as well. This is not a true client/server architecture; rather, it merely is a dispersed file service application.

True client/server database servers export views (processed subsets of data from a transaction database, GIS images, CAD displays, or scientific data sets) and partially processed client requests. Client/server file servers optimize those requests to generate significantly better performance than in a file server environment given the same hardware configuration and network transmission capacities. Distributed processing applications are supposedly a step further advanced in that remote processing is optimized on the fly to maximize available free resources and alleviate bottlenecks.

Adding more RAM

Most client/server operations occur on a machine with an operating system fundamentally different from single-user MS DOS. Typically, the OS will be OS/400, UNIX (or UNIX derivatives), NetWare, Windows NT advanced server, OS/2, or VMS. This differentiation is important because client/server tasks are queued and multitasked. CPU and bus time are shared between processes, and these concurrent operations are retained in both active and shared memory pages and virtual pages, which are temporarily written to disk. When memory is insufficient, the use of virtual memory increases. Since virtual memory is generally on a disk with millisecond access times rather than in RAM with nanosecond access times, performance can be substantially enhanced by augmenting RAM.

Before concluding that RAM is insufficient, try reducing RAM (physically or by reconfiguration) first to see if that has a detrimental effect. This is an easier task than adding more RAM to see if that improves performance. Consider what you will do (and the inevitable political consequences) if you add more RAM and it does not improve performance. If you have tools that track virtual memory usage in terms of paging, frequency of paging, and utilization, use those first.

Improper configuration of memory between RAM and cache or other system structures may also contribute to poor performance. Stacked caches could increase latency for accessing information. Cache could be slower than RAM. Also, the disk supporting the swapping operations between RAM and virtual memory may be overloaded, too full, or heavily fragmented. The data volumes might not all be appropriately cached.

Since sorts and indexing occur both in RAM and on the disk, it is important to have sufficient RAM and free disk space to complete the typical task. Insufficient resources may entirely prevent sorts from completing or just slow them to an unacceptable crawl. Large indexes and clustered (sparse) indexes require a good deal of RAM and swap space for adequate performance.

Faster I/O

Most client/server bottlenecks are caused by I/O jams at the server. The first possibility to check is network bandwidth and NIC bandwidth. While the network channel is unlikely to be jammed, it is easy to check utilization levels with a protocol analyzer or with server monitor software. Even if the bandwidth is not fully committed, review network latency times. It is possible that client/server performance is poor because of the time it takes to get the information around the network and through several routers or gateways. It is important to realize that the network delivery time can be poor even though the network is not very busy.

Servers with ISA NICs just cannot pump out enough traffic to saturate the network transmission bandwidth. Furthermore, the CPU load required to manage the network I/O may flow back to the bus and the server CPU itself. Coprocessing or bus-mastering NICs will improve I/O performance, and hence CPU performance.

Servers with 99 percent CPU utilization are CPU-bound. You will rarely see utilization at such extraordinary levels. Although servers with CPU loads averaging about 40 to 60 percent may not seem overloaded, assess the granularity of the CPU level readings. It is likely that 40 to 60 percent loading over a minute represents 100 percent loading during much of the analysis period. Compare this to a traffic jam on a highway. Although to drivers all lanes of the highway seem completely saturated with vehicles, someone standing on an overpass with a better vantage point might wonder why so there is much free space between the bumpers of adjacent vehicles. To the casual observer the highway might appear only 60 percent full. As with vehicular traffic, computer CPU saturation is caused by lags, processor interlocks, and wait times. The same mechanism can jam an apparently empty bus as well.

Disk I/O for client/server operations can be improved using the same methods outlined in Chapter 4. Increase the speed of the hardware and the disk controllers, optimize the disks, and remove dead files and data. Fundamentally, the current limit for most platforms is about 40 to 60 I/O events per second. This is mainly a function of hard disk head seek time, which averages about 15 ms. However, multiuser disk subsystems tend to provide higher performance than single-user disks. The disk storage requirements tend to be larger, and data tend to be split across multiple disks. Furthermore, systems that support RAID or some form of mirroring or data striping can in fact improve read performance about 400 percent. Since most client/server DBMS operations show read/write ratios of 20:1 to 100:1, do not consider only the beneficial reliability and integrity enhancements from RAID; factor in the performance improvements available as well.

One other factor can generally improve disk performance regardless of the platform and operating system. Raw partitions—that is, the real physical partitions on a hard disk—are more efficient than logical partitions. Do not create multiple logical disks on a single physical disk. The performance goal is rather to create one logical disk spanning multiple disks.

Also, solid-state disks can provide significant performance improvements for on-line transaction processing and client/server DBMS. Key record tables, master indexes, and other frequently accessed data can be accessed in about 1 ms instead of the usual 16 ms. Recall from Chapter 4 that a solid-state disk with the essential data will provide about 1000 I/O events/s instead of the normal 40. As a result, systems that represent an I/O bottleneck may see user response times decrease from 10 minutes to 10 seconds. The performance effect is a function of the operating system and platform architecture. It is also a function of the I/O queue and is very system-dependent. While NetWare and VMS may virtually stop operating when the I/O is a bottleneck, UNIX tends to attempt to perform other parallel, non-I/O-related tasks instead. Nevertheless, solid-state disk storage or storing key data on a RAM disk will improve performance for all these operating systems simply because I/O is the usual constraint on client/server processing.

Faster CPU

That a faster CPU will improve client/server performance is a common fallacy. Operations are usually I/O- or bus-bound. Operations that are CPU-bound will be improved. Number-crunching operations, CAD, and imaging are good candidates for faster CPUs. However, first you must know which CPU is the bottleneck. Faster client machines will not solve the problem of a slow-server CPU. Second, a faster CPU without a faster infrastructure does not always yield the expected gains. In fact, the Intel 80486 50 MHz with a 50-MHz data bandwidth will generally outperform the Intel 80486 DX/2 66 MHz with a 33-MHz data bandwidth in a server.

SQL effects

Structured query languages (SQL) provide a relatively uniform interface between different GUI platforms, different operating systems, and diverse database applications. While relatively uniform, the various versions of SQL are not all alike, interchangeable, or optimized for distributed computing. As a result, SQL represents several significant bottlenecks. This includes gateways between competing DBMS products, the interaction and messaging over the gateway, and the methods used to code actual SQL statements.

When it is clear that performance over the gateways between different DBMS applications is the problem—for example, between Sybase and Oracle—the only viable solution to the bottleneck other than adding more horsepower is to simplify the complexity of the DBMS environment. Consider leveling the field and simplifying the environment by eliminating one of the DBMS. A gateway represents an inefficient translation. Even when SQL statements can be passed cleanly between different RDBMS environments, statements that work efficiently in one environment may not work well in the other. Although the command may parse correctly and provide the appropriate results, the syntax might differ enough between the environments that results are delayed and overhead is dramatically increased. For example, one SQL command could deliver a substantial set of records that will require additional processing at the gateway and at the end-user station rather than providing single-record or value answers. While it might be desirable to split the CPU load between server and client, the extra gateway and LAN load is likely to be unwanted here.

Additionally, there are probably a dozen ways to code any data request. Some require fewer resources and are more efficient. When assessing DBMS bottlenecks in a client/server environment, review the code. Replacing two lines or five lines of code by a one-liner or replacing a loop by an index search or lookup may substantially reduce CPU, gateway, and network load. Programmers are usually evaluated in terms of getting the most accomplished in the least amount of time, and that does not mean machine CPU time. Getting the desired results may have been the main goal when the application was initially created. With the success and even enhancement of that application, it may have become widely disseminated through the organization. As a result, it might be wise to review the code and optimize it to reduce organizational bottlenecks.

Also, SQL is supported in two formats, *dynamic* and *static*. Static SQL is compiled and optimized at programming time or when an SQL script is initially loaded. On the other hand, dynamic SQL is reinterpreted each time a statement is executed and may run more than 20 times slower. If it is executed 1000 times for each procedure and called by 30 users dozens of times each day, the overhead for each reinterpretation is significant. You might compare the difference between static and dynamic SQL to the difference between a hard-coded reference and a macro substitution for a variable. SQL that is invoked across a gateway and is not optimized represents a particular source for trouble. Review the code and replace the dynamic calls with more efficient static lines. Note that some database vendors may call precompiled procedures or static SQL *stored procedures.*

Increase I/O channel speed

Increase the bus capacity of key servers. Avoid 8-bit and 16-bit ISA buses; install 32-bit EISA or MCA motherboards. Choose local bus PC servers carefully. It is not clear that optimized devices and device drivers are available yet to increase I/O performance. Upgrade to more capable platforms. DEC Alpha provides a 64-bit bus, as do Sun Microsystems and other UNIX vendors.

I/O channel speed can also be enhanced by installing parallel devices. If the disk is the bottleneck, install a striped RAID or create a partition that spans multiple disks. Install multiple I/O controllers. Sometimes the hardware is not the limitation. If the operating system does not support asynchronous I/O, consider replacing it with another one; this is possible with UNIX. Move from LAN Manager to Windows NT advanced server or stay with LAN Manager network and integrate asynchronous device and I/O support.

Decrease channel load

As stated throughout *Computer Performance Optimization,* the most reliable method of increasing overall performance is to decrease the overall workload. This is relevant for LAN or WAN bottlenecks too.

Network and server effects

Client/server operations include executable code, overlays (dynamic link libraries or .DLL files), synchronization, record or file locking, network management, data access, and user display of data. Often all but the user display of data occurs at the server. When server or network operation represents a bottleneck, move operations locally. If the WAN represents a bandwidth or latency bottleneck, make the software application locally available; minimize paging over the WAN linkage.

When possible, maintain data locally. There is a significant tradeoff between the increased complexity of distributed data management and the increased speed of access with local copies of data. However, when WAN performance becomes an issue, local data may provide the only degrees of performance freedom.

WAN bottlenecks are more common than LAN-based client/server bottlenecks, and thankfully more easily addressed. The easiest solution to a bandwidth limitation is to add more bandwidth. This represents a financial solution. If a connection is established by a 1200-bit/s modem link, move up to 2400 or 9600 bits/s. If you are using higher-speed modems, explore the quality of the dial-up line. You might find a high error level, or the link may not be functioning at 14,400 bits/s, but rather dropping to 1200 bits/s. If the connection is not retained at the higher speeds and drops to 1200 bits/s, most modems will not retry the connection or reset it to a higher speed; the transmission only goes more slowly. Acquire more advanced software that will reestablish a slowed connection or acquire modems which dynamically assign the highest possible connection speed.

If this performance level proves restrictive, try a data compression modem linkage which about doubles effective bandwidth. A dedicated 56-Kbit/s leased line or ISDN (two dedicated 56-Kbit/s lines) are other options. T-1 at 1.534 Mbits/s provides even greater bandwidth. Frame relay and fractional T-1 fill in the gaps between a 56-Kbit/s line and a full T-1 link. Data compression and data multiplexing can increase the effective bandwidths of even overloaded T-1-based WANs.

If the time for WAN transmission is too long, increasing bandwidth will not improve WAN performance. The issue is different. Review the transmission protocol. Dial-up modems require seconds to establish a connection. ISDN is almost instantaneous. A leased line is always available—it is a hard-wired linkage. If X.25 packet delays and frame relay are too restrictive for a real-time control process, establish a leased line. Explore the differences between a physical connection and a logical connection; the physical connection tends to be faster.

When a LAN is a bandwidth nightmare, there are fewer options. Client/server operations require significant maintenance and management overhead. First explore how to lower that workload. Disable network management functions, routing table updates, and routing broadcast storms. Do not gather real-time network statistics when the network is gridlocked; that only adds to the traffic jam. Segment the network. Increasing the network bandwidth is not always technically feasible or financially possible. Token-Ring is not easily upgraded to 16 Mbits/s from 4 Mbits/s, and an upgrade from Ethernet at 10 Mbits/s does not always provide the performance boost envisioned—the result may be even worse. As Chapter 7 explores, hub switching can alleviate some LAN bottlenecks by allocating the full bandwidth provided by the protocol to each network station. Also, FDDI and ATM are high-end possibilities, but even these protocols may only represent a tenfold enhancement in bandwidth and latency times. Explore your perceived LAN bottleneck carefully. See Chapter 7 for a complete discussion of network performance issues.

Diskless clients represent a significant network and server paging load for both LANs and WANs. When this is a problem, add more RAM for the local client. Add local disks for clients with cache, swap, and RAM paging. Move MS Windows and applications to the local disks. If you can control desktop management and what applications are available, maintain centralized server access to the .INI files and local executable files. There are ways to secure access to local applications.

Synchronous operations

Tasks which issue a synchronous request for data do not work well in a cooperative, networked, or multitasking environment. They tend to create logical performance bottlenecks when there really is no resource limitation. These tasks are locked until responses are provided because process control is retained. Specifically, SNA traffic, terminal connections, or any processes which maintain copious "keep-alive" messages are likely to work poorly when they are routed over a local area network. The time required for message delivery on LANs or across enterprisewide networks is not usually so predictable. It is better to replace a communications interface—that is, a terminal emulator or an SQL and GUI front-end interface—with one that is more robust and can provide other services or even provide continuous, simultaneous asynchronous tasks. Tasks which return control immediately after an information request provide a means for absorbing the full capabilities of available resources.

Although there is considerably more overhead in an application built with object-oriented tools, such an application is more likely to provide event interrupts, provide simultaneous processing, and continue to initiate more communication. For example, when an MS Visual Basic GUI requests data from a mainframe host, it issues an asynchronous call, immediately returns control to the user or subsequent task, and can potentially issue another request for information in the interim. An asynchronous, or *unlinked,* operation provides better performance, particularly over LAN and WAN channels.

Asynchronous operations

Asynchronous means that two or more operations can occur simultaneously and independently. Asynchronous events do not have to wait for prior events to complete. Most applications are coded sequentially and must be performed synchronously—that is, sequentially. However, this is not true of the actual CPU, bus, and I/O operations required to complete individual application tasks. For example, a user may request and change multiple records in a database; the read activity must occur when requested, but writes can be cached until a later time and performed all at once for improved efficiency. Furthermore, unrelated processes or applications are independent and can occur asynchronously. Since user login and

E-mail are unrelated to accounting, these operations can occur at the same time on different computers. When network operating systems cannot support true operational simultaneity, multiple machines may.

Split tasks

Break batch transactions that are massive jobs into smaller chunks that the user must invoke as separate functions. While this is unlikely to make the run faster, the user will be preoccupied by the need to watch and manage the new selections. This is a sneaky solution because it avoids real performance optimization. However, it can buy time and gloss over the performance problem.

This approach can, however, provide some real information. If a batch transaction involves several separable tasks, you can use this technique to discover which tasks run more frequently and if any of those tasks were deadwood. Accountants will frequently close the monthly books, generate the monthly accounts, and print out a list of all transactions, all ledgers, all customer accounts, and the P&L statement, the last of which is what they may really want printed out. Optimize the paper use. Optimize the system use. Provide the means to process only and exactly what the users want.

Speed up critical tasks

Some tasks may not seem important to software or system designers, but are important to the users. Ascertain what these hot buttons are, and fix those first. It may not even be an issue of the speed or quality of performance that must be resolved. Sometimes performance problems result from timing and access issues. Some client/server applications lock more than single records; they may lock entire files for long periods (in computer scale) of time and prevent others from getting their work done. You might be able to give the system a boost by changing the file-locking mechanism to a record-locking mechanism.

In a client/server LAN environment, little problems sometimes become performance bottlenecks. For example, printing labels may take an insignificant amount of CPU or system time, but the salespeople wait all day to get someone to change the paper and spool the label jobs to the label stock. They may do a slow burn. Set up a special printer so that labels and individualized promotional materials can be turned around faster. As you see, the bottleneck can be something as simple as understanding the user requirements, rather than poor system performance per se.

Some on-line tasks could be automated to run as batch jobs after hours in the middle of the night. Even graphical-based windows applications can be automated with key and mouse macros. These macros, in turn, could be initiated at certain times automatically. On the other hand, some after-hours tasks may actually be more important. Shift the times. Change the schedule. Revise the system.

Resource tradeoffs

Frequently speed can be increased by adding disk space, RAM, or other system resources. In fact, SunOS has an operating system extension called the *Database Excelerator* that provides superior performance on a database such as Sybase, Oracle, or Ingres with many concurrent users. This enhancement provides a greater number of transactions per second at the expense of memory usage.

Downsizing pitfalls

When you convert an existing application from a mainframe host or minicomputer to the target client/server environment, you must recognize that the architecture of the networked client/server environment is radically different. Typically, any direct transfer of code (platform porting) is likely to yield poor performance. For example, while conversions from CICS and DB2 in an IBM 39XX environment to CICS/2 or DB2/2 under OS/2 may go smoothly, the results are likely to be disastrous. The same thing is true when a mainframe COBOL and JCL application is recompiled for a PC environment or for a PS/2 with the IBM 39XX mainframe on a card. Yes, COBOL and batch files do work on a PC (or UNIX), but not within the same resources as on the mainframe. The fundamental design paradigms are different, and the OS/2 and LAN Server environment are emulating the functional performance of the mainframe.

Even the IBM adapter card, which provides a 39XX mainframe emulator that is installed inside a PS/2, does not provide the same infrastructure as the original mainframe. While emulation provides virtual processing of mainframe tasks, the PS/2 bus or any PC bus does not have the same significant communication capability as the mainframe. You are likely to experience bottlenecks on the bus, the NICs, and the disk storage subsystems. PC-based 39XX mainframe emulation may provide a viable downsizing or transition opportunity, but it is not the performance equivalent of the mainframe. Emulation usually provides inferior performance, as stated in Chapter 4. Instead, you will need to redesign and revise legacy applications to fit the paradigm of networking, RDBMS and DBMS, and the benefits and limitations of GUI interfaces.

Server I/O bottlenecks

Chapter 4 discussed most of the basic techniques for optimizing workstation performance. Fundamentally, servers are not too different from workstations. The load, however, is different. While a workstation might have GUI and CPU bottlenecks, servers are more likely to display I/O constraints. Refer to Chapter 4 for information on optimizing file space usage, optimizing file extents, installing faster controllers, disk striping, and RAID operations. Review information about RAM, CPU speeds, and bus issues. This section is strictly for client/server operations and techniques that are pertinent for optimizing the time that it takes to read, write, and seek data on a networked server. Although clients may have local disks for caching data, code, and network data packets, the substantial bottleneck for client/server data access will tend to reside at the data server. Such a bottleneck is a decreasing function of

- Server work request load
- Server storage seek time
- Server cache hit ratio
- Network signal propagation delay
- Server CPU(s) loading
- Network channel bandwidth load

- Server disk load
- Storage transfer rate
- Server cache miss ratio
- Server disk controller speed
- NIC load
- Server cache size

When server I/O seems to be a bottleneck, check the CPU load as well. If it is near capacity—even chronically at 40 to 60 percent—the server as a unit may be a bottleneck. Do not bother tuning it. You need precise tools to determine the root cause of server I/O jams. For example, System Performance Monitor for OS/2 will show where the bottleneck is on the server: whether it is queued up with requests or whether the problem is disk overload, CPU overload, or bus utilization. Many other servers provide performance tools as part of the database services or network management. Refer to Chapter 3 for other OS- or NOS-specific tools for evaluating server performance. When a server provides database services, look for tools to monitor the performance of the database as an entity with performance problems, with the server itself as a separate component.

Unless you can capture specific performance data about disk I/O, bus I/O, cache hit rates, network channel load, and CPU load in order to determine exactly why there is a I/O bottleneck, you may have to test solutions sequentially to see which one is the most effective. Faster disks do not provide much performance increase unless the seek and transfer times are sustainable by the controllers and CPU. Bus master disk controllers do not buy much unless the CPU is actually overburdened performing disk I/O. Solutions for a CPU overload include adding a faster CPU, installing coprocessors, or dividing the load among multiple buses or servers. If CPU upgrades alone are ineffective, the I/O bottleneck is more sensitive to bus conflicts than to CPU loads or disk performance.

The PS/2 model 295 supports asymmetric processing, with one CPU doing NOS and applications and the second CPU doing network and LAN Server processing. This is a nonasymmetric solution for this NOS only. On the other hand, NFS and Windows NT Advanced Server do support symmetric coprocessing or multiprocessing. Added RAM, faster disks, cache, and other techniques will not minimize the basic design constraints of the system itself. At that point, the only solution to improve performance is to divide the load among multiple servers. However, if the bus itself and not the CPU or disk access performance is the bottleneck, you have several options. Bus master boards (for disk and network) might dissipate CPU and bus contention.

However, if the bus itself is the bottleneck, you have several options. Create parallel channels for disk access; install multiple disk controllers. Install multiple storage disks. Most server CPUs can support asynchronous read and write operations, whereas a controller or disk cannot. The network itself can also limit access to the server. Typically, each NIC in the server can support 8 to 16 clients. Multiple network adapters provide access to more clients, but at a diminishing rate. Most server performance tests show that client/server network performance diminishes with 4 NICs and about 40 to 70 users per server. To a small degree the speed of NICs does matter. Although FDDI provides better performance by a factor of 4, the overhead for building the packets and controlling the process overwhelms most servers. However, the performance degradation is a systemic failure. Review your client/server design and see how the processing load can be divided among processors.

The most effective and available method for tuning server performance is not hardware-intensive. You will not need new hardware or more of it. Tune the cache and update the disk controller device drivers. Generally, better drivers are available from the controller manufacturer or the NOS provider. Recall that a driver represents 1 microsecond of system activity (1000 ms), whereas the replacement of mechanical disks with electronic drives represents only about 11 ms. Do not overlook the possibility that you could save at least 80 ms with optimized drivers. It may require extensive phone calls to find the right contact. Devices are effectively memory-resident; they are never removed from cache or RAM and run almost constantly. But cache is a built-in function for servers simply because it is so important. As discussed in Chapter 4, a cache hit provides nearly instantaneous access to the data, but a miss is even slower than bypassing the cache and seeking the data on the disk alone. Therefore, you will want to tune the cache algorithm, its size, and what can stay in cache and for how long. You may even want to flush the cache at intervals. The exact method of tuning the caches is very specific to the operating system and platform. For example, the NetWare "elevator" cache is very different from the Vines UNIX-based cache; each is detailed in its respective optimization manual or the vendor CD-ROM.

When there is a choice of cache products available for servers, test them in your environment. Caches tend to perform very differently and perhaps better than the original vendor-supplied cache depending upon data request frequency and average data request size. It is also possible that a new version or release provides features which are not automatically enabled. They may be risky or work only with special hardware configurations, as with the MS Windows 32-bit disk access. For example, IBM PC LAN release 1.3 and greater, support a disk requester and cache which detect sequential read-ahead requests. Two or three contiguous reads can be automatically fetched, and small files or multiple database records can be completely read into a 4k buffer before they are actually requested. This prefetch caching, if you will, represents important new technology for improving server performance by priming the CPU with the data that it will need next. This is critical technology for multitasking and parallel processing, both of which represent the next big technology wave for improving server performance.

Database and software design

Client/server applications based on databases and GUI front ends represent an attractive and leading effort to downsize and revitalize MIS operations. When host-based on-line transaction processing is moved to a client/server and LAN-based environment, the baseline workload is very likely to increase dramatically. First, applications which were optimized for a mainframe environment are not particularly portable to the new architecture. Second, the transfer of the operations to a new environment is also likely to include significant enhancements to the baseline applications. Third, the new environment itself is very likely to impose a substantial hurdle for designers and users alike.

Multivolume tables

When an on-line transaction processing database resides on a single volume (or worse, on a single disk), the bottleneck typically becomes the disk. This is an artificial barrier, but a very real constraint. Since each database update generally requires a read and a subsequent write operation, the I/O bandwidth of a disk drive will peak at around 40 I/O operations per second. This corresponds to about 20 transactions per second (TPS). The I/O bandwidth is different from the typical 1.3 to 16 Mbits/s data transfer rate because it includes the seek, read, chain, and other components of disk activity. TPS are significantly increased by partitioning a database over physical drives and even physical servers, as the next section shows.

Multiserver architecture

When I/O, CPU, or bus bandwidth constrains DBMS performance, consider moving the application to a multiple-server environment. Before assuming that this will resolve the TPS bottleneck, make certain that the DBMS engine can support this distributed architecture. It is possible that the DBMS would create 70 one-to-one processes for 70 users rather than one master DBMS process for all 70 users, for even more restrictive performance.

Log file bottlenecks

If a transaction log file is maintained for each transaction, a significant amount of overhead is committed to this activity. Since each log file update represents a data file transaction, the possible TPS is roughly decreased by half. This is not true when multiple servers or multiple disks support the database. In other words, optimize performance by moving log operations off the primary server or disabling log operations altogether.

Security bottlenecks

If security is maintained for each transaction by record and file or even by operation that a user can perform, a significant amount of overhead is committed to this activity. Since each security file verification represents at least one file read, the possible TPS are decreased by half or more. This is particularly true when security is implemented in SQL as a native part of the database design. The complexity of setting and assigning security rights in SQL can rapidly cause sluggish performance. Optimize performance by minimizing security operations and the need for them. It is far better to create separate tables or add the security at the functional menu level than it is to implement it at the data-record or file level.

Blocking reads and writes

Network operations frequently require that files or records be locked so that only one application or user has permission to modify them at any single time. The alternative is that two or more users get copies of a master record and make different changes simultaneously. If all users then rewrite the object, only the latest changes will be affected; other changes will be overwritten. This is complicated by caches. When master database records are locked, others cannot access them. This so-called *blocking operation* can bring a client/server to a standstill. It is necessary to lock records and files, but it is undesirable from a performance perspective.

Transaction commits

If caches or buffers of recently used database pages are forced to disk when a transaction is committed, consider enabling a write-through cache. Although this decreases overall writing performance, the bottleneck of a sudden series of operations is spread over a longer time period. This will provide a substantial performance boost. It is often desirable from a performance point of view to provide a group commit facility and defer writes without making changes to memory pages. Frequently used pages (master tables, for example) would stay in memory for improved performance.

Set task priorities

Tasks in client/server environments cannot all run at the same time. CPU time is sliced between the kernel (operating system), the client/server processes, and other operations running on the server(s). Since performance is really a perceptual concept to most users in the client/server environment and actually represents the total system time required to complete a task as seen by the user, set priorities of user activities higher than others. However, reports that require significant CPU, system, or network resources can be assigned off-hours or very low priorities. If at all possible, establish a time clock function for invoking these processes at off-peak hours. Furthermore, modify applications (if possible) to inform users that lengthy (and low-priority) tasks will be delayed. Reading and simple query operations can be given higher priorities, while creating new transactions can be assigned lower priorities. This will yield a perceptibly better response time.

Detuning

Relational database designs improve the integrity of a database by eliminating duplicate records and duplicated fields. The relational structure does not provide speed improvements. Typically, a single master record in a DB2 format may become four different records with multiple detail records in the relational and hierarchical format. This often means that a single record read under a flat data structure becomes 10 or more reads in a fully relational DBMS. The performance effect for writing information is usually not as pronounced, as only a single master or detail record is usually updated; however, several records could have to be updated instead of the original one.

Obviously, the means for improving relational database performance is to flatten out the database structure and eliminate the detail tables. Although this tends to create other problems, database designs that are significantly fragmented into detail records can be improved by detuning the relational record structure.

Pack and purge

The larger a database is, the longer it takes to locate records or add new records. Sequential lookups increase in proportion to the number of records in the database, whereas indexed searches increase less quickly (binomial increase only). Consider removing duplicated, dead, bad, or old records from the database. Search for detail records that no longer are connected to any master records. These are taking up disk space and increasing the time required for record searches. If it is necessary to maintain old data on-line in an archive for future reference, consider moving this information into a separate data set. Some organizations maintain accounting records for five years within the *current* database. This is a substantial performance hit that is easily fixed. Merely remove old master and detail records to another database and rename it.

Also, some databases, particularly dBASE and other similar PC-based DBMS engines, do not actually remove deleted records. They are merely marked as deleted and retain their original space within the data set. Deleted records can be recovered. Until the data set (or table) is actually *packed*, performance is suboptimal. Furthermore, the index usually contains references to these marked records, and this represents a performance hit as well. Scan your database and pack it. It will require less disk space for records and indexes and will run faster.

Data enumeration

Repeated data with inaccuracies decrease database efficiency in several ways. Not only is disk space bloated and search access time increased, mailings addressed and mailed to the wrong addresses, calls made to the wrong phone numbers, or inappropriate action taken because a partially duplicated record was referenced before the correct and up-to-date record represent expensive and wasteful efforts.

Run queries against single tables for duplicate and near-duplicate records. Consolidate and correct one of the records and delete and pack the dead records.

Data enumeration occurs when data are replicated across multiple platforms and servers. Before you pass judgment on the effects of data replication, realize that it is both a performance hit and a means for solving some complex performance problems. There is significant overhead involved in maintaining widely scattered databases in synchrony. The data must be copied and updated with predetermined frequency. However, the overhead required to copy the entire data set or just new and changed records may be significantly less of a bottleneck than serving out records as requested, when requested. The cost of data services may be extreme when the central server becomes overloaded or when the data requests saturate the LAN or WAN connection. Under those conditions, local data may be the only viable performance solution.

Data replication services

There is one other technique that is gaining acceptance, that of replicating the transaction groups on all distributed servers. By definition, a *replication server* copies the transactions across the distributed network. It does not copy the data sets or selected records themselves—just the activity. Replication supports near-time data updates sufficient for most backup and recovery operations. When transaction volume is low overall and all servers can support the combined transaction load, the replication process provides good performance enhancement. However, when the combined loads overtax any one server, the distributed data will not remain synchronized for long. Then, differences between the data need to be updated. This creates a double load, that of supporting the original replication process and also that of updating the databases to reflect the true state of the data.

Use files exclusively

Record locking is expensive in terms of CPU overhead. Open data files exclusively if users can have an exclusive copy of a data table or index, or if concurrent data access is not important.

Minimize file opens and closes

File operations are more costly than record operations. Minimize them. Open data sets or tables only when they are actually needed, and close them only when you are completely done with the problem. Opening indexes or detail files when these are not needed increases CPU, server CPU, and network load.

Index structures

Indexes are specialized data table columns in a database that speed up the search for information. An individual value in an index is often called a *key*. The lack of indexes or the use of improper indexes generally results in slow information searches. Indexing improves performance dramatically. Basically, a sequential lookup is replaced by a faster binary search or a comparison with a *hash* table which provides a referential record number. Although indexes require record and disk space, they usually represent a good tradeoff between disk space and data access time. The use of new indexes is not always a solution, however.

Basically, you want an index that is useful relative to operations. Names, contact names, customer numbers, telephone numbers, zip codes, and transaction types or codes are often better choices than addresses, customer types, or other less significant information. Furthermore, if there are too many indexes, when new records are added or existing records are updated, all indexes will have to be updated to reflect the new or changed information. This represents extra overhead that may be a performance hog.

Analyze the need for database indexing carefully. Choose the most significant information for indexes, or combine columns into a composite index for frequent searches and limit the number of actively maintained keys. It is always possible to occasionally update supplemental indexes or to create temporary indexes for infrequent operations. Often, DBMS performance is improved by optimizing indexing for the average day-to-day operations, such as customer queries, and building a new, temporary data table with all transactions in a transaction or customer sort order for month-end posting. It is also possible that sequential processing will be faster and more effective than keyed record processing. Indexes or better indexes are not always the performance panacea you expect.

If your DBMS supports clustered indexes—sparse entries—apply it. For many types of operations this will provide a significant overall performance benefit. These are very useful for static data sets—master customer lists—that change infrequently or not at all, since it is time-consuming to rebuild large clustered indexes.

Record structures

DBMS transaction speeds are generally limited to about 40 disk actions per second per disk device. This is mostly independent of record size, disk block and sector sizes, or complexity of the record structure. What does matter is the number of records that must be updated to complete a single user transaction. The more relational the DBMS, the more detail record updates are generally required per transaction. Also, when large logical record structures are artificially divided into multiple records in separate tables, the number of records written per transaction increases. On the other hand—depending upon the application and the workload—some types of information are not often updated and should be maintained in separate tables. For example, a customer billing list for an annual service contract is more stable than the address lists for a mail order house. The customer information, including name, contacts, addresses, and contract information, is optimally packed into a single record structure; whereas sales information for a mail order house is probably best referenced by a customer name or order number, and this is not included in a customer profile.

Optimal record structure is quite critical to DBMS performance. Not only does record structure redesign represent a detuning issue as discussed above, it also affects the complexity of the application code. In general, more complex record structures require more code, which requires more CPU, bus, and disk time.

Conclusion

It is important to recognize the objectives of client/server optimization tasks. High TPS is not always the goal. Optimizing client/server performance does not always means speeding up the operations. Furthermore, client/server technology is not a solution in itself. It does not function in an information technology vacuum. Develop appropriate goals, create benchmarks, gather data, and analyze them. Create an optimization plan that you can implement. As you do, track optimization progress against your benchmarks and the underlying objects.

In general, the most effective method of improving client/server performance is to reduce the workload. This is resource-wise and financially optimal. Workload reduction is accomplished by using better and more efficient software applications, dividing workloads between multiple CPUs or servers, or actually reducing processed workload. Not all client/server work is essential; some may merely be important or utilitarian. See what you can survive without.

When performance enhancement means decreasing processing time, increasing workload, or satisfying users, gather system information. Locate the bottleneck. Address the cause of that bottleneck with repairs, new or more hardware, better software drivers, or enhanced applications. Avoid generalized enhancements. These often will not address the relevant resource constraint and may only increase system complexity, decrease reliability, and even degrade performance. Define objectives. Create congruent goals. Gather data and analyze them. Devise a theory and a plan to test for the bottlenecks. Confirm those bottlenecks. Make a plan for easing those constraints. Gather data again and confirm that the bottlenecks have been bypassed and your initial objectives have been achieved.

7

Network Optimization

Introduction

Optimizing computer performance becomes significantly more complex when that system is part of a larger network. Basically, you now have a system of systems to optimize, and to compound the problems, the system of systems is usually interdependent. The network may be a small LAN, a WAN, or an enterprise network spanning many LANs and WANs. This chapter covers the issues of optimizing performance for LANs, WANs, host connections, and the networking aspects of client/server processing. For more information specific to the tuning of LANs, see the McGraw-Hill/Windcrest book by the author, *LAN Performance Optimization* (1993).

Typically, the network can consist of peer-to-peer connections, clients accessing one or more servers, or a mixed configuration of hosts, servers, clients, and interconnected systems (by using bridges, routers, hubs, gateways, or other services). Optimizing performance for networks entails optimizing the performance of the overall system and the larger processes; it also entails optimizing the hosts and servers within the context of the network, and ensuring that clients and interconnected systems perform well. For a thorough and complete network optimization, you might build a statistical model of the network process;

you might then optimize the model by minimizing the process completion times rather than by optimizing individual component performance. However, such a project is quite involved and beyond the scope of this book. The list below shows, in order of decreasing likelihood, sources of network bottlenecks. Note that this list represents LANs, WANs, and enterprise networks.

- Insufficient server capacity
- Insufficient capacity of host to serve network
- Slow software
- Suboptimal network configuration
- Network design violations
- Network installation flaws
- Misspecified network
- Suboptimal node configuration
- Connectivity devices configured improperly
- Connectivity devices with insufficient capacity
- Overloaded network channel bandwidth
- Overloaded network stations (peers and/or clients)

Although network transmission-channel bandwidth may seem the most likely network performance bottleneck, it rarely is the active constraint. It is, however, one of the most easily diagnosed bottlenecks and one of the most misdiagnosed bottlenecks. Connect a protocol analyzer to the network and track network load; this is the favored method for both LAN and WAN connections. While the channel utilization percentage is the key statistic, you might also test for response time. Statistically, response time is referred to as *latency*, the time required for a request to be fulfilled. In some cases, the network channel may be functioning at low load levels and still provide poor service. If error or collision rates are low, poor response time usually indicates that network components other than the channel itself are at fault.

Network optimization isn't merely a process of making each component run as optimally as possible, although that does help most of the time. This is one method of optimizing network performance when there are substantial resources available. However, it is important to recognize that the network itself represents an overlapping and competing series of projects that have complex and intertwined process paths. Some of these paths will have slack; other paths will be without slack and represent performance bottlenecks, as Figure 7.1 illustrates.

But, because projects and paths overlap, optimizing network performance will usually include making tradeoffs among projects. Network design, configuration, priority assignments, and allocation of resources to the different tasks represent optimization tradeoffs. It is simply not possible to create the "perfectly optimized" network environment unless the environment is partitioned in such a way that every task receives its own complete set of resources. That's rarely practical. Therefore, network performance optimization is the process of tuning the performance of the transmission channels and the key global components, while providing local resources selectively in order to meet the political and technically acceptable performance levels. This may often mean that full optimization is limited by available resources.

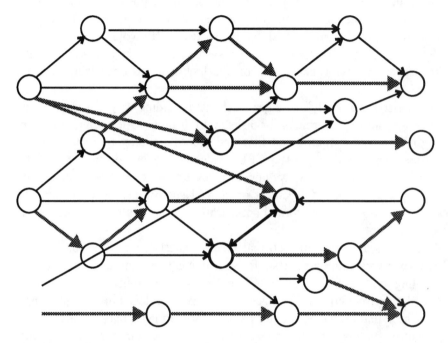

Figure 7.1 Network performance optimization represents adding slack to competing and overlapping tasks within multiple projects and making tradeoffs.

Optimizing the performance of a network rarely means replacing the network infrastructure with faster optical fiber or substituting a different transmission protocol, such as ATM or frame relay in place of 56-kB leased lines. Even ISDN doubles the performance of a leased line with bidirectional 56-kB throughput. Successful network tuning encompasses more than just the transmission channel. It requires revaluation of configuration and network architecture, as well as client, server, and host performance. In fact, substituting a crosspoint matrix switch (a telephone PBX-like technology) which is a switching hub allocating full protocol bandwidth for each node (much like ATM), or a 100-Mbits/s network such as TCNS and FDDI for a constricted 10-Mbits/s Ethernet rarely provides the 1000 percent gains imagined. While these matrix switches may provide full protocol bandwidth from the hub to each station, and a massive bandwidth within the hub on the order of 300 Mbits/s to 2 Gbits/s, this capacity is useful in only a few specialized environments. The computer infrastructure and NICs still need to approximate 10 Mbits/s, 16 Mbits, or 100 Mbits/s and not the 256 kbits to 3.2 Mbits/s most PCs and workstations can support.

Likely improvements in transmission throughput from substituting faster protocols could yield about a 45 percent overall improvement in performance at best. Reducing the network workload tends to provide the best optimization results; it is far easier to reduce workload than to augment the entire network infrastructure. For example, departments of transportation encourage car pooling as a method of reducing the load on the highway network. Sometimes they build new connections and widen existing roads, only to find that the system traffic volume has increased and that there are new bottlenecks in the system. You can probably see the similarity between relieving congestion on the highway and optimizing network performance.

By comparison, "unlikely" changes such as providing larger server disks, installing bus-mastering controllers for disks and NICs on a file server, establishing local disk caches, purging dead files and records, adding more memory or larger buffers, and substituting faster CPUs, video controllers, or buses with integrated high-resolution video may improve server response and workstation throughput by a factor of 2000 percent or more. Usually, merely reconciling the network configuration with the formal specifications enhances performance by as much as 100 percent.

Establish file search priorities so that client requests search the local drives first. Review network routing requests for spurious activity and unnecessary subnet or routing addresses (as in NetWare "hops"). Establish local swap or temporary files. Setting NIC buffer sizes to the maximum tends to strengthen performance. Check that bridge and router packets forward legal packets of all sizes. If the bridges or routers can filter packets based upon custom parameters in real time, apply these filters to relieve congestion. Make certain that routers send *source squelch* or *congestion* packets when a node or station reaches a preset threshold. Remove inferior devices from the network; many devices will ignore packets that exceed 512 bytes due to the influence of initial NetWare packet size limitations. Combining these changes often provides throughput improvements of at least 400 percent, and may yield performance gains of as much as 4000 or 5000 percent for GUI front ends interconnecting into client/server databases.

Optimize what you tune. If you tune the wrong component, that component is likely to perform better in the vacuum of a stand-alone setting, but perhaps no better within the network setting. If you tune the wrong component, any performance effect is likely to be less than anticipated or the reverse of the hoped-for results. Improper optimization, therefore, tends to be self-limiting. Consider this key recommendation: maintain a careful log of network performance, the exact steps taken to alter performance, and the consequences resulting from each step. You may have to reverse any performance dilution and diminishment.

Tuning network performance is a complex process, since the network is not a single device. Tuning can mean optimizing the performance of a single server, of a single station, of a network segment that performs poorly, or of the aggregate network. The complexity and sheer number of components in large networks make it difficult to optimize performance without modeling and project management techniques. Tuning can also mean the stepwise evaluation and enhancement of each subset. Correspondingly, this book espouses this stepwise refinement. Recall a basic message of this book: that the computer system and networks of systems are constructions which represent the aggregate of all devices and processes.

Frequently, attempts to optimize the performance of a single device that is performing poorly fail because that device is already performing at its peak within the context of the network. The device's performance is conditional upon its own attributes and configurations while subordinated to the limitations imposed by servers, hosts, and other stations, as Figure 7.2 illustrates. Within that setting, actual tuning proceeds first with elemental components such as stand-alone PCs and workstations, then progresses to more complicated and intertwined network stations and processes. Realize that even seemingly elemental and stand-alone components may impose limitations when optimizing performance of servers, segments, and the aggregate network. In spite of these complex interactions—network performance optimization is elusive and iterative—it is certainly worthwhile to master the bottlenecks and assess how performance on the network can be enhanced.

Tuning results	Station	Server or host	LAN	Network
Station	Optimum	No effect	Unknown	Unknown
Server	Better	Optimum	Unknown	Unknown
LAN	Qualified	Qualified	Optimum	Qualified
Network	Unknown	Unknown	Unknown	Optimum
Enterprise	Qualified	Qualified	Qualified	Optimum

Figure 7.2 Network performance goals and performance results.

Basic techniques

Before you can optimize a network, you will need to know its structure. The logical first step may be to document the structure of the network and inventory its components. Next, it might be helpful to model the network with a project management tool, such as Samantec TimeLine, Microsoft Project, or some other tool that supports the *critical path method* (CPM). You will need to add performance information in the form of task completion times. This is without question a complex and time-consuming task. The higher the quality of the information and the more information added into the CPM model, the more accurate the results. One of the disadvantages of a CPM model is that performing sensitivity analysis and accounting for burst loads is almost beyond the capacity of most project management tools.

Alternatively, you can run a network simulation using such tools as LANSIM from Internetix, Bones from Comdisco, or LANModel from Network Performance Institute. These tools provide confidence ranges and account for sporadic and burst traffic levels as experienced on most networks. Note that a version of LANModel is included on the tools disk with the McGraw-Hill/Windcrest book *LAN Performance Optimization*. These tools will indicate where channel transmission capacity lacks slack capacity and provide time estimates for network task completion. CACI and Comdisco also model server, host, and client processing capacities as well, so that you can model overall performance.

However, modeling and simulation are complex processes. Before you can get valid information, you first need to learn how to use the tools. Then, you need to design and model your network. Next, you need to understand the reports and how to evaluate this information. Because modeling tools are time-consuming, some MIS and network managers will decide instead to use available tools and run benchmarks. This does not provide as good information, but you already have the tools to find the bottlenecks, many of which are on the tools disk.

Bottleneck determination

When you think that there are bottlenecks on the network, you can run a benchmark. Network benchmarks, such as the previously described NetBench or Ghardenstone, will generate various types of workloads to provide an indication of channel and server capacities. If the network is transparent—in other words, if traffic is automatically routed to its destination—it will not matter whether the network is a LAN, a WAN, or a mix. However, the benchmark results will be useless without a basis for comparison, or if the benchmark is run in conjunction with a preexisting workload. Think about what the benchmark is telling you—very little about the network without a basis; you simply will not know the scale of the information. The best method for generating a basis for comparison is to run the benchmarks when the network and all attached devices are idle. Next, run the benchmarks when the network is running at or near peak capacity. Figure 7.3 illustrates network channel and aggregate server loads as a function of capacity.

The difference between these sets of results will show the base load and the effects of the peak load. Using that information and subtracting and adding values, you can make three general assessments. The first is the performance baseline for the network. How well does the network perform without workload? The second is the performance under current load levels. How well does the network perform with its normal peak workload? You can make very general assessments of what would happen if that load were increased. What happens when more load (stress) is added to the network? Could the network sustain increases in normal peak loads? Note that this method assumes linearity in network performance, which is hardly ever the case. Instead, as you add load to a network, performance tends to get disproportionately worse. Figure 7.4 below shows that Ethernet actually saturates as the traffic level increases while Token-Ring does not; however, response times become dramatically longer as the traffic level increases, as Figure 7.5 illustrates. These figures show why the models are more accurate than using benchmarks to make performance assessments beyond the scope of the benchmarks.

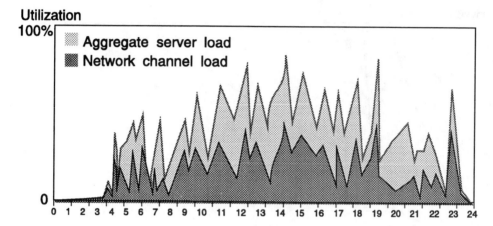

Figure 7.3 Network channel and aggregate server load as a function of capacity.

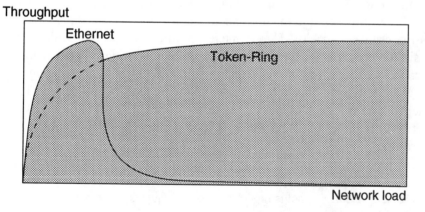

Figure 7.4 Network work accomplished is not a linear function of Ethernet network load.

In general, the LAN transmission channel is infrequently a performance bottleneck. However, WAN connections are slower—from 2400 bits/s to 1.536 Mbits/s—and often represent a performance problem. Most LAN channel widths exceed the performance capabilities of computer systems. This is true regardless of the LAN protocol bandwidth. The only time you are likely to experience a LAN channel bottleneck is when there are hardware problems with the network or when the number of devices on the network grows very large. Some client/server processing and intensive or large file transfers, as with graphic images or massive databases, will stress LAN transmission channels as well as WAN channels. Make certain that fatal embraces or DBMS record locks do not falsely emulate a bandwidth bottleneck.

Response time

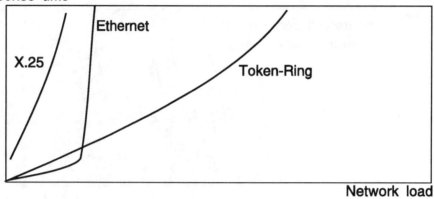

Figure 7.5 Network response time is nonlinear as a function of IBM Token-Ring network load.

Therefore, it is important to generate information about the network transmission paths. You absolutely need to know where the bottlenecks are. You can attach a protocol analyzer and compile network load and other performance statistics. This provides information about the traffic load relative to the transmission channel capacity. This is interesting information even without any other basis for comparison. It will show the absolute workload relative to the channel capacity. This is useful. For example, if the workload is pressing against the channel capacity, you have a bottleneck. You may need to consider providing greater network transmission capacity or lowering the traffic level to provide slack to the network. If the channel utilization is low, bottlenecks, *if any,* are located somewhere else.

Use the protocol analyzer to capture network packets and decode their contents. You may need to capture packets on each network segment and on individual LANs. Look for collisions, streams of requests to transmit again, or clear overload indications on individual segments. This process will show if any segment or LAN bottlenecks exist. For example, one LAN may be so busy as to be a choke point for routing packets from one segment to the next. That *path,* literally, represents a critical path lacking slack. As another example, an X.25 modem-based link, while configured for 56 kbits/s transmission, may be providing only 2400 to 9600 bits/s because the modem is not configured for the higher speed or is dropping to progressively lower speeds because of excessive line noise. Pairs of modems adhering to Microcom's MNP 10 standard for enhanced reliability over rural, cellular, radio, and international transmissions dynamically adjust speed and correct errors due to line noise. While the station may think it is configured for the higher speed, the modem and line failure is causing a bottleneck. The comparison of 3750 bits/s with the 56 kbits/s would erroneously suggest extra capacity, whereas careful comparison of the actual throughput of 3750 bits/s with the actual capacity shows full utilization. It may even show insufficient path capacity with significant delivery delays.

Similarly, WANs become bottlenecks because the full bandwidth may not be properly configured or allocated. For example, a T-1 point-to-point link may consists of 24 separate 56-kbits/s lines. T-1 may also consist of 24 separate 64 kbits/s digital lines. This is often shared with PBX-based voice services, facsimile, and data. It is common for one or more of those lines to be improperly configured and not be utilized at all. While voice management (telecommunications) groups could believe they are using 6 lines and MIS is using 18 lines, MIS could believe the same. As a result of this confusion, only 12 of the lines are actually employed. The carrier does not care or monitor how you use your lines; you must.

Frame relay is available on 56 kbits/s increments with minimum and fractional T-1 burst-load bandwidths. You may believe you have a 56/288 kbits/s capability, but have only two dedicated 56-kbits/s lines to the central switching office which limits you to 112 kbits/s. Check your WAN configurations for capacity from endpoint to endpoint and assume nothing. If the carrier provides 64 kbits/s of digital line capability rather than the older 56 kbits/s analog standard, expand your bandwidth capacity that 14 percent.

Large networks may have many active bottlenecks at the same time. The linkage points (completed steps in the CPM phraseology)—bridges, routers, repeaters, and gateways—can also represent *paths* of network service. While these devices may look like places for the network paths to end and thus complete a project path, they also are paths in themselves since they must process network packets. Look at their performance relative to their capacities. The devices should show if any packets were lost, rejected, or sent back to source; large numbers represent an indication of a bottleneck. Any device close to capacity should be considered suspect, and should be tracked if network load increases. It helps if these devices conform to a management protocol, such as CMIP or SNMP, or at least maintain performance statistics available from the device or a management support station.

Servers, hosts, and clients are the primary network bottlenecks. They tend to run out of RAM, then disk capacity, then bus capacity, and finally CPU capacity. The best method for benchmarking these devices is with a system monitor such as SysUse, PFM/2, DEKKO, or other such tools that show free RAM, free system resources, free disk space, and the CPU load. Free CPU capacity is the difference between capacity and the utilization level.

For example, a typical 17 percent CPU utilization level means that the CPU is waiting for work 83 percent of the time. High-server CPU load generally means anything above 50 percent. Although it is possible to see 100 percent loading, the measurement tools are often not that precise or sensitive to small time intervals. CPU load is a composite value that means the CPU is 100 percent loaded 15 percent of the time and only 10 percent loaded all the rest. Understand the granulation of the CPU load statistics and the implications. Consider as another example, that 40 percent CPU loading can mean that GDI and bus interlocks are using the other 60 percent. Analyze CPU load with care. Bus capacity usually is a hard statistic to gather without special oscilloscopes or hardware. You can make informed assessments by tracking the disk-drive lights, free RAM, and CPU capacity. If these values show adequate resources, you may assume a bus bottleneck when station performance is poor.

Optimization techniques

Optimization techniques begin with documentation and an inventory of the network. Next, run benchmarks on performance. It is interesting to measure performance on an idle network and a network running at normal peak capacity. Although it depends upon each environment, network load tends to peak about 11 a.m. and between 3 and 4 p.m. on many networks. That corresponds to people's peak productivity and attention levels. It also corresponds to when people effect trades, make transactions, and request information. It is typical to test the physical infrastructure, the network configuration, and the capacity of network devices. The next three sections detail these areas.

Physical infrastructure

The physical infrastructure of any network must be sound to achieve optimal performance. All transmission components—the cable, fiber, or wire; connectors; transceivers; hubs and MAUs; modems; public carrier circuits; interconnectivity devices; lobe or drop cables; NICs; and NIC drivers—can be tested for conformance to specification and proper installation. Basic network installation, infrastructure that matches specification, and acceptable installation and careful maintenance do improve network performance, but these basic techniques are outside the scope of this book.

A good infrastructure minimizes the effects of signal decay and distortion, timing errors, false signals, crosstalk, and random noise. Even networks that are poorly designed and improperly configured or balanced to match task workloads can realize 15 percent throughput gains through remedial physical infrastructure adjustments. Check configurations; make certain that devices match the values established in their hosts. Look for loose cables, broken connectors, transceivers, or other devices with error indicator lights. Replace suspected components. Test the infrastructure with voltmeters, TDRs, OTDRs, cable scanners, and signal injectors and correct any deficiencies as the initial step in the LAN performance optimization cycle.

Do not intermix components from different manufacturers. While this seems a small point, consider traffic rated at 16,000,000 characters per second on a 16-

Mbits/s Token-Ring with a network length of 2100 m. At a signal failure rate of 0.01 percent per 100 ft, the error rate will grow to 2.1 percent, or 42,000 characters each second at an average traffic load.

Network configuration

The actual physical layout of a network has a significant effect on network performance. This broad assertion is most relevant for enterprise networks. This represents client/server and distributed computing environments and interconnected LANs that have grown beyond small workgroups and now serve the needs of departments, larger divisions, and entire organizations.

For these flourishing networks, optimal performance is crucially dependent upon adequate design. The physical infrastructure must incorporate adequate file and application servers to match the workload and a cabling configuration to equal transmission channel throughputs, as Figure 7.6 illustrates. Divide overloaded LANs to balance workload, since the contention for each segment is less than that for the original combined LAN. This is particularly relevant for Ethernet, although it is also pertinent for other protocols, as fewer stations compete for a token.

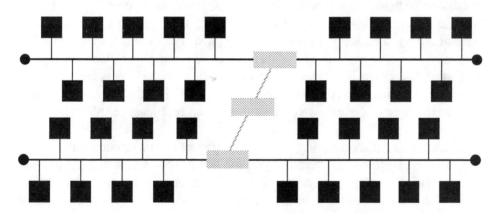

Figure 7.6 Divide overloaded networks.

Station placement tends to have significant effects on networks. Busy stations that talk to each other across WAN links or multiple LAN hops will experience poorer performance than those stations connected by local channels. Cumulatively, excess wiring and repeater delays can increase transmission times by 400 percent or more. Therefore, commensurate with the protocol and architecture, minimize network path lengths, hops, adjusted ring lengths (ARLs), lobe lengths, and node counts to provide faster response. While the overall load on a network may be very low, the transmission lags, strange (longer than necessary) routes, number of hops, and packet conversions add a significant delay to information delivery. This delay tends to be seen as poor network response time. When performance between certain pairs of stations is particularly bad, explore the delivery path between those two stations. It is possible that even though those stations may be 2 feet apart, the data packets are being misrouted through other segments on the network or even remote cities.

Asynchronous operations

As stated in the last chapter, synchronous communication can artificially create a performance bottleneck by denying and delaying access to resources. Tasks which issue a synchronous request for data do not work well in a networked environment. They tend to create logical performance bottlenecks when there really is no resource limitation. The limitation is really time. The problem can be compared to a hold up on an assembly line because one assembly station is missing the correct screws. Tasks are delayed until responses are provided because the necessary part—it is data in this example—is slow in coming.

Specifically, SNA traffic, terminal connections, or any processes which maintain copious "status messages" are likely to work poorly over a local area network. The time factor for message delivery on LANs is usually variable and unpredictable. Solutions for poor SNA network performance include increasing the data block transmission size, set the MAXOUT response to the largest possible value to minimize receipt confirmations, and reconfigure the PAUSE time limits to better handle network congestion. Virtual route pacing is also an issue, one that is very complex and not easily configured. For example, by establishing too many windows and increasing their sizes you can either flood or expand network traffic channels. SNA bottlenecks become even more pressing when the traffic is routed across WAN and LAN linkages. There is little hope for managing SNA traffic over LANs unless you can control and first manage the native SNA environment well.

It is better to replace a communications interface, that is a terminal emulator or an SQL and GUI front-end interface, with one that is more robust and can provide other services or even provide continuous, simultaneous asynchronous tasks. Tasks which return control immediately after an information request provides a means to absorb the full capabilities of available resources.

Network server optimization

Networks typically become bottlenecks when the server is overloaded, not usually because the transmission channel is overloaded. While it is possible to reach 100 percent of server CPU utilization—and some servers will—more likely cache or RAM is insufficient, the disk access is at capacity, or the server bus has reached saturation. The list below shows the reasons why servers become bottlenecks, in decreasing order of likelihood:

- Insufficient RAM
- Insufficient cache size
- Poor software
- Network access is a bottleneck

- Poor server configuration
- Insufficient disk capacity
- Server is overloaded
- Bus is saturated

Adding RAM is the most effective method of boosting the performance of an overloaded server. RAM can be used for maintaining more concurrent processes in RAM rather than paging to a virtual RAM on a slower hard disk, for caching data from disk, and for providing more room for better memory management. Also, Novell NetWare uses the extra memory very effectively for its elevator caching algorithms and for managing the NetWare Loadable Modules (NLMs).

The Novell DOS Requestor for NetWare 4.x can improve performance for both servers and clients. The CONN.VLM can be loaded low on the server for better speed, and the client requestor can actually be loaded into XMS memory on the client for performance parity with the requestor loaded into standard DOS RAM. However, the settings in the client NET.CFG file do affect performance. For best results, set CHECKSUM=0, LARGE INTERNET PACKETS=ON, SIGNATURE LEVEL=0, CACHE WRITES=OFF, and set the CACHE BUFFER SIZE to the largest packet you plan to transmit. On networks without big packet support, this is 512 bytes, on Ethernet it is 1500 bytes, and on Token-Ring it is 4096 bytes. This saves client RAM. However, do not make the buffer smaller than the largest packets as this will severely impede network performance.

Hardware is not the only means for improving performance. Often, server system settings affect performance significantly, and optimizing these settings usually requires nothing more than committing time. Analyze the current settings and revise them to better match the network parameters. Optimizing the configuration of a server is no science. Optimization is mainly by trial and error, testing performance with different configurations until one is found that is the best for that environment. However, some of this black art has been codified. Specifically, IBM engineers have created Lotus and Excel spreadsheets for calculating the optimal configuration for PC LAN and LAN Server; these are on the included tools disk. These spreadsheets generate RAM requirements, cache sizes, and network system settings based upon network size, station counts, and the networked applications.

Disk cache is a system configuration issue, and its size is determined in part by available RAM. Cache subtracts from available RAM. Although providing at least a minimal cache—512 kB—provides substantial performance gains for most user-level computer systems, the effects of increasing the cache size beyond the minimum are important for servers. Figure 7.7 shows the hit rate for a server as a function of the increasing cache size as compared with the hit rate for a client or stand-alone computer system. The difference between a client's efficiency with a cache and a server's is visible in the curve shape and overall hit rate. The client's higher efficiency is due to the number of concurrent processes and high cache turnover on a server. Note that some network operating systems make no distinction between RAM and a logically partitioned RAM cache; they use RAM for caching as needed and, as such, Figure 7.7 becomes a proxy for adding RAM.

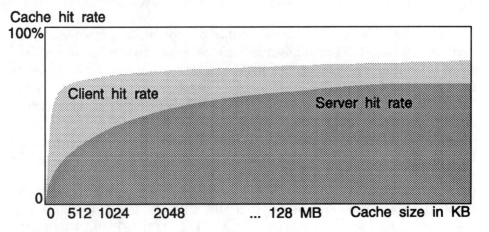

Cache hit rate

Figure 7.7 Increasing RAM cache size provides server performance gains that diminish less rapidly with increasing size than for client systems.

The cache hit-rate math is interesting. Increasing the cache hit rate from 60 to 99 percent decreases processing time for 100 requests from 806 ms to 29.9 ms. This is a 2596 percent performance improvement.[1] Realistically, cache hit rates can be increased to 95 percent from 70 to 85 percent. The math for increases in hit rates yields server performance improvements of about 200 to 800 percent. Before assuming that new hardware and faster CPUs are the answer, consider reconfiguring cache, installing a different cache, or testing a caching controller.

Review server configuration files. Remove unneeded .SYS and .INI files. References to functions or drivers that are not needed are best modified to prevent them from loading. For example, there is no need for the network CD-ROM driver to be loaded in LAN Server when there is no CD-ROM; indeed, it need not be on the system. Additionally, HPFS cache is a waste of 512 kB (up to 2 MB) when the file system is strictly FAT, although this is unlikely for OS/2 LAN Server. Do not load it. On the other hand, hard drives with more than 100 MB are faster under HPFS because it uses a sorted double-linked B-tree algorithm for locating files rather than the sequential lookup as supported by DOS FAT tables.

If a server is running multiple networks or supporting different networking protocols, consider minimizing the number of different network drivers required. See whether you can access all networks with a single ODI or NDIS driver. These support multiple protocols with multiple stacks and eliminate the need to load a different driver for each network. Also, if a server is functioning as either a router

---

[1]*Maximizing the Performance of Your Server*, Derfler, Frank J. Jr. and Schireson, Max, *PC Magazine*, October 26, 1993.

or a gateway, or providing dial-out or call-back dial-in communication in conjunction with other typical primary network activities, the configuration is very likely to be overly complex. Consider moving these communication functions to a secondary server and minimizing the configuration for both (or additional) servers.

Another server configuration issue is the device drivers. These operating system applications represent the single most frequently executed set of instructions on the server. *Every* disk access is funneled through the process control and task management functions before being passed in turn to cache drivers and finally to the disk controller drivers. These little pieces of code are running constantly. Optimization at this level has a performance effect disproportionate to its size. Make sure that your drivers are compatible with your server configuration, and that they are the ones with the best performance. In fact, there may be different device drivers which you can install depending upon the type of work the server performs. For example, OS/2 has an optional smart caching driver that looks for a pattern of sequential reads. When this driver sees sequential reads—as might happen when loading a Lotus spreadsheet or rebuilding a database index—the controller automatically reads the next sequential records into cache. This simple check can speed disk performance over 1000 times to yield a 20 percent overall gain to the user.

Server disk capacity becomes a bottleneck when seek and transfer times exceed the latency between data requests. In other words, too many requests exceed the capacity of the disk subsystems to fulfill them within the time allocated to that path. There is no slack. Since data requests fulfilled from disk take 100 times longer than those fulfilled from cache or RAM, expect to see no slack time in disk operations for a long time to come. The technology is expensive—electronic or solid state disks—and provides 1-ms response times. What do you do? If files are fragmented, make them compact. Add cache to raise the success rate for finding data in memory. Finally, increase the speed of the disk subsystem as cost limitations and availability allow. As described in Chapter 4, replace slower disks with faster ones on a per unit basis. Unchain multiple disks from controllers and install one controller per disk. Bypass the CPU and bottlenecks at the data transfer levels, if any, by installing bus-mastering controllers. Similarly, replace standard NICs with bus-mastering network controllers; standard NICs create a server bus bottleneck that impedes with data transfer. A secondary advantage of using bus-mastering NICs is that they increase the effective network data transfer rate. The network performance index, as described in Chapter 3, is a primitive though useful statistic for evaluating NIC performance. Servers supporting intensive disk activity or numerical processing will typically benefit from a bus-mastering NIC that reduces CPU load, while a workstation typically benefits with a faster NIC regardless of CPU loading effects.

However, do not overlook the performance effects of different NIC drivers. Many NOSs support native device drivers built by the card manufacturers. These tend to provide performance best tuned to the network adapter. However, sometimes it is necessary to run multiple protocols, IP, IPX, NetBIOS, NetBEUI, and SNA at the same time in separate protocol stacks. In such circumstances, native drivers are just not available for all these protocols, or the requirement in terms of RAM to maintain the multiple protocol stacks tends to prevent DOS or MS Windows from running anything else but the network. UNIX and OS/2 are better in this regard. The solution is to load generic drivers, such as Novell Open Data-Link Interface (ODI) or Microsoft Network Driver Interface Specification (NDIS). These drivers perform differently with different performance quotients depending upon the NOS, the machine, and the applications. The selection is particularly important for servers, less so for most workstations. It is preferable to use the native device drivers unless you are limited by RAM or must support multiple protocol stacks.

Cache configuration is also critical in server operations and the more complex operating systems such as Vines, NetWare, Windows NT Server, LAN Server, and PC LAN. Often the performance issue is not only about the cache size, but also about what is cached and how long data remains until it is flushed or replaced by newer data. Additionally, caching writes can provide more of a performance boost than caching reads because writes can require 10 times more time than read operations. Seek times and head movements tend to represent about 90 percent of disk activity, so it is desirable to minimize head motion. Some operating systems also *queue* disk I/O requests so that each sweep of the disk head across the spinning disks maximizes the number of requests serviced. For example, NetWare uses an "elevator" seeking mechanism to optimize the efficiency of disk reading and writing. It is called this because it picks up data "passengers" that are leaving and returning to the disks on all head movements, much like an elevator going from lobby to penthouse and back. Novell also caches entire disk directory structures to optimize reading and writing noncontiguous file extents.

As a result, the NetWare cache turns over frequently and contains "dirty" data, or block of memory, which have recently changed. By increasing the cache flush-delay time, you increase the efficiency of the disk activity. This also increases the chance—very, very slightly—that you might suffer data loss in the event of server failure. However, NetWare provides a transaction tracking system to protect mission-critical activities and balance the risk of increasing buffer flush times or dirty cache buffer times.

Install a redundant array of inexpensive disks (RAID); this has an extraordinary benefit where data is read more frequently than it is written—which is the norm for most servers. This is frequently stated in terms of a read-to-write ratio. Read-to-write ratios are usually presented in 1:1 to 100:1 format. Database activities tend to have higher read-to-write ratios than word processing. Some RAID designs provide multiple read accesses to the same files and even the same records simultaneously by allowing the disk controllers to read from whichever of the two or more disks holding the data is not currently busy. This tends to yield about a 30 percent disk performance improvement, according to the manufacturers of RAID subsystems.

The way to tell that a computer bus is a bottleneck is either with specialized software or hardware, or by proxy. The proxy method is one of elimination. Basically, ascertain that the network, CPU, and disk subsystems do not represent bottlenecks. You have tools to tell that. If those key components are not the bottleneck, the only significant component remaining is the bus. The bottleneck clearly is not the software, operating system, compatibility problems, or device drivers. If it were, you would see interrupt conflicts or a higher CPU load.

The functions of older ISA servers can be optimized by replacing them with MCA or EISA bus units. Bus bandwidth is nominally about four times higher, and sustained capacity is also about four times more with EISA or MCA. If an EISA or MCA server becomes bottlenecked at the bus, test the performance of a Tricord or Paradigm superserver. UNIX-based servers which exhibit bus overload can be upgraded with more powerful hardware, including UNIX superservers. OS/2-based LAN Server servers can be replaced by proprietary bus superservers and the IBM PS/2 295 servers. It is harder to upgrade a Macintosh-based System-7 server when you reach the top of the Apple product line, although it is possible to replace the NOS with NetWare, NFS, or Banyan Vines running on a superserver and connect this to the Appletalk clients.

It is rare that the server CPU is at capacity. If the CPU is overloaded, explore the possibility of decreasing its workload. Load fewer background tasks and fewer NLMs. Do not run the performance monitor that takes CPU time when you are short on CPU time. Get the games off the server. Remove marginally needed applications. Barring that, explore the possibility that insufficient RAM, cache, or disk throughput is causing the CPU to work harder, performing extra and unnecessary housecleaning. The computer project as represented by the critical path diagram previously in Figure 2.1 is simplified, of course. Paths tend not to be totally sequential or asynchronous; instead, computer system loads tend to be interdependent.

When benchmarks and computer system analysis clearly show the CPU at capacity, *first* consider how you can unload some of the work from the server. How much work is unnecessary? Does it need to be networked? Move it to the network server's clients. Get the clients to do more of their own work. Loading applications, overlays, and link libraries from the server may represent substantial server overhead. If the management is not burdensome, move the applications to the clients. When that is not practical or desirable, consider how the work that the server performs can be partitioned between two servers.

Split the workload by function. For example, construct one server that provides network login and application and file services, and establish a new, second (backup, slave, or secondary domain) server for database services only. Also, consider splitting the workload by functional user groups and establishing a server for each group. This approach is easier because the technology is already in place, the managers and users have experience with that environment, and it is cost-effective. It also provides a backup server in case of a primary server failure.

When E-mail, printing, modem communications, network fax, network backup, document scanning, and imaging reside on a primary server, consider setting up a secondary server for these functions. These functions are easily moved. Furthermore, while moving these support applications to another computer frees CPU capacity on the network server, secondary benefits include localized performance for disk- and bus-intensive activities and segmentation of functions.

Replacing a slow CPU with a faster unit (as provided by Kingston, AMD, or Cyrix) is an effective method of boosting CPU performance. Realize that swapping the CPU improves integer and floating-point performance, but provides no performance boosts for the computer system infrastructure. As stated previously, the interaction between system components is not strictly linear and sequential; as a result, you may find that the server still has a bottleneck with a new CPU. The critical path is just at a different component.

Coprocessing CPUs represents another option for some server environments. This is especially pertinent for threaded and multitasking operating systems that run within UNIX, Windows NT, or OS/2. Some will support symmetric multitasking, and since servers—even LANtastic and PC LAN, which are among the simplest NOSs— perform multiple tasks at the same time, coprocessing is a desirable option. One option for LAN Server is the IBM PS/2 295, which has dual CPUs. The workload is split between the two processors with each handling separate functions. The first CPU handles LAN Server and OS/2 functions, while the second CPU provides application services.

When the server is clearly the performance bottleneck, replace it with a faster model. While it has recently been realized that CPU performance is a major but not the most important performance factor in a computer system, the benchmarks and reviews that magazines print clearly show that system design and careful architectural tuning provide relative performance differences as high as 20 percent when vendor offerings with the identical CPU and system components are compared. Vendor offerings vary only in drivers, BIOS, motherboard design, and connecting circuitry. A server that provides 20 percent more performance than the server that is currently a bottleneck may provide enough slack so that overall network performance is adequate.

Recognize that vendors are creating more complex and specialized chips with internal communications speeds that are faster than the external bus speed. A server based upon the slower Intel 80486 50 MHz will outperform a system built with the 80486 DX 2/66 chip at the bus and disk level because the data transfer and bus speeds are 50 percent higher. Also note that some PC hardware that is optimized for MS Windows is unlikely to be the best for a NetWare server. Realize the limitations of the benchmarks and compare and contrast the basis with your computer requirements. Finally, realize that a system with a high-speed

VESA bus and VESA-compatible disk controllers may not provide as much disk speed and throughput as an IDE drive on a lesser bus with optimized drivers.

When server network access is a bottleneck—this means that the server cannot pump out enough packets to the network channel quickly enough—try a bus-mastering controller or a faster network controller card. Many PC-based servers have 8-bit or 16-bit NICs that are very slow when compared to 32-bit enhanced adapters. These cards easily double or triple capacity, and many EISA NICs can saturate the 10-Mbits/s Ethernet channel or the 16-Mbits/s Token-Ring limit, and provide as much as 40 Mbits/s on FDDI. That represents a substantial enhancement over older NICs with 1 Mbits/s of functional capacity. Also, consider installing multiple cards in the server. This will create parallel channels to transfer data, and when suitable bus-mastering cards are used, the CPU load corresponding to network communications will decrease.

Note that several trade magazine articles with benchmarks on bus-mastering controllers have made the incorrect assumption that these devices are not effective because they increase the CPU load rather than lowering it. Actual CPU utilization may nonetheless go to 100 percent, not because of the bus-mastering cards or because of the multiple cards per se, but because a bottleneck has been cleared from the I/O channel and the CPU now has more work to do. Nonetheless, you should test new components and make certain that they are tuned to your system requirements and optimize overall performance. Figure 7.8 shows the server contribution to a Token-Ring network overlaid by the CPU utilization levels for various types and numbers of NICs.

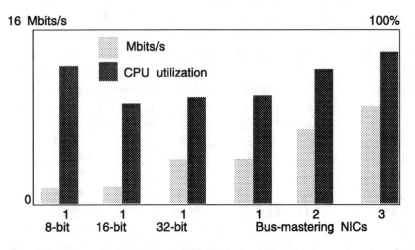

Figure 7.8 Server network throughput with CPU utilization levels for various types and numbers of concurrent NICs.

Client station optimization

When the client is a bottleneck and it is not waiting for the server to fulfill requests, the problem is usually too much work, too little RAM, and not enough horsepower. The most effective method for improving client performance is to decrease the workload. Switch from a GUI interface to a text-based one. Replace complex applications with more efficient ones. Reduce the number of background tasks or idled, iconized applications. Background and idled tasks all reduce available RAM and tend to increase the need to create virtual RAM on disk.

Consider moving secondary applications to a second client unit. A programmer could easily absorb the horsepower of several systems with code writing (development), source code compilation, testing and making bug fixes, and responding to E-mail in a timely manner. Some of those tasks do not require the latest and most expensive system; secondary tasks could easily be moved to a system with minimal resale value. After all, because these are network-accessible processes, they can be accessed from any system connected to the network such as an IBM XT clone with 640 kB of RAM, a bootable floppy, and network drivers.

When horsepower is the issue, see whether some of the processing can be moved to the server or to another client if the environment supports distributed computing. Under UNIX it is easy to spawn one of your own tasks on any other system to which you have access. Print servers that are not overwhelmed by sending output to printers at the leisurely rate of 4000 chars/min may well have extra capacity for another concurrent task. It is also easy to give a remote task a low priority so that it will not affect printing services; when there are no print tasks in the queue, the remote task will assume an active priority until it is displaced by other print tasks. The remote process need not run on a print server; any underutilized machine is eligible.

Adding RAM is the most effective method of boosting client performance. The exception is for DOS-based applications that are limited to 640 kB of standard memory and do not use enhanced or expanded memory. UNIX, OS/2, Macintosh, and MS Windows-based applications generally benefit from as much memory as can be provided. RAM can be used for maintaining more concurrent processes in memory rather than paging them to a virtual RAM on a slower hard disk, for caching data from disk, and for providing room for better memory management. If you are running DOS and MS Windows, consider loading FILESTAT to track disk access to the MS Windows swap file. Add memory until you minimize swapping. If the client does not have a swap file, create one. Consider, also, increasing the size of the swap file; recall that this file needs to be contiguous, installed on an uncompressed drive, and placed as close to the FAT directory as possible. You can do that by deleting from that drive all files but the boot files (COMMAND.COM, AUTOEXEC.BAT, IO.SYS, MSDOS.SYS, and CONFIG.SYS). If it is the boot drive, then create the swap file on a defragmented disk. It will have a name like 386SPART.PAR and will have the size that you specified when you created it under MS Windows. (If you are setting up multiple MS Windows clients over the network, you can speed up this process by merely copying these files with hidden system attributes over the network with a network copy utility that supports hidden files.)

Hardware is not the only means for improving network performance. Often, client system settings affect performance significantly. Tuning these settings usually requires nothing more than spending time. Refer to Chapter 4 for details. Analyze the current settings and revise them to better match the network parameters. This is no science. The tools that exist for benchmarking performance and providing configuration advice are primitive. Generally, minimize the number of drivers loaded. Do not load utilities. If you are running DOS, do not load TSRs, but try to load as many drivers into the 384 kB of high memory area (HMA) located above 640 kB and under 1 MB. This is basically dead space, except for IBM Token-Ring drivers, EGA, VGA, and other functions that may already have been circumvented with enhanced hardware solutions.

Disk cache is a system configuration issue, and its size is determined in part by available RAM. Cache subtracts from available RAM. Although providing at least a minimal cache—128 kB—provides substantial performance gains for most client systems, increase this for disk-intensive activities. Note that a local software disk cache will possibly cache client requests to a *network* disk. On the other hand, a hardware disk cache on a local controller will not buffer network reads. This is basically the result of the local cache performing as a logical entity. Network disks tend to be faster than local client hard drives. When this is not the case, consider relocating applications and data to the local drive for a performance boost. You should be more concerned with files that are repeatedly accessed than with files that are loaded once or twice per day. Data that are accessed by many network users should be retained on a network disk for control, security, and management reasons. If they are accessed often, they will be retained in the network server's cache. This is true for NetWare, LAN Server, SUN NFS, and most other NOSs. This performance improvement is a function of the cache and the demand for these data, not of the operating system or anything else.

Client stations with slow NICs, network drives, or servers benefit from local workstation cache that can cache network drives as well as local drives. CacheAll from C&D Programming Corporation buffers removable drives, local hard disks, CD-ROMs, and network devices too. It buffers both read and written data. Local caching of network drives is pertinent when the same data is frequently read from the network. For example, this includes loading application .DLLs or overlays from the server, frequently refreshing CAD drawings or images, or rereading a master database from the network.

Another configuration issue, as with servers, is the device drivers. These operating system applications represent the single most frequently executed set of instructions on client computers. *Every* disk access is funneled through the process control and task management functions before being passed in turn to cache drivers and finally to the disk controller drivers. These little pieces of code are basically running constantly. Optimization at this level has a performance effect disproportionate to its size. Make sure that your drivers are compatible with your client, server, and NOS configuration, and that they are the ones with the best performance. In fact, there may be different device drivers which you can install depending upon the type of work that the client performs. Clearly, different video drivers can have a significant performance effect.

It is rare that a client CPU is at capacity. The client is more likely to experience an architectural bottleneck than a CPU crunch. Counterexamples are CPU-intensive graphics, CAD, and floating-point processing. Text entry and keyboard activity will not overtax even the oldest microcomputer. If the CPU seems overloaded, explore the possibility that insufficient RAM, cache, or disk throughput is causing the CPU to work harder performing housecleaning. GUI activities tend to benefit more substantially from fast NICs, an adequate video card and driver, sufficient RAM, and local resources than they do from additional CPU power.

When benchmarks and computer system analysis clearly show the CPU at capacity, *first* consider how you can unload some of the work from the client. How much work is unnecessary? Does it need to be networked? Can more load be moved to the network server? Split the workload by function and move it to different CPUs. This approach is easier because the hardware may already be in place. When background tasks such as E-mail, printing, communications, Rolodexes, and games sap CPU and computer system resources, set limits. Assess what the organization is willing to support, and then make it clear that resources are limited to the main network applications. If a user wants more than that, the consequences become either that user's decision or something negotiated with network or MIS management.

Replacing a slow CPU with a faster unit (as provided by Kingston, AMD, or Cyrix) is an effective method of boosting CPU performance. Realize that swapping the CPU enhances integer (and sometimes floating-point) performance but provides no performance boosts for the computer system infrastructure. As stated previously, the interaction between system components is not strictly linear and sequential; as a result, you may find that the client still has a bottleneck with a new CPU. The critical path is just at a different component, often the network server. When the client is clearly the performance bottleneck, replace it with a faster model.

Peer-to-peer

Peer-to-peer networks represent a special case of servers and clients combined into one heterogeneous environment. When every system is likely to be both a client and a server at the same time, performance requirements tend to be uniformly more significant than when network devices are split between high-powered servers and minimally configured clients. Since peer-to-peer networking is mostly a PC, DOS, and MS Windows phenomenon, most 386- and 486-based PCs will provide sufficient horsepower.

When bottlenecks are observed at specific peer-to-peer stations, upgrade those units. Classify network nodes as clients and servers based upon primary node usage. Optimize performance as if those nodes were true servers or clients. When the infrastructure becomes fundamentally insufficient, replace the network with a more traditional client/server network. Note that security, network management, and control tend to be more difficult issues when there are no clear demarcations as to who owns what. Performance optimization tends to become as muddled an issue as hardware management and security.

Drivers

Not all network drivers and multiprotocol stacks are the same. This becomes an important performance issue for internetworks and complex networks; it is relevant not only for complex networks that the latest drivers be tested. The four performance issues usually are reliability, compatibility, performance, and memory consumption. You need to know that some load as TSRs, as .DLLs, and others swap in and out of memory as requested. Some require as little as 40 kB of RAM, others as much as 400 kB. Transfer times vary by a factor of two. If your network provides considerable internetworking and mixes protocols, NDIS, ODI, or TCP/IP drivers, you should explore the effectiveness and efficiency of different vendor products.

Furthermore, when a server or client is supporting a multiprotocol stack—that is, it is supporting different types of network operating systems, different types of protocols, different types of NICs, or even multiple NICs—it may be possible for the same .DLLs, buffers, sockets, and protocol stacks to load as a single instance rather than loading redundantly. This saves RAM and processor overhead and simplifies the interrupt tables created to support these network processes and hardware devices.

Evaluate software upgrades

When LAN bottlenecks have definitely been traced to software, more server and workstation horsepower is usually the best recourse. Migration to Windows, OS/400, Windows NT, UNIX, or UNIX derivatives which support parallel processing and multiple processors may overcome the software constraints. However, when the dispersed application has other serious flaws, consider upgrading that dispersed application software with something supporting client/server optimization. Slow client/server applications can be upgraded to a distributed computing version. In some (few) cases, the software upgrade may be more straightforward, particularly when the applications are based upon a generic standard, such as ANSI C or SQL. However, note that bottlenecks attributed to slow applications actually could be precipitated by slow disk searches through large data sets, poor index selection, lack of indexes (relying instead upon sequential lookups), as well as many dead files and deleted (but not purged) records. In some instances, poor software execution can be improved by moving the application to a local disk on a network workstation. Also, note that software upgrades typically require more disk space and the upgrade process may leave unnecessary files which are associated with the prior release. You may want to install the upgrade to a test directory and reconcile the differences between old and new, particularly with regard to performance.

Realize too that a software upgrade can be a feature-bloated performance fiasco because the software is more demanding of network and client resources. While the upgrade may seem to provide enhanced functionality, this can be at the expense of speed of performance. Furthermore, the features may not be pertinent to organizational needs and may also represent a significant training and support issue. Upgrade carefully and realize the possible compatibility problems arising with new upgrades or releases; network performance means many things.

Data compression

When network paths are overloaded and the cost to increase their capacity is high—as with leased lines and dedicated digital or analog connections—consider compressing data prior to transmission. While it is possible but awkward to compress individual files for transmission using an application such as PKZIP or LHARC, there are not only modems but also communications terminal packages that automatically compress data on the fly (asynchronously) for transmission with only a few milliseconds additional delay. The modems apply a run length encoding or a Zempel-Zev conversion technique to double or quadruple the efficiency of the transmission line. This will add slack to critical paths. Similarly, some remote control or terminal emulation programs will transmit only bits or bytes that have changed from screen to screen and will pack these changes for transmission savings. Packed bits also optimize performance in terms of delivery cost per information unit for frame relay, X.25, or ATM connections where you pay for packets by the packet.

Note, however, that you will gain no performance improvement—and perhaps experience poorer performance—if you stack compression technologies atop one another. A packed file cannot be compressed further, and the time required to discover that this is so dramatically lengthens the process. Pick one process, whichever one you find easiest or fastest, and implement it.

Load distribution

The most economical method of lowering network usage available is to charge for network service at graduated rates and offer users incentives to avoid prime-time network access. This is what telephone companies do to reduce daytime traffic and encourage off-peak usage. Since any network is built to handle a peak load, and since a peak load might be several times larger than off-hour usage, there is a built-in network excess capacity. Unfortunately, that extra capacity is available during nonwork hours. Figure 7.9 illustrates this principle by graphing the network load during the progress of a normal day. Harried users often implicitly understand this principle and reorient their work schedules to reduce the impact on the overloaded network. Publish a graph of daily network loads to encourage off-peak usage if financial incentives are impractical.

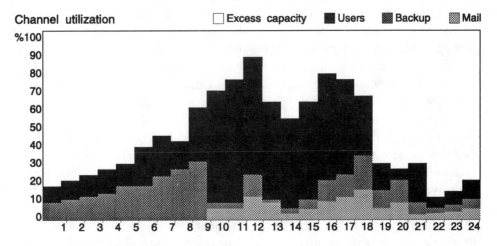

Figure 7.9 Network load during a typical workday.

When this last option is unavailable, the next-easiest method for reducing traffic levels is to filter the traffic and not allow certain vehicles on the network during peak usage periods. The network administration group, for example, doesn't need to perform data backups when the network is overloaded. Electronic mail can be stored and forwarded when the network shows a lull, or else saved for distribution during off-peak hours. Other processes can be hogs of network resources. Curtail such processes. Figure 7.10 illustrates a typical distribution of network traffic. Note that this display represents volume percentages for each hour of a typical day. Collision traffic parallels the peaks of the last figure, but most traffic is disk access. Mail and graphics is a minor component in this sample.

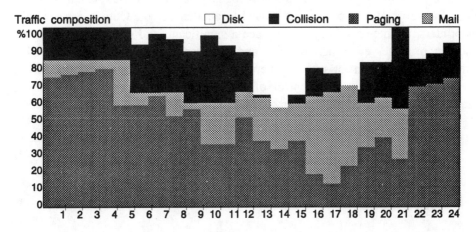

Figure 7.10 Network traffic by major networked application.

E-mail often starts as a 10-line memo containing 1000 characters, but this memo is then directed to 150 users. Since each user receives a separate copy, 150,000 characters plus the mail addressing information and delivery packet overhead must be included. That simple mail message therefore requires upward of 300,000 characters of network transmission. A bulletin board with a single posting reduces this "junk mail" load almost entirely. Side benefits include a reduction of "temporary" mail disk storage—temporary because each day's new mail will require that old space. Recall from Chapter 4 that many small E-mail messages can also fill a hard drive's directory or i-node space and make that disk prematurely full. It is poor performance to fill a "600"-MB disk with only 30 MB of mail message files, whereas that same disk could have three partitions, one of 540 MB for normal use and two 30-MB partitions just for the mail files.

Remote data backup could be banned from the network and performed exclusively from each client, with network data on servers being backed up from the servers themselves. Such a policy might entail additional backup devices; it shifts financial costs from network communication channel improvements (infrastructure) to node-specific upgrades (depreciable usage-specific equipment).

Local resource substitution and load balancing

Excessive loads on any single LAN component will undermine performance. Providing additional parallel capacity is one solution to these bottlenecks. Bottlenecks best solved with this technique include network file servers, overloaded LAN output devices, transmission channels, and internetworking devices such as bridges, hubs, routers, and gateways.

As previously stated, work from an overloaded server can be allocated among several intermediate, subordinated stations. Overloaded departmental file servers often simultaneously and concurrently provide file services, mail, print services, routing to other subnetworks, user login, and security functions. When the network operating system supports backup and secondary network servers, one or more of these fundamental services can be moved to another server. Output devices such as printers and network fax servers place a significant load upon their file server and the print server. When the file and print server are the same, the CPU overhead is significant for spooling, network output redirection, temporary storage of the output to disk, and control of the output devices; instead, farm these facilities out to different servers, as shown in Figure 7.11.

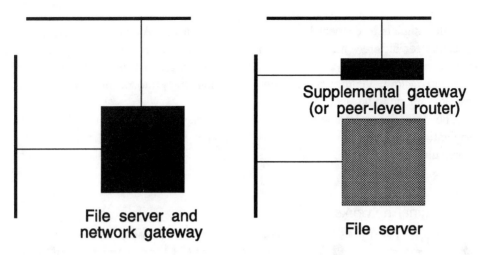

Figure 7.11 Add resources to enhance server facilities and overall network performance.

Network growth configuration

Massive networks—LANs started as test projects or as ad hoc resources to bypass the traditional MIS department and have since grown explosively—may actually saturate the transmission channel. They are best optimized by a process sometimes termed "load leveling" and by segregating workgroups on linked segments. This effectively amounts to identifying workgroup units and constructing separate segments adequate to match the requirements for each individual unit. Since E-mail, shared resources, shared access, and communication are fundamental to the success of the network, each subnet needs a central connecting backbone.

This subnet approach has the advantages of simplicity, immediacy, and control. Subnetworking also provides isolation from LAN failures in other workgroups and a global failure in the central backbone. Ideally, each subnet could function adequately without the central backbone. This is a traditional and acceptable approach that has proven effective for overloaded Token-Ring and Ethernet LANs. These "firebreaks" increase reliability while isolating traffic to the subnets for improved performance. Bridges, hubs, routers, and gateways actually interconnect the workgroup LANs. There are three shortcomings to this approach.

The first of these shortcomings includes the overhead and bottlenecks imposed by the routing software (traditionally at servers) or by the stand-alone connectivity devices. When stations perform double duty as file servers, mail servers, print servers, and gateways, the usual performance bottlenecks tend to occur at these CPU choke points.

The second shortcoming is that stand-alone connectivity devices may not match the traffic requirements. A repeater is not the appropriate device for interconnecting high-traffic subnets; a repeater is best used to extend signals for servicing physically dispersed areas. Repeaters increase the collision and dropped packet rate on Ethernet while increasing the TRT on token-based networks. Bridges, in the traditional definition of course, merely repeat LLC-layer protocol and filter signals to connect LANs with different media. As such, they are signal repeaters for different media. MAC-layer routers that filter packets are protocol-dependent. Routers are complex to install, configure, and maintain. They are frequently slow. Gateways performing routing or protocol encapsulation or translation tend to be slower still.

The third shortcoming is that internetwork traffic—that is, the traffic originating on one subnet and routed to another subnet—often traverses many other subnets, as Figure 7.12 illustrates.

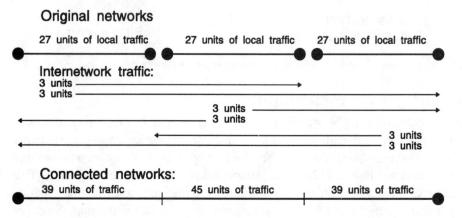

Original networks

27 units of local traffic   27 units of local traffic   27 units of local traffic

Internetwork traffic:
3 units
3 units

3 units
3 units

3 units
3 units

Connected networks:
39 units of traffic   45 units of traffic   39 units of traffic

Figure 7.12 Avoid routing internetwork traffic through local subnets. Not only does this adversely affect local traffic performance, it also has a significant tendency to create an internetwork bottleneck.

These other subnets are used merely as links; the local traffic increases significantly, sometimes to the saturation point. The intermediate links also increase the transmission latency, which often causes problems with multiprotocol networks. Latency is a serious problem for networks supporting synchronous terminal services or SNA.

The solution to these network configuration flaws is threefold. First, subnets should be intelligently designed, with some purpose other than merely cable length minimization or convenience of installation. Each subnet should be balanced for load as an individual resource. Servers, when overloaded, can be partitioned to distribute their processing loads to other subordinated devices. Standard PCs or UNIX workstations can provide at least as good performance as specialized, single-purpose bridging and routing hardware—in some cases. Moreover, standard station hardware obviates the need for learning how to operate another type of device or stocking specialized replacement parts.

Second, bridges, hubs, routers, and gateways should replace repeaters for enhancing performance. The MAC-layer packet forwarding and filtering capability of bridges, routers, and gateways reduces transient and irrelevant traffic. Note, however, that performance characteristics of bridges, routers, and gateways from various manufacturers differ. Some can handle high-volume traffic without losing packet header bits or completely dropping packets. Some optimize routing. Routers also vary in routing algorithms or can support several routing algorithms at the same time; what is best depends upon your environment and the internetwork load.

Some routers also create their own traffic in the form of *broadcast storms* as they maintain and update routing tables or distribute management information and performance statistics. When typical routers and gateways become LAN subnet bottlenecks, there are two solutions: reassess the configuration and install bridges, or install a higher-performance device called *cross-point matrix switch*. These switches are specialized computers with high-performance data buses; they route packets from multiple subnetworks at traffic volumes from 340 Mbits/s to 2 Gbits/s in their parallel multiple backplanes. However, realize that a matrix switch is not always the solution to a transmission channel overloaded with traffic. It establishes an exclusive point-to-point connection between communicating stations and thereby restricts access to other stations, highly demanded servers included.

Routing information update is also true for "domain" networks such as LAN Server, LAN Manager, Vines, Windows NT Advanced Server, NFS with yellow pages, and for networks supporting X.400 and X.500 global naming services. Domain networks distribute service, user, and activity information to all servers on the network in order to maintain up-to-date tables. On extensive networks, not only is it a management burden to maintain all this information, domain services also add to network traffic. When domain services create performance bottlenecks, the only effective solution is to manually update naming tables and to create a single domain network. You could also consolidate the many separate domains into fewer sets. The disadvantage is that network service changes will not always propagate throughout the network and that security is weakened.

Break network connections

Repeaters, bridges, hubs, routers, and gateways generally create performance problems by extending the transmission delivery time. This increases the likelihood of increased latency and poor response times. These devices simply increase the potential for too-large, too-busy network configurations by extending the network architecture to the statistical breaking point. In situations where a network is grossly overloaded, disconnection of repeater units might solve the traffic bottleneck, as shown in Figure 7.13. This obviously defeats the purpose of the network by cutting intercommunication channels. There are other alternatives, but this iconoclastic solution can be implemented quickly to solve short-term overloading problems until more reasonable (and expensive) options can be implemented. A router with a filtering technology, a high-speed packet switch, a spanning tree, or a backbone in a bus are superior alternatives.

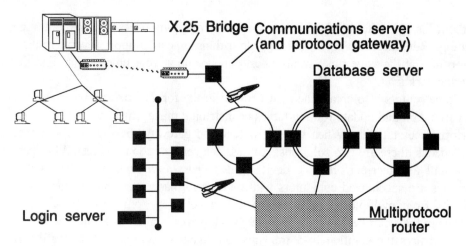

Figure 7.13 Divide LANs and WANs linked to an overloaded enterprise network for immediate bottleneck relief.

Some newer-model bridges can be configured through software as routers; similarly, some routers can be configured as bridges for faster execution. Bridges tend to be several times faster than routers. 3Com, Retix, and Synernectics provide these configurable devices. Forwarding throughput can reach 95 percent or more of full channel capacities. One point is that vendors are aware of subnetwork interconnectivity bottlenecks and requirements, and seek to address these needs. The other point is that older-model bridging and routing equipment may be insufficient to match current LAN performance needs. The technology has improved; unit-for-unit replacement of substandard components may resolve the obstruction.

Third, design a configuration so that all stand-alone subnets are connected to a hub (backbone) rather than chaining into other LAN segments. Even FDDI cannot support the intensive loads from many LANs. In other words, set up parallel channels for segmenting traffic or establish single-purpose router-to-router links. Servers or mainframe hosts that must communicate with every subnet can reside on the hub or else connect into each LAN segment where these stations can support multiple NICs. In this configuration the enterprise hub serves no other purpose than to facilitate communication among the various LAN segments.

Fourth, check that network addresses and routing addresses are correct to minimize internetwork traffic and prevent unnecessary hops. When LANs are connected via WAN links, supply sufficient bandwidth to carry all real-time activity within acceptable response times. When that is not feasible—usually for economic reasons or lack of availability of a particular service—minimize the traffic that crosses the network. Otherwise, consider installing inverse multiplexing to dedicate one base line to service, and thereafter access as many additional lines as needed to meet bandwidth requirements. This is *bandwidth-on-demand*, and it is available in packet switching technologies served by ISDN, frame relay, ATM, and X.25. Service is not cheap, but it is more cost-effective than oversubscribing based upon worst-case bandwidth scenarios. Bandwidth-on-demand with standard dial-up lines is also a feature provided by some newer routers.

Remote access operations

A *remote procedure call* (RPC) provides another method to offload processing to network servers or clients. Although this technique is a built-in feature of SunOS, NFS, UNIX, and OSF, it is lacking as a standard feature in many other network operating systems. It can be added to most NOSs including, NetWare, Vines, LAN Manager, OS/2 LAN Server, Windows for Workgroups, Windows NT Advanced Server, LANtastic, and others. Remote access to other workstations, as with PC Anywhere from Symantec, Proxy from Funk Software, WINview from Citrix, and RPCs, allows a user to control another machine over a local network or remote WAN. This means that idle workstations on a network can be commandeered and the idled CPU can be put to use.

In the case of Citrix WINview running as a communication server with LAN Manager, LAN Server, or NetWare, this also means that DOS, Windows, and OS/2 applications will appear to run on a 8086 or 80286 machine; instead, such applications are tasks computed on the communications server which usually has more horsepower than these 8086 or 80286 chips. Only screen changes, keystrokes, and mouse movements are transported over the network. This is true for both LANs and WANs. The performance hit is only to the WINview communications server, not to the network itself or the network bandwidth. By the way, if you have skipped Chapter 5 or Chapter 6, this technique provides an excellent solution to poor performance of client/server or applications run from a server at a remote WAN site. Proxy provides a maximum of 254 remote DOS or MS Windows 3.x sessions with 10 MB of free RAM on the user machine, or the limit of available RAM (190 kB base plus 37 kB per remote session).

Because the application actually runs at the remote site on a communications server, performance is the same as though the remote user were on that local LAN. However, information that is transferred by a wide area network—screen updates, keystrokes, and mouse movements—tend to be jerky due to the latency of the WAN connection and hops. Because you need local CPU resources to handle each such remote connection, the disadvantage to this technique is that high-powered GUI and database applications could well require parity of resources with those needed to run the applications at the remote site. On the other hand, remote high-powered stations could be doing multitasking in the foreground and running the local application as a simple background window.

Buffer networks with store-and-forward gateways

The store-and-forward mechanism duplicates some of the filtration functionality of the router. It will store a message packet for an unlimited amount of time until network slot time is available; it might save the message packet until off-peak hours. This store-and-forward technology is used for long-haul optical fiber networks, microwave, and VSAT links. Store-and-forward mechanisms require that network protocols be decoupled from a return receipt message (ACK/NAK) so as to free applications from timing out.

This is an expensive technology, usually installed as an ISO gateway. It is, however, suitable for low-volume, low-priority transmission. It is dependent upon the robustness of the network software, since the typical TCP/IP or IPX transmission confirmation is not supported in real time. In fact, receipt confirmation might not be supported except at the mechanical level of the store-and-forward gateway. The concept is akin to a receptionist taking a message when the telephoned party is already busy; no message receipt confirmation is provided to the caller, and the intended recipient of the call never knows that he or she was wanted until a message is received or a follow-up call is accepted.

Provide alternative channels

When a network carries a traffic volume in excess of design capacity, performance deteriorates nonlinearly for Ethernet and linearly for token protocols; this is a function of protocol persistence, as previously explained. If performance is already degraded, higher loads degrade performance disproportionately. Alternative channels provide additional communication paths, much as local side roads and highway "shoulders" relieve a highway bottleneck after a traffic accident. While the same volume of traffic is transported, waiting time is decreased. An alternative channel might provide specialized high-speed disk-to-disk file transfers, imaging information transfer, or terminal services.

Terminals (DTE) require full packet transmission for each keystroke and are an overlooked resource hog. A fast typist on a networked word processing terminal can create 480 packets per minute, and another 2560 with every screen page (requests, keystrokes, display echo, and ACK/NAK). Terminal equipment transmissions reveal efficiencies of less than 2 percent, whereas most network traffic will experience 60 percent efficiencies or higher. RS-232 lines—twisted-pair serial connections, for example—yield a better match for such low-speed transmission than LAN protocols. Conversely, an imaging camera or scanner often digitizes upward of a megabyte of information from a single picture. At LAN speeds, 1000 or more packets will need to be built and transmitted. Such a load could jam an unloaded network completely for 4 s, or a network at capacity for several minutes. You can imagine the bottleneck at typical WAN transfer speeds. Direct device-to-node bus connection improves transfer rates and transfer success rates. Many managers recommend hybrid networks and tune performance in just this manner. Figure 7.14 shows how to construct a *spanning tree* and augment traditional communication channels with *dual homing* connections.

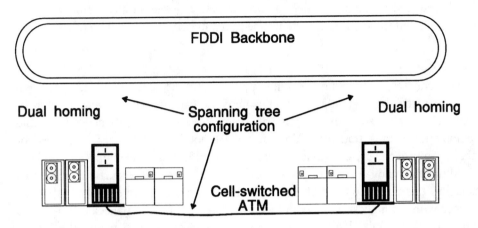

Figure 7.14 A spanning tree and dual homing connections provide performance amplification for complex networks.

Try better solutions

Sometimes, increasing speed with better configurations and more or superior hardware does not provide optimal results. Performance may be better, but not even by an order of magnitude better. As you recall, replacing an Intel 80486 with a Pentium merely provides 1.4 times faster system performance. Instead, consider that a better operational solution may solve the performance problem.

For example, network facsimile provides a better solution than most mechanical fax machines. Specifically, it really is not busy; a person can "send" a fax at any time without waiting in line for another person to send a fax or waiting until an incoming transmission is complete. Instead, network fax queues these jobs without delay. Additionally, transmission can be delayed until off-peak rates begin. The network fax will automatically retry lines that do not answer or are busy. One major problem with network fax is routing the incoming transmissions. Incoming facsimile transmission opens a security loophole and it usually requires a person to read each fax and make routing decisions. If every fax—which is a large graphic image, anywhere from 70 kB to 250 kB—is viewed in order to make a routing decision, the system is slowed by this significant process overhead.

Although some network fax servers use OCR technology to read incoming transmission to convert the image into more compact text, there is often no net disk space and viewing time savings. Specifically, the original pages are retained as images in case the conversion was not 100 percent accurate—as is normal. Furthermore, a person will usually still need to make routing decisions.

Instead, some fax applications can capture the remote terminal identification (RTI or RTID) and the caller subscriber identification (CSI or CSID). Incoming faxes can be routed based upon this information which is traded between mechanical and software-based fax machines. However, not all machines transmit this information, or this information can be missing or fabricated. Some network fax applications can additionally capture the caller ID (CID) or direct inward dial

(DID) header with the originating phone number. This essentially entails an extra line charge, but the labor and system time saved may be more than justified.

Conclusion

As you can see, optimizing computer performance becomes more complex and involved when the system is part of a network because you have a system of systems to optimize. This system of systems is usually interdependent, and optimization entails tradeoffs. You simply do not have the time, resources, or labor to improve every component to its theoretical performance limit.

Although many network bottlenecks are blamed on insufficient channel capacity, this is rarely the right answer. It is somewhat counterintuitive that the devices with the highest bandwidth tend to create the most bottlenecks. Protocol is rarely the flaw. Only WANs tend to impose signal delays and bandwidth limitations. This is due in part to current technical limitations or WAN costs. More likely, network design, installation, and configuration flaws create performance bottlenecks. Host-based and client/server networks tend to saturate at the host or the servers, but for different reasons. Host-based bottlenecks tend to be caused by network access speed limitations. Server-based bottlenecks tend to be caused by RAM, disk, or bus bottlenecks.

Tuning network performance is a matter of running benchmarks and performance tests, locating the bottlenecks, matching these constraints with the underlying causes, and then developing effective appropriate solutions. Without adequate information, you will make improper assessments; tuning will be ineffective or, worse, counterproductive.

8

Tools Disk

Diskette contents

The material on the enclosed tools disk includes an MS Windows help file, performance benchmarks for various operating systems, and some specialized optimization tools. Most of this material is freeware, shareware, or vendor material. All is copyrighted. Installation and the usage for each tool on this disk is explained in this chapter. The tools disk directory is shown in Figure 8.1.

```
   Volume in drive B has no label
   Directory of B:\

   WINBEN    EXE    124041 07-15-90    4:03a
   DRYSTO    EXE    293776 07-15-90    3:58a
   QBENCH    EXE    176843 05-20-93    1:28p
   OPTIMUM   EXE    249295 07-15-90    4:09a
   OPTIMIZE  BAT       480 07-15-90    3:53a
   SERVER    EXE    122616 05-20-93    2:27p
   WINBEN    DOC       261 07-15-90    4:05a
   DRYSTO    DOC       482 07-15-90    4:05a
   QBENCH    DOC       312 07-15-90    4:07a
   OPTIMUM   DOC       799 07-15-90    4:11a
   SERVER    DOC       577 07-15-90    4:12a
   HELP      EXE    355147 05-20-93   10:19p
          12 file(s)    1324629 bytes
                         130560 bytes free
```

Figure 8.1 File contents of tools disk.

Unpacking the software

These files are packed and compressed into self-extracting files. Some were extracted and compressed to save space on the distribution diskette. The DOS batch file will create a target directory on the hard disk and extract the target files. The unpacked files require approximately 2 MB of disk space to completely install. (You can also install a subset of the tools disk by typing the name of a source .EXE file on the tools disk from your target directory.) The .DOC files merely contain the names of files which are extracted from the self-extracting executable files. Invoke the batch file on the distribution diskette. If your 3.5 in disk drive is A: type A:OPTIMIZE.BAT from a DOS prompt. If your 3.5 in disk drive is B: type B:OPTIMIZE.BAT from a DOS prompt. This runs the following DOS batch file shown in Figure 8.2.

```
REM This assumes installation to a hard disk named c:
REM change this to the network drive or network path.
REM You may need authorization or rights for network installation.
c:
cd \
md optimize
cd optimize

REM If your 3.5" floppy drive is b: or c: or e:, replace "a" with that
REM letter.
REM These are self-extracting compressed files. When run, the contents
REM are extracted to full file size.
a:HELP.EXE
a:WINBEN.EXE
a:DRYSTO.EXE
a:QBENCH.EXE
a:OPTIMUM.EXE
a:SERVER.EXE
```

Figure 8.2 The contents of OPTIMIZE.BAT on the tools disk, which create a target directory and extract packed files on the distribution disk to the target directory.

MS Windows executable code can be run by double-clicking on the file name in File Manager or by typing the full path and file name from the File/Run menu item in either Program Manager or File Manager. DOS applications can be run within a DOS compatibility box under MS Windows, OS/2, or UNIX. You may also be able to double click on DOS programs under other GUIs from your Program Manager or File Manager and have them execute if DOS support is enabled through the native GUI (this does include MS Windows, OS/2, and SunOS). OS/2 programs will not run except under OS/2. MS Windows applications will run under OS/2 2.2, and SoftPC, or WABI compatibility boxes.

Hypertext book

The text for *Computer Performance Optimization* is included on the diskette in an MS Windows hypertext help file format. This format was chosen for several reasons. First, MS Windows help is available on more systems than any other format. Second, the help file can be compressed into a smaller size than other packaging technologies. Third, Doc-to-Help optimized what generally is a painful and difficult task for programing a help file; using Wextech's templates in Word for Windows (WinWord) made the task possible. Fourth, a hypertext file provides various mechanisms for searching, exploring, and finding information in a nonlinear fashion. Books are linear. It is hard to jump between chapters, indexes, footnotes, terms in a glossary, and related concepts. Hypertext provides this facility. These choices represent a process of optimization.

The help file is called OPTIMIZE.HLP. It is compressed on the distribution tools disk in a self-extracting file called HELP.EXE. There are two methods of viewing this help file. The first method is by brute force, the second applies the automatic File Manager double click association. Either invoke Help from Program Manager or from File Manager by selecting the Help menu item. Select the Contents menu item. When the help application appears, select File and Open. Type OPTIMIZE.HLP. Figure 8.3 illustrates these steps.

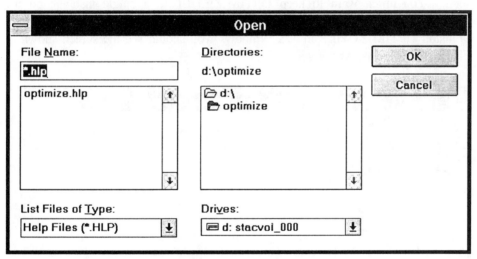

Figure 8.3 File box for opening OPTIMIZE.HELP.

The second method of viewing the help file is more elegant. Run File Manager and Program Manager in Windowed, noniconized modes. Locate this help file, OPTIMIZE.HLP in File Manager. Highlight it by clicking on its name. With the mouse button pressed and held down, drag this file into Program Manager. Place it in the group folder of your choice. You should now see a yellow question mark with the file name beneath it. Fifth, double click on this icon to view the help file. Figure 8.4 illustrates the icon in Program Manager. Note that you can also double click on the file name itself, OPTIMIZE.HLP in File Manager, to invoke the help system with this file.

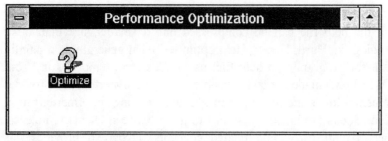

Figure 8.4 Icon for OPTIMIZE.HELP in a Program Manager group.

MS Windows help contains information on using help. If you have trouble with this process or want to learn more of hypertext help, Microsoft provides a good tutorial and overview. Note that help for MS Windows is large. Once you understand applications, you might consider deleting the on-line help from the hard disk to free space, as Chapter 4 suggested. Network users probably will gain a substantial amount of local disk space by installing a single instance, or just one copy, of each different help file or on-line documentation on the network file server. You might want to keep OPTIMIZE.HLP in a single instance on the network as well; multiple copies would not be optimal. No matter how you choose to install OPTIMIZE.HLP in MS Windows, you should see the screen shown in Figure 8.5 when you first invoke it.

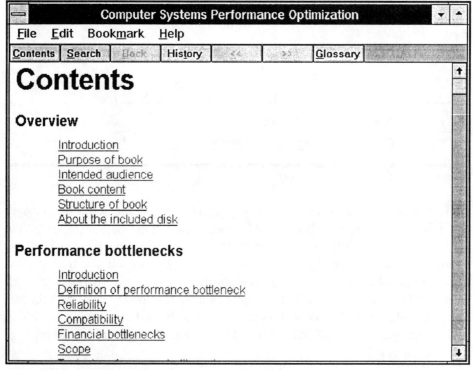

Figure 8.5 The initial help screen with table of contents for OPTIMIZE.HLP.

Benchmarks and utilities

If you highlight all the executable files extracted to c:\optimize in File Manager, and drag them into a Program Manager group (named *Performance Optimization*), you should see a program manager group, as shown in Figure 8.6.

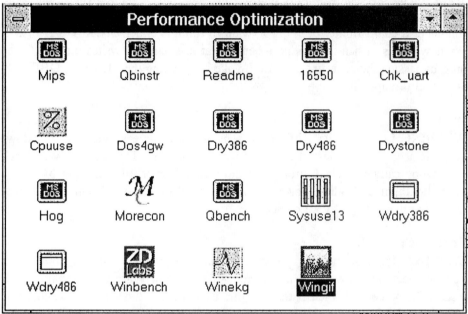

Figure 8.6 The group of executable programs contained on the tools disk.

Dhrystones

DRY.C is the source code for the Dhrystones benchmark. Included within the comment lines are benchmarks for various systems including PCs, minicomputers, mainframes, and engineering workstations. Compile this code with a C language compiler. It is platform independent. Performance should vary very little by compiler. DRY386.EXE, WDRY386.EXE, DRY486.EXE, WDRY486.EXE, and DRYSTONE.EXE are executable versions that run on MS DOS or MS Windows. DRYSTONE.EXE is the author's information file. To run the DOS versions, type either DRY386 or DRY486. To run the Windows versions, double click on the file name, either WDRY386.EXE or WDRY486.EXE, in File Manager.

MIPS

MIPS.COM is a DOS benchmark from Chips and Technologies, Inc. that will run on any Intel-compatible PC that generates a value for millions of instructions per second (MIPS), but does not provide that value except in relation to an IBM XT, an IBM AT, or a Compaq 386 computer. This is a general-purpose performance evaluation tool for measuring horsepower. Invoke it by typing the file name, MIPS, at a DOS prompt. It will run in the MS Windows DOS box.

Quantum Data Access Time

This is a DOS performance measurement utility from Quantum, a disk drive manufacturer, that measures the seek time for a disk controller and hard disk. When you have reason to believe that the disk subsystem is a bottleneck, this is an appropriate tool for measuring disk performance. This is a utility that should not run under a compatibility box; if you want to run this under UNIX, OS/2, or MS Windows, do so when there is no other disk access, since it writes directly to the disk, bypassing the operating system. Invoke it by typing the file name, QBENCH at a DOS prompt.

WinBench

WINBENCH.EXE is the Ziff-Davis benchmark for measuring MS Windows performance. It includes the WinMark evaluation. The actual WinBench application can be invoked through Program Manager or File Manager by typing the full path, or by loading it as an icon in the Startup group in Program Manager or any in other group of your choice.

BenchTech for OS/2

BenchTech for OS/2 allows you to measure integer and floating-point math performance, data movement, and memory access. There are three separate disk tests, and you control whether the program uses the OS/2 system disk cache. The program allows you to determine relative video and application-oriented test performance. There is support in the commercial version for DOS or WIN-OS/2 tests and 25 benchmark tests. Two higher-level benchmark tests are included for comparing systems. To invoke the demonstration, highlight BTECH.EXE in the OS/2 File Manager and double click.

System information

System information is crucial for assessing system configuration, hardware and software health of a computer, and for initiating a logical method for measuring performance. Included on the tools disk are some MS DOS and MS Windows utilities for measuring performance in ways missing from these systems. These tools include SysUse, CPUuse, WinEKG, and HOG. The reason similar tools are not provided for OS/2, Macintosh, or UNIX is that these operating systems provide a more robust set of basic performance measurement utilities. For example, PS, PSTAT, NFSTAT, and similar tools are built into UNIX, Windows NT Advanced Server, and OS/400.

SysUse

SYSUSE13.EXE is an MS Windows application that shows CPU, disk, system resources, and RAM utilization levels. This information is necessary for making assessments of CPU, RAM, and disk bottlenecks. It is also useful as a proxy for assessing bus bandwidth bottlenecks. When system resources, an object-table size limitation, falls below 20 percent, performance will be poor or erratic. There is little you can do about system resources except to close applications or exit and restart Windows.

This application can be invoked through Program Manager or File Manager by typing its full path or by loading it as an icon in the Startup group in Program Manager, or any other group of your choice. SYSUSE13.TXT provides installation and shareware details. Additionally, this utility provides an interesting feature. It will compact memory; it calls the GlobalCompactWindows function to compact global memory. Select this when MS Windows reports there is insufficient memory to run an application even though there appears to be a lot. It may be that the free memory is just not contiguous. Figure 8.7 shows what happens when MS Windows is run without a disk cache. The bottleneck is the I/O channel, and it is a persistent constraint. You might notice, in fact, that CPU levels and memory levels are nonactive paths.

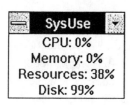

Figure 8.7 SysUse shows that CPU speed is not the generic bottleneck you might expect. The lack of a functioning disk cache creates a disk performance bottleneck in this screen-shot example.

CPUuse

CPUUSE.EXE is an MS Windows application that shows CPU utilization levels as an iconized application. This information is necessary for making assessments of CPU bottlenecks. This application can be invoked through Program Manager or File Manager by typing its full path or by loading it as an icon in the Startup group in Program Manager, or any other group of your choice.

WinEKG

WINEKG.EXE is an MS Windows utility which provides a real-time graphical display of CPU utilization within a window and a numerical display of remaining free memory as the window caption (similar to the OS/2 Pulse). The advantage of displaying utilization in a window is better resolution. The advantage of using a dynamic icon is minimal memory utilization and size. This application can be invoked through Program Manager or File Manager by typing its full path or by loading it as an icon in the Startup group in Program Manager, or any other group of your choice. WinEKG is shown in Figure 8.8.

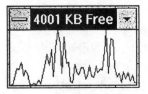

Figure 8.8 WinEKG shows CPU load over time during intervals. It provides different information from SysUse in that CPU utilization is the key indicator and is not averaged over longer time periods.

File space hogs
HOG.EXE is an MS DOS utility that creates a colorful pie chart of disk space usage at the directory level. It will show major directory usage from the root if the program is invoked at C:>. It will show subdirectory disk usage contribution if you change to a subdirectory and invoke the program from that current directory. Type the file name from the DOS prompt to invoke it. This application runs under MS Windows in the DOS box set to full-screen mode. Type ALT-ENTER to switch between a windowed DOS session and a full-screen DOS session.

Hardware tests
Poor modem communication could seriously impede WAN linkages. This is particularly relevant for client/server communications, remote dial-in connections, and even remote debugging. The acquisition of high-speed 14,400-bits/s modems with error correction and data compression are easily defeated by slow serial ports. The modem and connecting line may work perfectly, but nonetheless be impeded by a serial port that cannot accept bits any faster than 4500 bits/s. Although many vendors and Intel have tried several times to correct several defects in the original Universal Asynchronous Receiver/Transmitter (UART) chip, not all PCs include the correct chip set. Even late-model PCs may include the older, defective UARTs, high-performance servers included. The test is very simple, and two are included.

Test for UART chip
CHK_UART.EXE is a DOS-based PC-compatible application that tests to see what type of Universal Asynchronous Receiver/Transmitter (UART) chip is present. Type the program name from the DOS prompt to invoke it. This application runs under MS Windows in the DOS box. CHK_UART.DOC provides background information on the UART series and limitations of each chip.

Enable UART 16550

16550.EXE is a DOS-based PC-compatible application that tests for the presence of a UART 16550 chip for all communication ports. It enables the on-board FIFO buffer if this chip is found. Type the file name from the DOS prompt to invoke this application. This application runs under MS Windows in the DOS box; however, it may disable serial communications if already in progress. 16550.DOC provides background information on the UART 16550 chip and how to use this application. 16550.TXT provides an initial overview of this shareware.

Windows utilities

Although this book covers a broad range of platforms and operating systems, from DOS to UNIX, OS/2 to VMS, from AIX to Macintosh, the stunning success of MS Windows begs for inclusion of two utilities that help you configure and use it. Since GUIs are so complex and require considerable tuning, MORECON.EXE is included to help you view the system configuration files. WINGIF.EXE is a nice utility for capturing and converting bitmap images into other formats. Of note, WinGIF will resize and crop large images, convert true-color images into more condensed 16-, 4-, or monochrome images, and will create compressed .RLE files. WinGIF does not provide the outstanding JPEG compression as found with the Matrox video boards or the Lead Technology compression software discussed in Chapter 4, nor will it enhance the outlines of a bitmap as Raydreams's Jaggies are Gone with anti-aliasing features. However, it is very useful for reducing a 350,000-byte MS Windows bitmap screen image into a more manageable 175,000-byte run-length encoded file. The compressed bitmap will load faster and use less space.

More Control

MORECON.EXE is an MS Windows .INI viewer and configuration modification utility. You can establish file name and application associations to improve point and click performance. You can modify the colors of the desktop and view fonts. This application is included here because it provides a simple means for modifying some complex components of WIN.INI and SYSTEM.INI configuration files. MORECON.TXT explains integration of this function within the control panel.

WinGIF

WINGIF.EXE is an MS Windows bitmap conversion utility. It will compact .GIF, .BMP, .PCX, and .RLE image formats into lower-resolution or monochrome images. It will convert the larger .BMP and .PCX images into smaller .RLE formats. Additionally, this utility provides some effective tools for altering the contrast, gamma, and brightness. It is provided here mainly as an example of a good tool that reduces file space and image loading times. This application can be invoked through Program Manager or File Manager by typing its full path or by loading it as an icon in the Startup group in Program Manager, or other group of your choice.

Optimization utilities

IBM provided two sets of spreadsheets which are very useful to optimize the performances of LAN Server and PC LAN. SoftLogic Solutions provided an MS Windows help file with some optimization tips and information about their MS Windows optimization tool. These spreadsheets from IBM are provided in MS Excel and Lotus 1-2-3 formats. Basically, you would enter network node counts, available memory, disk space, special processes you expect to run, and other numerical information to the spreadsheets to calculate settings for critical server configuration files. Proper configuration of the server will turn a marginal operation into one about 10 percent faster. The configuration will show what new or added resources (memory, disk space, etc.) are required to turn a poor server into a stellar performer.

Since Chapters 4 and 6 stated that system configuration does affect performance of stand-alone user systems, client workstations, and servers, it seemed only appropriate to include some tools that will help you configure them. Although the LAN Server information is specifically intended for the IBM LAN Server product, you might note that it nonetheless shares characteristics with Microsoft LAN Manager and Windows NT Advanced Server. If you are so inclined, generate system configurations and extrapolate these settings to the Microsoft environment. Do so carefully, however, as these sibling products have six years of diverging enhancement. On the other hand, the fact that there are tools which embody expert knowledge might encourage you to contact your vendor. See if the vendor has spreadsheets, technical notes, performance patches, or installation instructions pertinent to the latest release of the network operating system, client operating system, client drivers, server drivers, or hardware platforms.

DLRSETUP

DLRSETUP is an MS Excel and Lotus 1-2-3 spreadsheet which will generate a DOSLAN.INI file, a DOS CONFIG.SYS file, and AUTOEXEC.BAT parameters which are required to run a PC LAN workstation. It may be used for an initial setup of a user DOS workstation. It takes into account any system requirements for communications, NetBIOS programs, and both mail and spooler programs as well as MS Windows 3.x. It will show memory requirements and optimize the client workstation for your requirements. All you have to do is answer a few simple questions via dialog boxes and the system will be defined for you. It will even copy the files to the required location via a menu pull-down. Full vendor documentation as provided by IBM is found in DLRSETUP.DOC.

CNFGLS30

CNFGLS30 is a spreadsheet to generate a starting point for LAN Server 3.0 configuration. It is provided in both an MS Excel V2.2 or Lotus 1-2-3 V3.0 and 1-2-3/G spreadsheet formats. The spreadsheets generate a LAN Server configuration, an IBMLAN.INI file, and NTS/2 NetBIOS, 802.2 PROTOCOL.INI, and NETBEUI.NIF parameters which are required to run the server. It may be used for an initial setup of a domain controller or additional server. It will take into account NTS/2 802.2 requirements for other functions in addition to the server software which might be running on the server machine. These include other NetBIOS applications, CM/2 SNA Gateway, APPC, RDS, IBM LAN Network Manager, and 802.2 applications. When the generated .INI file is complete, it may be cut from the spreadsheet, pasted into an editor session and saved directly into the IBMLAN subdirectory if you use Excel. Lotus 1-2-3 users can copy the generated parameter settings and enter them into the IBMLAN.INI file manually. Full vendor documentation as provided by IBM is found in CNFGLS30.DOC. Note that this information is specific to the LAN Server. If you are running other NOSs or have OS/2 clients, configuration tuning for those devices is best provided by a tool such as Clear & Simple's OS/2 performance kit.

WinSense

The BOOK.HLP file is a subset of the MS Windows 3.x optimization tool sold by SoftLogic Solutions called WinSense. The help file is included here because it has valuable information. It shows what an automated optimization product, such as WinSense for MS Windows, Help! for Macintosh, or the OS/2 performance tuning kit Performance 2.1 can do. The help file information in the full WinSense product is extensive. Specifically, almost all the possible .INI settings are described and the relationship of each to system performance is defined. While this tool is useful for no other reason than this help facility, it also analyzes and evaluates system performance of MS Windows and offers useful suggestions for improving performance. WinSense will implement these suggestions if you so choose. Many of these suggestions relate to insignificant issues of windows sizes, border thicknesses, or double-click speeds. However, this tool is disproportionately effective for optimizing .INI values on complex configurations and high-end PCs with SCSI drivers, network connections, and with enhanced modes enabled. While it makes references to SMARTDRV and the permanent swap partition, WinSense cannot tune these items; it also does not recognize other disk cache options or other vendor cache software. Figure 8.9 shows some of the useful help information provided by WinSense.

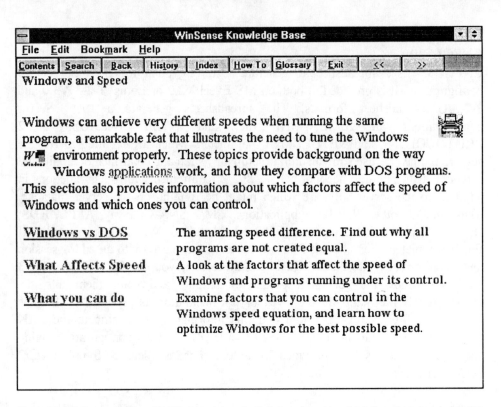

Figure 8.9 WinSense optimizes MS Windows automatically but also provides detailed configuration and tuning information in a hypertext format.

Tool and product sources

The uncompressed, ASCII file, SOURCES.TXT on the tools disk contains company names, addresses, phone and facsimile numbers, along with product names. These companies provides me with documentation, product information, samples, loaner equipment, or demonstrations relevant to the topic of performance optimization, productivity, and system benchmarking.

Sources

AIX 3.2 RISC System/6000 Introduction to Performance Tuning, AIX National Technical Support Center, IBM Corporation, Southlake, TX.

AIX 3.2 RISC System/6000 Advanced Performance Analysis and System Tuning, AIX National Technical Support Center, IBM Corporation, Southlake, TX.

AIX 3.2 RISC System/6000 Performance Monitoring and Tuning Guide, IBM Corporation, Austin, TX.

AIX Performance Monitoring and Tuning, Virgil Albaugh, *AIXpert Journal*, Winter 1991.

AMIDiag, American Megatrends, Norcross, GA.

Analyzing Performance Problems on Internets, Mark Smith, *Networking Management*, January 1992.

Research Methodology, Computer Performance Benchmark Survey, Business Applications Performance Corporation, (BAPCO.), Santa Clara, CA, 1991.

Barlow, Brian, Future Systems Solutions, Angola, IN.

Bodkin, Richard, Account Representative, Magnetic Software, Mount Airy, NC.

Box, Mark, VP Sales and Marketing, Pure Software, Sunnyvale, CA 94087.

Bump, Dodie, Marketing Communications Manager, ColorAge Inc., Billerica, MA.

Burress, Randy, Public Relations Specialist, Intel Corporation, Hillsboro, CA.

Conklin, Dick, Editor, *OS/2 Developer Magazine*, IBM Corporation., Boca Raton, FL.

CPU Upgrade Easiest Route to Faster Speeds, MacWeek, November 2, 1992.

DBMS Optimizations for Transaction Processing, 1993, Ingres Corporation, The ASK Group, Alameda, CA.

Doc-to-Help, version 1.1, WexTech Systems, Inc., New York, NY.

Denedepti, John, Technical Support Specialist, Epson America, Carlsbad, CA.

Diskeeper/Plus, Executive Software, Glendale, CA.

DrivePro, Micro House, Boulder, CO.

Eaken, Kennith, Vice President, Marketing, MapLinx Corporation, Plano, TX.

Epson Wingine, Epson America, Carlsbad, CA.

FileStat, File Activity Usage Monitoring Software for IBM PCs and Compatible Computers, Solid Oak Software Inc., Santa Barbara, CA.

Freedom of the Press, ColorAge Inc., Billerica, MA.

Heise, Russell A., Performance Team Leader, AIX Performance Consultant, IBM AIX National Technical Support Center, IBM Corporation, Roanoke, TX.

Hughes, John, Technical Support, Ingres Corporation, The ASK Group, Alameda, CA.

IBM OS/2 LAN Server Version 3.0 Network Administrator Reference, Volume 2: Performance Tuning, IBM Corporation, Austin, TX.

Liposuction Your Corpulent Executables and Remove Excess Fat, Matt Pietrek, *Microsoft Systems Journal*, July 1993.

Local Area Network Server Version 2.0, Information and Planning Guide, 1991, IBM, White Plains, NY.

Lough, Mike, Caere Corporation, Los Gatos, CA.

Management Solutions for Commercial Open Systems; Guide to Vendors and Products, Sun Microsystems, Mountain View, CA 94043.

MapLinx, MapLinx Corporation, Plano, TX.

Matrox Electronic Systems, Ltd., Dorval, Quebec, Canada.

Maximizing the Performance of Your Server, Frank J. Derfler, Jr., and Max Schireson *PC Magazine*, October 26, 1993.

Maximizing Memory Under DOS 6.0, Jeff Prosise, *PC Magazine*, August, 1993.

Microsoft Guide to Optimizing Windows, Dan Gookin, Microsoft Press, Redmond, WA. 1993.

Monitoring and Optimizing Vines Performance, Banyan Systems, Westborough, MA. 1992.

The Need for Speed, *MacWorld*, June 1992.

Neshamkin, Paul, Technical Support Coordinator, WexTech Systems, Inc., New York, NY.

Network and File Servers: A Performance Tuning Guide, Sun Microsystems, Mountain View, CA 94043. December 1990.

Neuenschwander, Bill, LasterMaster Corporation, Eden Prairie, MN.

Optimizing your Mainframe, Rusty Weston, Corporate Computing, June 1993.

OS/2 2.1 Performance Tuning, IBM, International Technical Support Center, Boca Raton, FL.

OS/2 2.1 Performance Tuning for End Users, IBM, OS/2 System Performance Department, Boca Raton, FL.

OS/2 Productivity through Multitasking, Pat Scherer, IBM OS/2 Developer, IBM, Austin, TX. Fall 1992.

OS/2 V2.1 Redbook, IBM, IBM Corporation, International Technical Support Center, Boca Raton, FL.

Ostrow, Gail, IBM Independent Vendor League, Greenwich, CT.

Parr, Diana, Product Marketing, Ingres Corporation, The ASK Group, Alameda, CA.

PC Sentry, System Activity Monitoring, Logging, and Security Software for PCs & Networks, Solid Oak Software Inc., Santa Barbara, CA.

Performance Enhancers, *MacUser*, 1993 Annual Review.

Performance 2.1, A Tuning Kit for OS/2, Clear & Simple, Inc., West Simsbury, CT.

Performance Tuning: A Continuing Series, Russell A. Heise, */AIXtra*, IBM's Magazine for AIX Professionals, September/October 1992.

Performance Tuning: Theory and Practice, Elizabeth Lewis, */AIXtra*, IBM's Magazine for AIX Professionsal, March/April 1993.

Peterson, John, Business Applications Performance Corporation, (BAPCO), Santa Clara, CA.

Pittman, Robin, Marketing Specialist, Epson America, Carlsbad, CA.

Product Overview, Intel Corporation, Mt. Prospect IL. 1993.

Roarabaugh, Virginia, Advisory Programmer in OS/2 Systems, Performance, IBM, International Technical Support Center, Boca Raton, FL.

Scherer, Pat, Industrial Engineer, IBM Personal System Line of Business, Austin, TX.

Shulman, Richard, Laserprint, Pompano Beach, FL.

Skylight, RenaSonce Group, Inc., San Diego, CA.

Speedcache+, Future Systems Solutions, Inc., Bluffton, IN.

Sun Performance Tuning Overview, Sun Microsystems, Mountain View, CA 94043.

Supercharging Your Mac, MacUser, April 1993.

System Performance Tuning, Mike Loukides, O'Reilly Books. ISBN 0-937175-60-9. 1991.

This Old PC, Dale Lewallen, Ziff-Davis Press, 1993.

Tuma, Wade, President, Disk Emulation Systems, Inc. Santa Clara, CA.

Tuning DOS and WIN-OS/2 Sessions under OS/2 2.x, Joe Salemi, *PC Magazine,* September 28, 1993.

Tuning NCP To Improve SNA Network Performance, Ted Ernst and David Schwee, IBM Corporation, Technical Support, February 1993.

Tuning NetWare File Server Performance, Michael Day, *LAN Times*, November 18, 1991.

Tweaking the Tail of the Beast, Windows Tech Journal, May 1991.

Wade, Virginia, Technical Support Specialist, WexTech Systems, Inc. New York, NY.

Warmbrod, Bruce, Intel Corporation, Norcross, GA.

Whitfield, L. Kenneth, Advisory Systems Analyst, IBM, Austin, TX.

Wilson, Brian, Eastern Area Systems Engineer, Sun Microsystems, Mountain View, CA 94043.

Windows Resource Kit, Microsoft Corporation, Redmond, WA.

WinGIF, SuperSet Software Corp., Provo, UT.

WinJet, LaserMaster Corporation, Eden Prairie, MN.

WinMaster, PC-Kwik Corporation, Beaverton, OR.

X Performance, Kevin Reichard and Eric Johnson, *UNIX Review*, Volume 9, Number 9.

Glossary of Terms

Adapter board

A PC board that plugs into any computer: mainframe, minicomputer, personal computer, or workstation. Within the networking context it often refers to the network access unit, a network interface card (NIC), or a network controller adapter.

Address generation interlock

A processor gridlock caused when a memory address or register referenced by an instruction is unavailable because it is being affected by a previous instruction that has already begun but has not yet finished processing. It also occurs when both pipelines reference the same memory locations or chip registers. Generally *referred* to as an AGI.

Adjusted ring length

The driving transmission path length for a ring architecture when a station or segment fails and the ring wraps to provide network service without interruption.

Agent

Software or a combination of software and hardware that gathers information about a network device and executes commands in response to a management console's requests. In SNMP, the agent's capabilities are determined by the MIB.

AGI

See Address generation interlock.

American National Standards Institute

A governmental agency that maintains standards for science and commerce, including a list of acceptable standards for computer languages, character sets, connection compatibility, and many other aspects of the computer and data communications industries. Better known by the ANSI acronym.

ANSI

Abbreviation for American National Standards Institute (q.v.).

ARL

Abbreviation for Adjusted ring length (q.v.).

Arrival

A technical term referring to a request for service in a queueing model. *See also* Birth.

Asymmetric processing

Workload distributed among multiple CPUs by some prearranged assignment.

Average

The most likely value in a set of numbers; the *mean* in a probability distribution.

Backbone

See Bus.

Bandwidth

The range (band) of frequencies that are transmitted on a channel. The difference between the highest and lowest frequencies is expressed in hertz (Hz) or millions of hertz (MHz).

Benchmark

A measuring standard. Network performance benchmarks include Mbits/s, throughput, error rates, and other less formal definitions.

Birth

A technical term referring to a request for service in a queueing model.

Bits per second

A rate at which data are transmitted over a communications channel; sometimes abbreviated as bits/s or bps.

Bits/s

A rate at which data are transmitted over a communications channel. *See* Bits per second.

Bottleneck

1. Any obstruction that impedes completion of a task.
2. The critical path in task completion; the path without slack time.
3. The task or process in a larger system that has no slack time or is the task which delays subsequent and sequential tasks, so that system completion is delayed.

BPS

See Bits per second.

Bridge

A device that interconnects networks using similar protocols. A bridge provides service at level 2 of the OSI Reference Model. *See also* Gateway and Router.

Broadcast

The transmission from one station on a network to two or more stations on the network, or a frame with a destination broadcast address.

Buffer

A temporary storage area that is used as a staging area when moving memory between RAM, applications, and storage disks.

Burst-mode protocol

A NOS enhancement implemented in Novell NetWare that optimizes the performance of intensive file transfer operations.

Bus

The main communication transmission channel for a computer system. A computer system may have more than a single bus; the bus may refer to either the I/O bus; the I/O adapter bus (such as ISA, EISA, MCA, Multibus, VMEbus, or a proprietary design); the memory bus; and a utility bus as found in PCs supporting the VESA, PCI, and VL communication adapter standards.

Bus width

The size of the data units that the computer system needs to move through I/O; usually represented by 8-, 16-, 32-, 48- or 64-byte units.

Bus master

A specialized CPU and interface unit that controls the data transfer path and bypasses the computer CPU.

Bus-mastering controller

A specialized device controller which bypasses the normal CPU access process and bus access controller to move segments of memory between RAM and the device which it controls.

Cable scanner

A testing tool which verifies the integrity and performance of network wiring and cable. It tests for electrical breaks, shorts, impedance, and capacitance, as well as for signal crosstalk and signal attenuation. These tools are sometimes called pair or ring scanners when designed for FDDI.

Cable tester

A testing tool which verifies the integrity and performance of network wiring and cable. It tests for electrical breaks, shorts, impedance, and capacitance, as well as for signal crosstalk and signal attenuation. These tools are sometimes called pair or ring scanners when designed for FDDI.

Cache

A temporary storage area, generally a memory cache where data are retained for possible reuse or subsequent movement to a permanent storage medium.

Caching controller

A specialized disk controller that enhances performance by buffering data, reading data ahead, or caching (delaying) data that are to be written to the disks or other storage media.

CCITT

See Consultative Committee for International Telephone and Telegraph.

CDDI

A trademark by Crescendo for FDDI over twisted-pair copper wire.

Channel

An individual path that carries signals.

Client

1. A network user, often a device or workstation.
2. A secondary processor which relies upon a primary processor or server.

Client/server processing

The establishment of a host computer (server) to provide end-user (client) services.

Clusters

A stream of blocks or a collection of related blocks on a storage device. References to clusters usually occur when fragmented files are chained together on a storage device.

CMIP

See Common Management Information Protocol.

CMIP over Logical Link Control

A network-independent version of CMIP jointly developed by IBM and 3Com. While CMOL can run on any network regardless of transport, it can't pass through routers, limiting its usefulness to LANs.

CMIP over TCP/IP

A version of CMIP that runs on TCP/IP networks.

CMOL

See CMIP over Logical Link Control (q.v.).

CMOT

See CMIP over TCP/IP (q.v.).

Collision

The Ethernet protocol mechanism by which simultaneous or overlapping network access requests are handled.

Common carriers

Companies which provide communication networks (like AT&T).

Common Management Information Protocol

A hierarchical, secure management protocol; an alternative to SNMP. Usually *referred* to as CMIP.

Common Management Interface Protocol

A contender for standard network management protocols specified by ISO. This protocol provides a standard for managing large networks across bridges, routers, and gateways.

Computer virus

Man-made software designed to disable, damage, or destroy computer hardware or read/write storage systems; sometimes incorrectly called worms, Trojan horses, and trap doors.

Concentrator

A wiring hub.

Confidence interval

A statistical range surrounding the average value based upon a multiple of the standard deviation.

Congestion

A slowdown in a network that is due to a bottleneck.

Consultative Committee for International Telephone and Telegraph

An international organization that makes recommendations for networking standards such as X.25, X.400, and CCITT facsimile data compression standards.

Controller

The device in a network node that physically connects that device to the network media.

CPM

Abbreviation for Critical path method (q.v.).

Critical path

The task or process in a critical path model which delays completion of the system process; the tasks which must occur sequentially between the projects start and finish; the path without float or slack time; the bottleneck.

Critical path method

1. A project management method that determines project duration based upon the duration of all critical tasks and the sequential dependencies. 2. A method for determining the tasks within a project that represent the limiting factors for completing the project.

Crosstalk

A technical term indicating that stray signals from other wavelengths, channels, communication pathways, or twisted-pair wiring have polluted the signal. It is particularly prevalent in twisted-pair networks or when telephone and network communications share copper-based wiring bundles.

CSU/DSU

Abbreviation for Customer server unit/data service unit (q.v.)

Customer server unit/data service unit

A device which attaches between computer equipment and digital data lines (not voice telephone lines) to convert data bits into the appropriate data signal technology. Usually *referred* to as CSU/DSU.

Data compression

1. A method of reducing the space required to represent data, as either bits, characters, replacement codes, or graphic images.

2. A reduction in the size of data by exploiting redundancy. Many modems incorporate MNP5 or V.42bis protocols to compress data before it is sent over the phone line. Dual compression (at the file- and modem-level) actually increases the transmitted size. For compression to work, data must be sent over a clean, noise-free telephone line. Since common error-correction protocols are synchronous, there is usually a throughput gain there as well.

Data terminal equipment

A computer terminal which connects to a host computer. It may also be a software session on a workstation or personal computer attaching to a host computer. Usually *referred* to as DTE.

DCE

Abbreviation for Distributed computing environment.

DLL

Abbreviation for Dynamic link library; the file extent for an MS-Windows or OS/2 application overlay and executable code library.

Death

A technical term referring to the fulfillment of a request for service in a queueing model.

Decouple

A gateway (OSI application layer) process to notify an application that transmission will not be completed within the roundtrip delay limitations of a network protocol. Instead, a completion message (for transmission success or failure) is given at some later time. This feature is critical for WANs, heterogeneous networks, and enterprisewide facilities.

Defragmenting

The process of rewriting files stored on disk in discontinuous blocks into a contiguous format to improve disk performance.

Desktop Management Task Force

A coalition of companies led by Intel, and including Novell and Microsoft, with the charter of creating a standard method to manage networked desktop computers and applications. Refered to by DMTF acronym.

Device

Any item on the network. This includes logical addresses that refer to software or hardware processes. A device can be any physical station, including a PC, workstation, mainframe, minicomputer, bridge, router, gateway, remote probe, repeater, or protocol analyzer.

Direct memory access

The process in which a bus-mastering controller or CPU accesses memory directly and moves it, rather than referencing that memory logically. Generally *referred* to by acronym, DMA.

Disk mirroring

See Mirroring.

Disk rotation speed

The speed at which the disk storage media rotate.

Disk shadowing

See Shadowing.

Disk striping

A technique in which sequential data blocks are written over several physical storage units simultaneously to provide greater integrity of data and faster read and write access to the data.

Disk transfer rate

The amount of data that can be transferred from a disk storage unit into memory on a sustained basis. It is presented in bytes/s.

Distributed computing environment

A network management protocol that distributes computing tasks in parallel and shared fashion to other CPUs on a network. Proposed by OSF in 1988, it is still only partially defined.

Distributed management environment

A network management protocol that will allow both SNMP and CMIP to exist within one framework. Proposed by OSF in 1991, it is still only partially defined.

DMA

Abbreviation for Direct memory access (q.v.).

DME

Abbreviation for Distributed management environment (q.v.).

DMTF

Abbreviation for Desktop Management Task Force (q.v.).

Downsizing

The replacement of computer equipment (and the operating environment) with a less expensive version.

Driver

A software program that controls a physical computer device (such as an NIC, printer, disk drive, or RAM disk).

DTE

Abbreviation for Data terminal equipment (q.v.); a computer terminal.

Duplex

The method in which communication occurs: either two-way as in full duplex or unidirectional as in half duplex.

Dynamic link library

Code overlays and function sets loaded into memory as requested by application programs or operating systems. Generally *referred* to as DLL or .DLL file extension.

EISA

Enhanced industry standard architecture.

Electromagnetic interference

Signal noise pollution from radio, radar, or electronic instruments. Generally referred to as EMI.

EMI

See Electromagnetic interference.

Erratic

A general term used to describe a probability distribution with a large variance.

Error correction

When sending files, it is generally best to let the computers at each end do the correction, using a protocol like Kermit or UUCP. However, the ability of MNP4 and V.42 to send data synchronously may make them worthwhile to use. Error correction detects when received bits are garbled and automatically asks for a retransmission of the data.

Ethernet

A popular local area network from which the IEEE 802.3 standard was derived. Ethernet applies the IEEE 802.2 MAC protocols and uses the persistent CSMA/CD protocol on a bus topology. Transmission rate is a maximum of 10 Mbits/s. Ethernet is a persistent transmission protocol. 100BASE-T, 100BASE-VG, or 100BASE-X are developing standards supported by LANModel providing a maximum transmission rate of 100 Mbits/s.

Facility

A WAN connection provided by a common carrier (such as Sprint, MCI, or AT&T).

FDDI

See Fiber Data Distributed Interchange.

Feature detector

A device for measuring lengths, objects, scatter, and probable performance in optical fiber.

Fiber

Optical fiber; a network signaling medium in which plastic or glass transport optical signals.

Fiber Data Distributed Interface

An optical fiber network based upon the ANSI X3.139, X3.148, X3.166, X3.184, X3.186, or X3T9.5 specifications. Abbreviated as FDDI. FDDI provides a 125-Mbits/s signal rate with 4 bits encoded into 5-bit format for a 100-Mbits/s transmission rate. It functions on single-, dual-ring, and star networks with a maximum circumference of 250 km, although copper-based hardware is an option. *See also* CDDI.

File server

A device that provides file services for other stations and nodes. It is a shared resource that often has higher speed, larger capacity, or better economies of scale than remote data storage.

Firewall

A mechanism to protect network stations, subnetworks, and channels from complete failure caused by a single point.

Firmware

Software which is encoded into a ROM, BIOS, or PROM chips.

Float

The difference between the length of a task and when it must be completed to meet the critical path.

Flow control

The protocol that ensures that the modem or computer is not supplied with more data than it can cope with (based on a signal to the data source to stop sending). Ideally, every link in the communication path should have a way to manage flow control with its peers, otherwise data can be lost.

Frame

A self-contained group of bits representing data and control information. The control information usually includes source and destination addressing, sequencing, flow control, and error control information at different protocol levels.

Frame relay

A packet switching device. A switching interface to get frames or packets over parts of the network as quickly as possible. *See* Packet Switching Network.

Freeware

Computer applications which are available on disk or by downloading from bulletin board services for which no cost or compensation is requested. *See also* Shareware.

Garbage collection

The process of collecting no longer used portions of RAM and recycling them as memory pages for symbol tables, data space, disk buffers, or application code.

Gateway

A device that routes information from one network to another. It often interfaces between dissimilar networks and provides protocol translation between the networks. A gateway is also a software connection between different networks; this meaning is not implied in this book. The gateway provides service at level 7 of the OSI Reference Model. *See also* Bridge and Router.

GIS

Abbreviation for Graphical information system (q.v.).

Global resource

Any hardware, software, server, or other resource generally available to all processes and users on a network.

Graphical information system

Generally a database of graphical data, although the term also can refer to an image storage and retrieval system. Abbreviated as GIS.

Graphical user interface

A reference to application display shells including DOSSHELL, OS/2 Program Manager, MS Windows, Solaris, and X Windows. Abbreviated as GUI.

GUI

Abbreviation for Graphical user interface (q.v.).

Heap management

The process of collecting no-longer-used portions of RAM and recycling them as memory pages for symbol tables, data space, disk buffers, or application code.

Hit rate

A ratio found by dividing the number of times requested information is found in the cache by the number of requests made to the storage disk (or CD ROM).

Hub

A network interface that provides star connectivity for FDDI nodes.

Hub adapter

A network interface board that provides access for additional network nodes. This network interface unit (NIU) essentially doubles as a concentrator unit.

I/O channel

See Bus.

IEEE

Abbrevation for for The Institute for Electrical and Electronic Engineers (q.v.).

IEEE 802

An IEEE standard for interconnection of local area networking computer equipment. The IEEE 802 standard describes the physical and link layers of the OSI Reference Model.

IEEE 802.1

A specification for media-layer physical linkages and bridging.

IEEE 802.2

A specification for media-layer communication typified by Ethernet, FDDI, and Token-Ring. *See also* Logical link control.

IEEE 802.3

An Ethernet specification derived from the original Xerox Ethernet specifications. It describes the CSMA/CD protocol on a bus topology using baseband transmissions.

IEEE 802.5

A token ring specification derived from the original IBM Token-Ring LAN specifications. It describes the token protocol on a star/ring topology using baseband transmissions.

IETF

Abbreviation for Internet Engineering Task Force (q.v.).

Institute for Electrical and Electronic Engineers

A membership-based organization based in New York City that produces technical specifications and scientific publications.

Integrated services data network

A digital data network based upon two 56-kbits/s bearer lines and a 16-kbits/s session control line which provides asynchronous service. Better known as ISDN.

Intelligent hub

A hub device that connects Ethernet, FDDI, and Token-Ring nodes and manages nodes and traffic while also isolating failing lobes, trunks, and nodes.

Interface

A device that connects equipment of different types for mutual access. Generally, this refers to computer software and hardware that enable disks and other storage devices to communicate with a computer. In networking, an interface translates different protocols so that different types of computers can communicate. In the OSI model, the interface is the method of passing data between layers on one device.

International Standards Organization

The standards-making body responsible for OSI, a set of communications standards aimed at global interoperability. The United States is one of 75 member countries. Abbreviated as ISO.

Internet Engineering Task Force

The standards-making body for the Internet; the arbiter of TCP/IP standards, including SNMP.

Interpacket delay

The time in milliseconds between arrivals of packets on the network.

ISA

Abbreviation for industry standard architecture.

ISDN

Abbrevation for Integrated services data network (q.v.).

ISO

Abbreviation for International Standards Organization (q.v.).

kB

Abbreviation for kilobytes (1024 bytes) of memory.

LAN

Abbreviation for Local area network (q.v.).

LAN operating system

See Network operating system.

Latency

1. The delay or process time that prevents completion of a task. Latency usually refers to the lag between request for delivery of data over the network until it is actually received.
2. The period of time after a request has been made for service before it is fulfilled.

Lazy-write

A reference to a write-behind cache process, or a storage cache system that holds requests to write until there is a lull in disk utilization.

Linkage product

Any unit that provides an interface between network segments. This includes gateways, bridges, and other specialty components.

Local area network

A network limited in size to a floor, building, or city block. Better known by the acronym, LAN.

Lossful compression

See Lossy compression.

Lossless compression

A reversible data compression technique applying a run length encoding (RLE) or lookup table method to remove redundancies from within the data.

Lossy compression

A nonreversible data compression technique that removes redundancies and actual data from within the object.

MAN

Abbreviation for Metropolitan area network (q.v.).

Management Information Base

A database that defines what information can be gathered and what aspects can be controlled for a network device. Referred to as MIB.

Mbits/s

Abbreviation for Megabits per second. Sometimes abbreviated as Mbits/s or mbps.

MCA

Abbreviation for IBM Microchannel Architecture.

Mean

Technically, the sum of a set of numbers divided by the number of set members. The mean is the expected value of a probability distribution. It is also called the *average*.

Medium

1. The physical material used to transmit the network transmission signal. It is usually either some form of copper wire or optical fiber. However, wireless networks use infrared, microwaves, or radio frequency signals through the ambient air as the medium.
2. A reference to a data storage device such as a hard disk, tape unit, or CD-ROM.

Metal oxide varister

Typical electrical device included in backup power supplies, surge suppressors, and power filters to protect electronic equipment from electrical surges. It loses potency with usage and can become a fire hazard when it finally fails. Abbreviated as MOV.

Meter

Unit of measurement equivalent to 39.25 SAE in, or 3.27 ft. Meter is abbreviated as m.

Metric

A formal measuring standard or benchmark. Network performance metrics include Mbits/s, throughput, error rates, and other less formal definitions.

Metropolitan area network

A network that spans buildings, or city blocks, or a college or corporate campus. Optical fiber repeaters, bridges, routers, packet switches, and and PBX services usually supply the network links. Abbreviated as MAN.

MIB

Abbreviation for Management information base (q.v.).

MICR

Abbreviation for Magnetic ink character recognition.

Mirroring

The process of writing data to multiple disks for increased reliability and data recoverability, and also for increasing the performance of reading data from storage.

MNP

Abbreviation for Microcom network protocols. A set of modem-to-modem protocols that provide error correction and compression.

MNP2

Error correction using asynchronous transmission.

MNP3

Error correction using synchronous transmission between the modems (the DTE interface is still asynchronous). Since each 8-bit byte takes 8 rather than 10 bits to transmit, a 20 percent increase in throughput is possible. Unfortunately the MNP3 protocol overhead is rather high so this increase is not realized.

MNP4

Introduces data phase optimization, which improves on the rather inefficient protocol design of MNP2 and MNP3. Synchronous MNP4 comes closer to achieving 20 percent throughput.

MNP5

Simple data compression. Dynamically arranges for commonly occurring characters to be transmitted with fewer bits than rare characters. It takes into account changing character frequencies as data flows. Also encodes long runs of the same character. Typically compresses text by 35 percent.

Mode

Technically, the area of a probability distribution with the greatest contribution to its density. In other words, this is the number or single range of numbers that occurs most frequently.

Modem

A device which converts digital to analog signals and restores analog signals to digital signals for transmission over a network. Abbrevation for modulator/demodulator.

Monitor

See Protocol analyzer.

MPS

Megabits (1,000,000 decimal units) per second (Mbits/s). This is a channel bandwidth. *See also* Bandwidth and Mbits/s.

μs

Abbreviation for a microsecond.

Multicast

The ability to broadcast to a select subset of stations and nodes.

Network computing

The ability of underutilized workstations to broadcast their status and provide automatic, parallel computing power.

Network interface card

The network access unit which contains the hardware, software, and specialized PROM information necessary for a station to communicate across the network. Abbreviated as NIC.

Network management console, network monitor

The administrator's window into the network. The console is the control panel through which network devices, such as routers, are monitored, configured, and reset.

Network management platform

A set of management services upon which specific management applications, such as consoles, can be built.

Network monitor

See Protocol analyzer.

Network operating system

The software required to control and connect stations into a functioning network conforming to protocol and providing a logical platform for sharing resources. Abbreviated as NOS.

NIC

Abbreviation for Network interface card (q.v.).

Node

A logical, nonphysical interconnection to the network that supports computer workstations or other types of physical devices on a network. Alternatively, a node may connect to a fan-out unit providing network access for many devices. A device might be a terminal server or a shared peripheral such as a file server, printer, or plotter.

Noise

Electrical signal interference on a communications channel that can distort or disrupt data signals. Generally, this refers to electromagnetic interference (EMI) or radio-frequency interference (RFI).

NOS

Abbreviation for Network operating system (q.v.).

Abbreviation for a nanosecond.

Object

A distinct type of management information or variable for a network component. For example, the on/off status of a router is an object. In SNMP, MIB objects can be read (Get objects) or read and written (Get and Set objects). Operators can manipulate these objects to gather information and change configurations.

OCR

Abbreviation for Optical character recognition.

Open Software Foundation

A Cambridge, Massachusetts-based nonprofit organization responsible for assembling the DCE and DME specifications.

Open Systems Interconnection

The suite of communications standards mandated by ISO and the U.S. government. CMIP is part of this suite.

Open Systems Interconnection Reference Model

A specification definition from the International Standards Organization (ISO). It is a data communication architectural model for networking.

Operating system

The software required to control basic computer operations (such as disk access, screen display, and computation).

Operation research

A branch of statistics related to performance modeling and event frequencies.

OSF

Abbreviation for Open Software Foundation (q.v.).

OSI

Abbreviation for Open Systems Interconnection Reference Model (q.v.).

Overhead

CPU, disk processing, and/or network channel bandwidth allocated to the processing and/or packaging of network data.

Packet

A self-contained group of bits representing data and control information. The control information usually includes source and destination addressing, sequencing, flow control, and error control information at different protocol levels. *See also* Frame.

Packet burst

An overwhelming broadcast of frames requesting network and station status information, requesting source or destination addresses, or indicating panic error messages.

Packet switching

The process by which data transmission packets are routed to separate channels. Most LANs and WANs utilize a packet switching technology.

Pair scanner

A testing tool which verifies the integrity and performance of network wiring and cable. It tests for electrical breaks, shorts, impedance, and capacitance, as well as for signal crosstalk and signal attenuation. These tools are sometimes called cable scanners when designed for Ethernet or ring scanners when designed for FDDI.

PCI

Acronym for the Intel 64-bit accessory bus, peripheral component interface.

PCMCIA

Acronym for Personal Computer Memory Card International Association. A standard for a computer plug-in, credit card-sized card which provides about 90 percent compatibility across various platforms, BIOS, and application software.

PDN

Abbreviation for Public data network (q.v.).

Peer-to-peer exchange

The ability of computer workstations from the same or different vendors to interconnect and communicate.

Performance evaluation and review technique

A project management technique for estimating and evaluating costs, materials, and time frames for completing projects. Abbreviated as PERT.

PERT

Abbreviation for Performance evaluation and review technique (q.v.).

Physical channel

The actual wiring and transmission hardware required to implement networking.

Physical device

Any item of hardware on the network.

Print server

A device that provides print services for other stations. It is a shared resource that often has higher speed, larger capacity, or better economies of scale than local printers.

Private MIB

Also called extended MIB. A standard MIB to which proprietary extensions have been added in order to monitor or control network device functions not included in the standard MIB specification.

PROM

Abbreviation for programmable read-only memory; a computer chip with software designed into its structure.

Protocol

A formal set of rules by which computers can communicate. They cover session initiation, transmission maintenance, and termination.

Protocol analyzer

Test equipment that transmits, receives, and captures data frames to verify proper network operation.

Queue

A waiting line with requests for service.

Queueing model

A statistical model describing a system of event arrivals (such as frames or transmission requests) and service times (such as transmission delivery times, network channel loading, and performance levels). An example is the LANModel application from Network Performance Institute.

Radio-frequency interference

Electronically propagated noise from radar, radio, or electronic sources. Abbreviated as RF or RFI. *See* Electromagnetic interference.

RAM

Abbreviation for Random access memory (q.v.).

Random

A technical term (here) referring to events that have no formal interrelationship; events that occur with equal probability.

Random access memory

The large block of memory which contains the executable code for the operating system, device drivers, application software, and user data. Abbreviated as RAM.

Read-ahead

The process whereby a disk controller reads blocks of information subsequent to the one actually requested on the slight chance that they will be requested later.

Redirector

A software driver that diverts commands to access local devices and routes them to network devices for data storage, retrieval, and printing.

Relative measure

A measurement system without a clear physical basis; a logical measuring system.

Remote Monitoring MIB

An extended MIB that delivers statistics about data packets and network traffic to an SNMP console.

Repeater

A device that boosts a signal from one network lobe or trunk and continues transmission to another similar network lobe or trunk. Protocols must match on both segments. The repeater provides service at level 1 of the OSI Reference Model.

Replication server

A process which duplicates transactions rather than the data itself across a distributed database environment.

Requester

What IBM calls a network user, often a device or workstation. *See also* Client.

RLE

Abbreviation for Run length encoding (q.v.).

RMON MIB

Abbreviation for Remote Monitoring MIB (q.v.).

Router

A device that interconnects networks that are either local area or wide area. Routers often provide intercommunication with multiple protocols. Routers provide service at level 3 of the OSI Reference Model. *See also* Bridge and Gateway.

Run length encoding

A common method for encoding streams of data with repeating patterns into a more space-efficient representation. It is a common data compression method used for compressing entire disk volumes (as with Stacker), individual files (as with PKZIP), or the native MS Windows format for bitmapped images.

Saturation

An occurrence on Ethernet when packets arrive on the network and create new collisions faster than collisions can be resolved and the transmission pressure can be handled.

Scanner

A testing tool which verifies the integrity and performance of network wiring and cable. It tests for electrical breaks, shorts, impedance, and capacitance, as well as for signal crosstalk and signal attenuation. These tools are sometimes called cable, pair, or ring scanners.

Seek time

The time required for the moving read/write heads on a magnetic disk storage unit to move from the current location to the location specified by the disk controller in order to locate the record, sector, or file required.

Sensitivity analysis

The practice of making small or large changes to data and model specifications to test the stability and variability of results.

Server

1. A dedicated processor performing a function such as printing, file storage, or tape storage. *See also* File server and Print server.
2. A technical term referring to the service completion mechanism in a traffic queueing model.

Shareware

Computer applications which are provided on disk or by downloading from bulletin board services for which payment is expected from the recipient if the software is used beyond a trial period.

Simple Network Management Protocol

An IETF-defined protocol that runs natively on TCP/IP networks. Considered the de facto standard for network management, it is used to monitor the status of devices, but because of its lack of security, is rarely used to control network devices.

Simulation

A technique for modeling or representing a real-world situation using computerized tools (such as LANModel or Bones).

Slack time

The time after completion of a task in a system of other sequential or parallel tasks that is extra or underutilized; the unscheduled time in a project path.

Slot time

The time during which the protocol allows a node or station to transmit.

SPM/2

Acronym for System Performance Monitor/2, a network administration tool for OS/2 LAN and LAN Server.

SNMP

Abbreviation for Simple Network Management Protocol (q.v.).

SNMP version 2

The next generation of SNMP. It will add security (encryption and authentication), support a hierarchical management scheme, and run on network transports other than TCP/IP, including AppleTalk, IPX, and OSI.

Solid state disk

The emulation of a mechanical hard disk with dynamic random access memory (DRAM). A device which provides about 100 to 500 times faster data seek and access times.

Spanning-tree algorithm

IEEE 802.1 standard that detects and manages logical loops in a network. When multiple paths exist, the bridge or router selects the most efficient one. When a path fails, the tree automatically reconfigures the network with a new active path. Abbreviated as STA.

Spectrum analysis

A technique that tests the radio, electrical, or optical signal frequencies to ascertain that the transmission signal conforms to requirements.

Splice

A mechanical connection in optical fiber made by fusing the media together with heat.

Standard deviation

The square root of the *variance*.

Station

1. A logical, nonphysical interconnection to the network that supports computer workstations or other types of physical devices on a network.
2. Alternatively, a station may connect to a fan-out unit providing network access for many devices.
3. A station might be a terminal server or a shared peripheral such as a file server, printer, or plotter.
4. A station can also be a single addressable device on a network, generally implemented as a stand-alone computer or a peripheral device such as a printer or plotter. *See also* Node or Workstation.

Subnet

A ring that is a portion of a larger network.

Symmetric processing

Workload is balanced evenly among multiple CPUs.

Telnet

A part of the TCP/IP protocol suite that allows managers to control network devices, such as routers, remotely.

Terminal server

A computer device that provides low-speed DTE network access; a device for connecting terminals to a network.

Token

The protocol-based permission that is granted to a station in a predetermined sequence. The permission allows that station to transmit on the network.

token ring

A physical networking configuration.

Token-Ring

1. An IBM network protocol and trademark.

2. A popular example of a local area network; the IEEE 802.5 standard was derived from original IBM working papers. Token-Ring applies the IEEE 802.2 MAC protocols and uses the nonpersistent token protocol on a logical ring, although it uses a physical star topology. Transmission rate is 4 Mbits/s, with upgrades to 16 Mbits/s and an option to release a token upon completion of frame transmission, as well as an early token release and burst mode option.

Topology

Layout of a network. This describes how the nodes are physically joined to one another.

TPS

Abbreviation for transactions per second (q.v.).

Traffic

A measure of network load which refers to the frame transmission rate (frames per second or frames per hour).

Traffic queueing model

A statistical model that simulates traffic levels, queue service waiting times (protocol response time), total system waiting times (user response time), and system load.

Transaction Control Protocol/Internet Protocol

A common communication protocol servicing the network and transport layers that provides transmission routing control and data transfer. This represents logical connectivity at levels 2 and 3 of the OSI Reference Model, although the protocol does in fact not conform to this model. Also known by its acronym, TCP/IP.

Transactions per second

The number of discrete data entry, data update, and data requests processed by a system each second; a measurement of performance capacity or measure of work accomplished generally applied to on-line transaction processing environments. Abbreviated as TPS.

Transmission Control Protocol/Internet Protocol

Developed by the U.S. Department of Defense to internetwork disparate computers, TCP/IP is the most popular protocol for multiplatform networks. Abbreviated and generally referred to as TCP/IP.

UART

See Universal asynchronous receiver/transmitter (q.v.).

Universal asynchronous receiver/transmitter

The chip in a PC that allows the computer to communicate through the serial port with mice, modems, and light pens, and directly with other computers.

UPS

Uninterruptable power supply; a backup power supply in case the main electrical source fails.

V Series protocol

A set of standards published by the CCITT for data communication over telephone networks.

V.32

V Series protocol with transmission at 9600 bits/s with fall back to 4800 bits/s.

V.32bis

V Series protocol with transmission at 14,400 bits/s with fall back to 12,000 bits/s, 9600 bits/s, 7200 bits/s, and 4800 bits/s.

V.42

V Series protocol with transmission supporting error correction with asynchronous to synchronous conversion, which eliminates the start and stop bits, reducing each burdened character from 10 bits to 8.

V.42bis

V Series protocol with transmission applying data compression using a Lempel-Ziv-Welch or Shannon-Fano technique, which detects frequently occurring character strings and replaces them with tokens. Typical compression for text is 50 percent or better, with a nearly 20 percent gain from synchronous conversion that reduces transmission time by almost 60 percent.

Variance

The sum of the squared differences of all point values from the mean value, divided by the number of point values. This is the squared value of the *standard deviation.*

Virus

See Computer virus.

VSAT

Very-small-aperture terminal; synonymous with satellite data communication.

WAN

Abbreviation for Wide area network (q.v.).

Wide area network

A network that spans cities, states, countries, or oceans. It usually provides PBX or internetwork links.

Wiring concentrator

A central wiring concentrator for a series of Ethernet, FDDI, and Token-Ring nodes. *See also* Wiring hub.

Wiring hub

A central wiring concentrator for a series of Ethernet, FDDI, and Token-Ring nodes.

Workload characterization

The study that observes, identifies, and explains the phenomena of work in a manner that simplifies how resources are being used.

Workstation

1. Any computer device.

2. Any device on a network.

3. A station can also be a single addressable site on FDDI that is generally implemented as a stand-alone computer or a peripheral device, connected to the ring with a controller. *See also* Node or Station.

WYSIWYG

Acronym for what you see is what you get, or an indication that the screen display will mirror the corresponding output.

Index

About the Author

Martin A. Nemzow is director of product development with the
Network Performance Institute where he is involved in helping MIS
managers optimize their ROI on computer investments. He is the
author of *The Ethernet Management Guide, LAN Performance
Optimization, FDDI Networking* and *The Token Ring Management
Guide,* all published by McGraw-Hill.

DISK WARRANTY

This software is protected by boh United States copyright law and international copyright treaty provision. You must treat this software just like a book, except that you may copy it into a computer to be used and you may make archival copies of the software for the sole purpose of backing up our software and protecting your investment from loss.

By saying, "just like a book," McGraw-Hill means, for example, that this software may be used by any number of people and may be freely moved from one computer location to another, so long as there is no possiblity of its being used at one location or on one computer while it is being used at another. Just as a book cannot be read by two different people in two different places at the same time, neither can the software be used by two different people in two different places at the same time (unless, of course, McGraw-Hill's copyright is being violated).

LIMITED WARRANTY

McGraw-Hill warrants the physical diskette(s) enclosed herein to be free of defects in materials and workmanship for a period of sixty days from the purchase date. If McGraw-Hill receives written notification within the warranty period of defects in materials and workmanship, and such notification is determined by McGraw-Hill to be correct, McGraw-Hill will replace the defective diskette(s). Send requests to:

Customer Service
TAB/McGraw-Hill
13311 Monterey Avenue
Blue Ridge Summit, PA 17294-0850

The entire and exclusive liablility and remedy for breach of this Limited Warranty shall be limited to replacement of defective diskette(s) and shall not include or extend to any claim for or right to cover any other damages, including but not limited to, loss of profit, data, or use of the software, or special, incidental, or consequential damages or other similar claims, even if McGraw-Hill's liability for any damages to you or any other person ever exceed the lower of suggested list price or actual price paid for the license to use the software, regardless of any form of the claim.

McGRAW-HILL, INC. SPECIFICALLY DISCLAIMS ALL OTHER WARRANTIES, EXPRESS OR IMPLIED, INCLUDING BUT NOT LIMITED TO, ANY IMPLIED WARRANTY OF MERCHANTABLILTY OR FITNESS FOR A PARTICULAR PURPOSE. Specifically, McGraw-Hill makes no representation or warranty that the software is fit for any particular purpose and any implied warranty of merchantability is limited to the sixty-day duration of the Limited Warranty covering the physical diskette(s) only (and not the software) and is otherwise expressly and specifically disclaimed.

This limited warranty gives you specific legal rights; you may have others which may vary from state to state. Some states do not allow the exclusion of incidental or consequential damages, or the limitation on how long an implied warranty lasts, so some of the above may not apply to you.